D0551535

THE DALESMAN
A Celebration of 50 Years

THE DALESMAN
A Celebration of 50 Years

Edited by
DAVID JOY

PELHAM BOOKS
STEPHEN GREENE PRESS

PELHAM BOOKS

Published by the Penguin Group
27 Wrights Lane, London W8 5TZ, England
Viking Penguin Inc., 40 West 23rd Street, New York, New York 10010, USA
The Stephen Greene Press Inc., 15 Muzzey Street, Lexington, Massachusetts 02173, USA
Penguin Books Australia Ltd, Ringwood, Victoria, Australia
Penguin Books Canada Ltd, 2801 John Street, Markham, Ontario, Canada L3R 1B4
Penguin Books (NZ) Ltd, 182–190 Wairau Road, Auckland 10, New Zealand

Penguin Books Ltd, Registered Offices: Harmondsworth, Middlesex, England

First published 1989
Reprinted 1989

Copyright © The Dalesman, 1989

All rights reserved. Without limiting the rights under copyright reserved above, no part of this publication may be
reproduced, stored in or introduced into a retrieval system, or transmitted, in any form
or by any means (electronic, mechanical, photocopying,
recording or otherwise), without the prior written permission of both
the copyright owner and the above publisher of this book

Typeset 11/12pt Goudy Old Style by Goodfellow & Egan Ltd, Cambridge

Printed and bound in Great Britain by Butler & Tanner Ltd, Frome

A CIP catalogue record for this book
is available from the British Library

ISBN 0 7207 1865 1

CONTENTS

FOREWORD

It is a mere pocket-sized publication of less than a hundred pages. Yet it is Britain's biggest-selling regional magazine, bought by almost 60,000 folk every month and borrowed by at least five times that number. It was once described as being produced by amateurs for amateurs. Yet it is cherished as a well-loved friend by a huge family of readers who pounce on its every word. It regularly ignores great events and high-society. Yet it is revered by all true Yorkshiremen and women, including over three thousand expatriates in every country of the globe. Putting people before things, *The Dalesman* is comprehensible to both Dalesfolk and Dales lovers. Staunchly and devotedly Yorkshire, it could exist in no other county.

At celebrations in 1964 to mark the magazine's twenty-fifth anniversary, a visiting journalist asked the rhetorical question, 'Why **do** people read *The Dalesman?*' His answer went straight to the heart: 'Many who see it for the first time may well wonder, for its contents often seem inconsequential, or merely nostalgic, or of limited local interest. In these days of mass markets, monopolistic journalism and superficial television, probably the reason for *The Dalesman's* success is its air of individualism. It is a magazine for the lover of the countryside; for those interested in a dialect or little-known lore, or those who feel they belong to a family of readers with similar interests. It is a magazine for the little things of life – and how often do the little things give the greatest pleasure.'

After those self-same celebrations, a letter was received from Sir Linton Andrews, then recently retired as editor of the *Yorkshire Post*: 'In sending congratulations to *The Dalesman*, I have two dominant thoughts. One is that you have built up the magazine as one of the great institutions of Yorkshire. The second is that you have done it by determination, unusual talent and a love of the Dales which you have shared with many thousands of readers. I little thought when I heard of the enterprise you proposed to start that it would become the most popular regional magazine in this country, but you have created a magazine so good and with such personality that I am sure it arouses nothing but affection among its subscribers. Long may it flourish!'

The letter was addressed to Harry J. Scott, who back in 1939 had finally been persuaded by Linton Andrews – then more familiarly known as W.L.A. – that the time was right to start a magazine for the Yorkshire Dales. The two of them had already discussed the idea at length over the years, for until 1934 Harry Scott had been a Leeds-based journalist on the *Yorkshire Post* group of newspapers. Yet his dream was to leave behind the city life and unsocial hours of newspapers and work in the country. One day he went down to Burford in Oxfordshire seeking a job on *The Countryman* magazine, and then on the way back decided he would instead start a similar publication just for the Dales which would reflect his own style and interests.

Shortly afterwards, Harry was looking through the *Yorkshire Post* property page and saw advertised a 'little house' at Clapham. That weekend he bundled Mrs Scott and their two

children, Martin and Margaret, into the car, drove to Yorkshire's north-west frontier and agreed with the local estate agent to rent the house for ten shillings a week – the amount he was still paying when he left in 1968! So the move to Clapham was made, Harry arguing that if he could earn four guineas a week from freelance journalism then he could survive until the magazine was off the ground. Fellow journalists thought he must be mad – they had seen the shoebox where he kept the pile of documents relating to his pet project!

Hope finally became a reality when Linton Andrews and another half-dozen friends each put up loans of £50 to enable the first issue of the *Yorkshire Dalesman* to be published in April 1939. Compiled in the front parlour of what was now known as Fellside, its twenty-eight pages were hand-set and printed by Lamberts of Settle and it cost just three old pence. Alas! There could scarcely have been a worse time to launch a new magazine and it was so nearly strangled at birth. The dark days of war saw its size shrink to a mere twenty pages with monthly sales dropping to as low as 2,500 copies. Even then there were moments of light relief as instanced by the magazine's first colour advertisement – a breakthrough achieved by obtaining a batch of coloured labels from a tea manufacturer and then sticking them by hand into a blank space left in each copy.

Harry Scott eked out an existence through the war years by becoming a sub-editor on the *Craven Herald* weekly newspaper in Skipton. In 1943 an opening for a junior reporter on the paper at a wage of 12s.6d. a week was filled by W.R. ('Bill') Mitchell, who had just left school at the age of fifteen. He has never forgotten his first meeting with Harry, who, reeking of peat, tweeds and pipe tobacco, greeted him, 'Hail to thee, blithe spirit!' Life on the *Craven Herald* was not over-hectic and the two of them frequently worked together on the magazine. In 1948 Bill joined Harry Scott at Clapham as editorial assistant on what was now known simply as *The Dalesman*, its coverage having expanded to embrace the whole of the Yorkshire countryside.

Once recovered from the rigours of war, the magazine grew steadily both in size and readership and by 1955 its circulation was over 25,000. A sister magazine *Cumbria* had been started for the Lake District and a growing volume of book publishing meant that the floor of Fellside was in danger of sinking beneath the combined weight of paper and parcels. Crisis was averted by acquiring the former vicarage coach house and estate workshops in the village and converting them into offices.

Yet many of the old ways still persisted, as recalled by Dennis Bullock, who in 1961 joined what had now become the Dalesman Publishing Company Ltd and is today its Managing Director: 'When I started, one of my first tasks was to take over the sorting of the morning mail. I was invited up to Fellside to see how it was done – it was really quite amusing as all the letters were opened among the toast and marmalade during breakfast. For some years, Mr Scott always took all the spare cash and postage stamps out of the mail and put them to one side. He used to leave the auditors and myself to sort out what were his drawings at the end of each financial year. The library was the current accounts department and what books were in print were piled all over the place – under tables, on tables, round the walls. There was no stock control. If someone did not pay a cash-sale bill for books after they had been sent, then it was ripped up and thrown in the waste-paper basket!'

In the spring of 1965 another journalist with a yearning to live and work in the countryside joined the fold when I left the *Yorkshire Post*, beating a path to an editorial desk where sounds of sheep and curlews replaced city-centre noise and stress. Later that summer *The Dalesman* had a distinguished visitor: J.B. Priestley was commissioned by *Life International* to write an article on the Dales and called in for a chat with Harry Scott. The result was a dense fug as both men consumed prodigious amounts of pipe tobacco. It proved more than worthwhile for Priestley's article in what was then one of the world's great magazines made generous reference to *The Dalesman* and also foretold its future destiny: 'Harry Scott is one of those rare and fortunate newspapermen who have made a familiar dream come true. He founded and edited his own monthly magazine. And if he is worried about its future – and he is – that is simply because various publishing combines in London would like to take over *The Dalesman*. If this should happen, he feels, though it might increase circulation and advertising, *The Dalesman* might also begin to lose its character. He has a very cosy and personal set-up there in Clapham. While we were talking I could hear girls laughing and giggling in a neighbouring room. It was dispatch day, he explained, and the girls always got a bit out of hand. Perhaps the girls laugh in Fleet Street, but I have never heard them. *The Dalesman* must stay in the Dales.

So it was that Harry Scott semi-retired to Grange-over-Sands, Bill Mitchell assumed editorial control and a scheme was devised to secure the company's future by transferring its ownership to the four longest-serving employees. *The Dalesman* stayed in the Dales.

Harry Scott died in January 1978. He remained to the end an unassuming man, his love of people shining through all his utterances and writings. Bill Mitchell later commented: 'He was a man with a flair we like to think we have inherited. He was in many ways an individualist and an innovator. Above all, he had a great sense of fun; he used to enjoy telling stories against himself, and he hated pomposity.'

A decade later Bill opted to retire as Editor, having taken the magazine to new heights and contributed some one-and-a-half million words to it over a forty-year period. This end of an era was marked by major articles in newspapers all over the land as well as a half-hour television programme, narrated by playwright Alan Bennett, which ended on a high: '*The Dalesman* has proved to be something of a river; it just goes flowing on – and like a river it is, I hope, unstoppable.'

In April 1988 I thus became only the third Editor in nigh on fifty years. The magazine is in no danger of succumbing to current trends and becoming 'The Dalesperson' but it is certainly moving with the times – my editorial colleague is now Hilary Gray who called in at the office one day in the winter of '87. Fresh from an editorship in Scotland, she was unknowingly maintaining a long tradition, for no journalistic post on *The Dalesman* has ever been advertised! Somehow the two of us manage to produce two magazines each month and some two dozen books a year; I am enormously grateful for her cheerful and enthusiastic help and support.

Yet a successful publishing operation requires far more than just a pair of wordsmiths. I acknowledge a deep debt of gratitude to my two co-directors Dennis Bullock and Tony Jefferies; the three of us have collectively given seventy-five years' service to the company! I thank also Allan Brooks, our Advertisement Manager, for ensuring that the 'bread' on either side of the editorial sandwich maintains its very special flavour which

W.R. Mitchell (front row, left), Editor of *The Dalesman* for twenty years from 1968, alongside David Joy, the present Editor. Behind are Tony Jefferies (left), Sales Director, and Dennis Bullock, Managing Director.

The entire *Dalesman* staff – all fourteen of them – photographed specially for this book in July 1988.

helps to give the magazine its unique character. And I am equally grateful to all the *Dalesman* staff who collectively appear in the photograph on this page.

Many of them have helped in the preparation of this anthology as I have delved back into the distant past. It has been a long but rewarding journey, embracing fifty volumes, six hundred issues, some 18,000 pages and over 15 million words. It has revealed the immense riches that lie waiting to be re-discovered in the earlier numbers of the magazine. It has confirmed that one of the great virtues of *The Dalesman* is that each and every copy still retains its freshness ten, twenty or more years after original publication.

This is not a bumper issue of *The Dalesman*. Rather, it is primarily a personal selection of articles not too long and not too short that I felt have stood the test of time, have extra-special appeal or have proved milestones during half-a-century of the magazine's gradual evolution. With its broad themes, it is intended both to commemorate our fiftieth birthday and form a bedside book of Yorkshire in all its glorious and infinite variety. I hope these pages both inform and entertain and may even inspire my successor when in 2038 he or she begins to compile our centenary anthology. Have a good read!

David Joy,
Editor, The Dalesman
Clapham, July 1988

OUR FIRST HALF CENTURY

SUCCESS TO *THE DALESMAN*

J.B. Priestley

introducing the first number, April 1939

I AM GLAD to learn that our beloved Dales are to have their own magazine and I wish the venture the success it deserves.

The Dales are associated with some of the very happiest memories of my life. Oddly enough, after I was demobilised from the army in the spring of 1919, the very first writing job I was given was to do some articles on a little walking tour in the Dales, and I went, treading on air, a civilian again, a free-lance journalist at last, through Upper Wharfedale and then roaming about in Wensleydale. I shall never forget beginning that little walking tour.

I have never found again – no, not even in the romantic islands of the West Indies or the South Seas, not in the deserts of Egypt or Arizona – the sunlight that set all the dewdrops glittering about my path that morning. And though many places have disappointed me when I have returned to them, the Dales have never disappointed me. I still consider them the finest countryside in Britain, with their magnificent, clean and austere outlines of hill and moor, their charming villages and remote white-washed farms, their astonishing variety of aspect and appeal, from the high gaunt rocks down to the twinkling rivers.

As far as my present life is concerned, the Dales have only two faults: they are not easy to get at from London, to which I am anchored for a good part of my year; and they have never offered me yet a country house suitable in size and type and cost to a family like mine. But I believe that one day I shall return to their high hills and grey-green valleys and lovely peace. So please see that your new magazine fights to keep them all unspoilt.

THE BIRTH OF *THE DALESMAN*

Harry J. Scott

I T ALL began in the far-off days before the war. I had lived and roamed about in the Dale country of Yorkshire for many years, and had jotted down for my own interest my finds and discoveries, impressions of people and things, stories and notes of encounters – a bit of that buried treasure which lies deep in every

Harry J. Scott.

it then was, into the troubled seas of 1939 amid the raucous shouting of Hitler and the sabre-rattling of Mussolini. Their anger was hardly directed at us, for we were so small and frail a vessel, with a first print order of only 3,000 copies and a first printing bill of £25. Yet it all seemed staggeringly large then, and we waited somewhat fearfully for the first response from folk who have a reputation for being 'tight wi' ther' brass'. For many months before we had been collecting material, cajoling a few advertisers to take space, and organising the distribution of copies. Even then it might never have come into existence but for the practical encouragement and valuable advice of W.L.A., then Editor of the old *Leeds Mercury*, now Sir Linton Andrews, Editor of *The Yorkshire Post*. He had been privy to our hopes and plans. He knew our hesitations. His was the injunction to 'get on with it now, or it may be too late.' It was the start of much friendly help he was to give us during the difficult years to follow.

One of our first tasks was to devise a cover, and Godfrey Wilson, of Stainforth, produced the design – the first of much art work he was to do for us down the years. Incidentally, this cover brought us an early hint of Dales' realism. An old Dalesman, to whom we proudly showed this cover, commented: 'Ay, them's grand fells, that's a grand road, and (pointing to the little flock in the picture) them sheep's all right. But if Ah'd been yon chap (pointing to the shepherd) Ah'd a' sent t'dog for them few sheep. Ah wouldn't a' gone missen.'

countryside. And I found the treasure so rich and inexhaustible that my gathering shaped itself into the project of a monthly magazine into which all these discoveries – my own and other people's – could be poured.

There were head-shakings, of course, and pointed reminders that Yorkshire folk were 'tight wi' ther' brass,' that 'tha'll loss more ner tha addles', and that North-country folk were too hard-headed to be interested in a magazine about themselves. But the idea grew. It was to be a friendly little magazine, a simple monthly record of Dales life and ways, with photographs, and drawings and paintings, if we could afford them, and full of the genuine stuff of Dales life, created in the Dales for Dales folk.

We launched *The Yorkshire Dalesman*, as

We received much other friendly help in our launching. J.B. Priestley gave us an encouraging first article. William Riley (the author of *Windyridge*), C.J. Cutcliffe-Hyne (the creator of Captain Kettle), Leonard and Lettice Cooper (both Yorkshire novelists), Ella Pontefract (author, with Marie Hartley, of the Dales books), Donald Boyd (then Talks Director of the B.B.C.), Marmaduke Miller (of Arncliffe), and A. Creech Jones, M.P., all contributed. With Norman Thornber, of Settle, who shared in our early adventures, we toured the Dales trying to dispose of little bundles of copies 'on sale or return' to unenthusiastic newsagents. We received good counsel from Guy Schofield, who some years before had founded *The Yorkshire Monthly*, and who later became Editor of the London *Evening News* and of the *Daily Mail*.

The first response to the new magazine was encouraging, and we began to indulge in pipe dreams of the future as the circulation grew in those early months. Alas, September 1939 dashed those hopes. Almost at once our supplies of paper were reduced to a continually curtailed proportion of what we had used in our first six months – which meant cutting our circulation to a maximum of 4,000 copies with a minimum number of pages of inferior paper. Our costs rose far beyond what we could ever hope to secure in revenue on our tiny sales, and it looked as though we should have to close down almost before we had reached our first birthday. And then came the first trickle of that great flood of letters which poured into us every week of the war, from men and women in

Early cover designs for *The Yorkshire Dalesman*.

the Forces scattered over an ever wider area of the world, begging us to keep the magazine alive as a link between them and the Yorkshire countryside they loved and knew so well. Copies went in devious ways to France, to Africa, to the Middle and Far East. They went to men in the Navy, to lonely outposts in the desert, to air stations round the world. Somehow we had to stay alive to keep faith with our loyal readers.

Incidentally, 'we' is not used in this connection as the editorial 'we' of the newspaper leading article. It embraced the Editor and his wife, who, in addition to normal editorial tasks, addressed labels and envelopes, tied parcels, kept the accounts and wrote hundreds of letters to correspondents in every continent. It included also the Editor's children, who trundled letters and parcels to our village post office in the garden wheelbarrow. And from time to time it included much valued help from assistants who could give whole or part-time help at rush periods.

The loyalty of our readers – and would-be readers, for in those days we had a 'waiting list' of subscribers – the goodwill of our wartime friends, the determination to keep going, come what may (and often we felt that nothing was coming in), and the kindly forbearance of J.W. Lambert and Sons, of Settle, our then printers, who themselves had many difficulties to face, saw us into the brighter days of peace. Inevitably through all this we have ourselves learned much about the countryside and the people we have sought to portray. We blush a little as we think back to our earliest days, when we felt that one of our qualifications for publishing this magazine was that 'we knew our Yorkshire'. How little we really knew, and how little we still know of this vast county and the folk who live in it!

There have been very many lighter moments to compensate for the headaches. Many of them have come from the very friendly – we might almost say family – relationship we have always had with readers. Many times it has happened that two postal subscribers have notified us that in future one subscription only will suffice for both, 'as a wedding is to take place shortly'. More than one reader has asked for an extra copy containing a particular picture, 'as that was where I proposed to my wife'. One subscriber apologised for a delay in the renewal of her subscription 'because she was supporting the church roof'. Another, a schoolteacher, had overlooked hers because 'the schoolroom ceiling' had fallen on her head. An overseas reader was very angry that his copies had ceased to arrive each month. Didn't we know he had had an accident and therefore could not send us a cheque!

We have had requests for back numbers 'because the dog chewed up ours', 'because my boss always takes my copy home and sometimes forgets to return it', and, from a doctor, 'my patients take them from the waiting-room'. During the war such requests for copies came frequently from men who had lost everything when their ship sank under them, or when their possessions were bombed, or because they were so often on the move that their copies failed to keep up with them. One copy went each month to a group of Yorkshiremen in the Middle East known as 'The Yorkshire Pudding Club'. It was read and re-read 'until all the print was worn off the pages and the magazine practically fell to pieces'.

Some of our vicissitudes were grim at the time, even though we can smile at them now. There was a winter when we were literally snowed up for a week; posts were delayed, buses were off, and we were awaiting proofs for correction with only a few days to go to press day. A friendly corn merchant's wagon, which managed to get through to the village with fodder, brought up the proofs. We corrected them in a frenzied haste, and sent them back to the printer on the return trip. There was one exciting day when the postal rate on all printed matter was due to be increased (was it from ½d. to 1d. per copy?). That increase meant a great deal to a magazine then living from hand to mouth. A group of young people rallied round to help us address and pack copies and rush them to our post office in time for the last collection before the rate changed. On another occasion the whole of our staff – total three – were down with 'flu, and we compiled that issue with shivery hands between sneezes and wheezes.

We have received many reader-requests, from ideas for holidays (one from four young ladies who insisted on 'respectable' lodgings) to enquiries about homes for returning exiles. One correspondent wanted 'a list of all the guide books published on Yorkshire', and a woman reader wanted us to find her a Dales farmer for a husband. We have provided recipes, witnessed legal documents, passed on enquiries (often from America) for family trees, and hunted up obscure facts to settle arguments. We have had no high-flown aims. We have had no ambition to reform the world, or found a party, or revolutionise the countryside. We have preached no gospel and led no crusade. Our purpose has been simply to serve as a chronicle of our countryside, to picture the Yorkshire scene in words and photographs and drawings, to provide a link between Yorkshire folk at home and all over the world, and by these things together to enlarge and deepen the appreciation of our county of the broad acres in its infinite variety among all who know it.

A compilation of editorials which appeared in the 'Dalesman's Diary' section of the magazine on the occasion of its tenth and twenty-first anniversaries (March 1949 and April 1960).

FIFTY YEARS WITH *THE DALESMAN*

An Introduction by W.R. Mitchell

WHEN HARRY SCOTT, founder of the magazine, rented his new home in the Dales from the Ingleborough Estate in 1934, the agent said there would be no objection to him changing the name. Harry thought of calling it Beckside, after the watercourse that divides the village of Clapham into two. It is a lively beck, rising on Ingleborough, and having many adventures before merging its waters with those of the Wenning. But Harry Scott's first love was for the limestone hills, and so he called his house 'Fellside'. When the magazine began in April 1939, the name 'Fellside' was incorporated in the official address.

The estate agent, Claude Barton, had described the property as a 'little house'. Early in the war, Harry Scott was asked to contribute a series of articles about Dales life to the old *Yorkshire Evening News*, and he wrote as though from 'The Little House'. For over thirty years, this every-week chronicle of country folk acted as a balm to city minds. I maintained the series for about half of that time, and it was a constant reminder of our good fortune in being able to work in such a glorious setting. Local characters, like Ben Hudson and Arthur Tennant, unknowingly provided us with a host of amusing tales and accounts of traditional Dales life.

For many years *The Dalesman* was devised and produced in the front room of the Scotts' house, to which came a procession of contributors and readers. Bertram Unne, the photographer, took some charming photographs of the family in the garden at the front of the house. 'Garden' was perhaps too grand a name for the modest plot in which Mrs Scott raised a few plants despite intrusion by the voracious and ever-hungry Ingleborough sheep. Their favourite food was a freshly-planted wallflower. Nothing annoyed the normally gentle Dorothy Scott more than the sight of sheep droppings on the slate path and severely-pruned rows of wallflowers.

Professor Joad, of B.B.C. Brains Trust fame, appeared, sopping wet, on the doorstep after climbing Ingleborough and was allowed to have a bath while his clothes were dried. In later years, the artist Ionicus descended from those self-same heights, where he had been seeking caves to draw for a feature that would appear in *Punch*. The Scotts welcomed him and we found him some photographic references to augment the sketches. For sixteen years he provided us with cover illustrations, based

'Ionicus' (J.C. Armitage), who for sixteen years provided *The Dalesman*'s cover illustrations.

on a fictionalised Dales community called Ghylldale. A. Wainwright visited us with our printer, Harry Firth, before the first of his unique Lakeland guide books had been published; we marvelled at the original artwork for the first guide, a most imaginative production.

Autumn brought the russet flare of discoloured leaves on the creeper that spread over most of the facade. Winter saw the return of the sheep. The spotted flycatchers returned to nest in spring. I would see one of the pair flying from its perch to catch

OPPOSITE
Many of the 'Ionicus' covers pictured the fictionalised Dales community of Ghylldale.

passing insects. Summer's glory was in the garden that Dorothy Scott painstakingly maintained.

I remember the main passage of Fellside because of its ever-changing appearance. When the printer delivered copies of the magazine, the parcels were dumped here to await packing and posting. A man would have left them as they lay, but Mrs Scott contrived to make them attractive by covering them with cloths and, several times, adding vases of flowers!

Turn right at the end of the passage, and you would enter the dining room which held the archaic telephone. The breakfasting Scotts also contrived to open the *Dalesman* mail here. At the time of which I am thinking, the cost of an annual postal subscription to the magazine was 10s.6d. What Harry Scott could do that day depended largely on how many postal orders were received. Sometimes, he would set off to Leeds for a haircut, by courtesy of money that came in the morning mail. At other times of the year, the trickle of postal orders was a flood and the surplus could be banked.

Walk through the dining room and you entered the office of the Dalesman Publishing Company, the nerve-centre of the operation. Progress through the room was limited to narrow walkways, flanked by files, books and the huge desk that was the room's central feature. Harry Scott was fond of relating that when the magazine was first published, all the relevant documents were kept in a boot box. Soon there was a grave risk of avalanches of paper overwhelming visitors. Having been a journalist on Leeds daily newspapers during the 1930s, the founder of *The Dalesman* was addicted to newspaper cuttings. Whenever he read a newspaper, he neatly snipped round any item worthy of being

filed and kept it for future use. A visitor, looking at a desecrated copy of *The Yorkshire Post*, described it as the 'filleted' edition. New cuttings joined old and yellowing ones, either in loose heaps, second-hand envelopes or special files, which it was my job to keep up to date. In this process, gallons of Gloy were used.

Harry Scott blended the past and the present as he picked up really old newspapers and read them with no less interest than if they had just been printed. In this way, he re-lived the period of the Abdication – over thirty years after the event. He knew Bishop Blunt, who was a fellow governor of Bentham Grammar School. He once showed me a letter he had received from the Bishop in 1939, in response to one sent from *The Dalesman* asking for 'memories' of the Dales. The Bishop wrote with cordiality, regretting that he did not know the Dales too well but suggesting that his Registrar's knowledge was considerable, especially if Mr Scott was interested in the interiors of Dales inns!

The office was heated by a coke stove. Harry Scott's chair stood immediately in front of it, and he developed a system of slipping pieces of cardboard between himself and the stove – a simple but effective way of controlling the heat. In my distant corner, I had the benefit of any warmth that was not absorbed by Harry's back or the desk. Across at Bentham, a lady clerk had a huge room above a grocer's shop in which to deal with *Dalesman* subscriptions. There she developed a novel way of restricting the warmth from an electric fire to the area where it would do most good – her body. That heat was fed into a tunnel formed of packets of books, with corrugated paper above. The tunnel led directly to her desk.

Harry Scott's approach to publishing had

about it some of the Edwardian grace. If he became ruffled, he kept it to himself. He was inclined to base complicated business decisions on hunches and he once set the price of a *Dalesman* book rather lower than the cost of production. After years during which the magazine was hand-set and printed by Messrs Lambert at the Caxton Press, Settle, we went to Dixon and Stell of Cross Hills, thence to Messrs Atkinson and Pollitt of Kendal. I never saw Harold Lambert in the office, but Harold Dixon and Harry Firth called to be welcomed amiably by Harry Scott. He did get a little 'prickly' when he had to negotiate a new printing to take allowance of rising costs and rising expectations by the printers.

Most days, we did editorial work and then we engaged in some other activity – a campaign for new advertising, or the production of a book; a round of letters aimed at ensuring a supply of review copies of books or the tedious but essential task of sending out subscription copies of the magazine to interested folk. Harry Scott's special ambition was to get a copy of the magazine into the waiting room of every dentist in the land.

Dominating the staircase at Fellside was a large painting by Constance Pearson of Malham – a study of the clints at the head of Malham Cove, with a prospect of Malhamdale, painted in cloudy weather. The soft greys and greens made a strong appeal to me. We had seen so many paintings of the Dales brought in by amateur artists – paintings as garish as chocolate box covers – that it was a delight to see the work of poor-weather practitioners for whom lowering clouds and lack-lustre moorland offered a challenge. Constance Pearson's paintings adorned one of our first major books, *Malham and Malham Moor*, the text for which was written by Arthur Raistrick.

From a deep window on the landing, one might look into the back garden. Here Mrs Scott laboured hard and long at her gardening. Here the family relaxed on old-fashioned summer days. I recall an article written by Harry Scott that began: 'My small nephew knows that summer has arrived – he has just been stung by a bee!' In wartime, the garden housed a pig that helped the Scotts to supplement the meagre food rations, though this batch of pork had poor keeping qualities, caused – said the butcher – because the pig had been handled rather roughly when it was being driven up some steps. 'It must have got het up,' he added.

In the running of the house, Dorothy Scott had the considerable help of Doreen Shaw, whose breezy personality enlivened many a day. She shared the responsibility of keeping us supplied with coffee in the morning and tea in the afternoon. In this respect, it was a normal office. When the Scotts were away from home, I had to be especially vigilant to ensure that no sheep placed its cleaves in the garden. I would attend to the morning mail and then saunter to the post office, pausing on the Brokken Bridge to watch the local dipper 'curtseying' on a rounded boulder or entering the clear water to search the bed of the beck for food.

When the postal business was done, I had to wait for the morning bus to Bentham, handing over a parcel of completed subscription forms that would be collected at the other end by Elsie Dickinson. It was during the wait that I could catch up with local gossip, which Harry Scott once described as 'the small change of village life'. Once, Ben Hudson, a local farmer, and his wife Dora were waiting for the bus, intent on going on holiday. When I inquired about their destination, Mrs

Hudson said it was Morecambe, 'but after half an hour, Ben will be asking the way to Lancaster auction mart'. Much later, when Mrs Vant was in residence at Clapham, she had a pet duck which travelled with her on the bus.

In autumn, another break in the editorial routine occurred when a load of logs arrived for the winter fires. Harry Scott included in his list of pleasures the act of 'lighting fires in cold rooms'. He went into a state of semi-hibernation during the winter, devoting most of his time to reading. The sitting-room came into its own – its snugness off-set the effects of the wild weather. With the curtains drawn, and

with the heat from a coal fire seeking out every chilly recess, Harry Scott plodded steadily through the latest books or joined a little group in playing Canasta. His wife was rarely still. Even when the snack meal had been made, her fingers moved restlessly with the latest item of knitting or she scribbled names and addresses on $9'' \times 6''$ envelopes, into which would be slipped specimen copies of the magazine, to be posted far and wide in the hope of attracting new readers. There were times when a working party was organised, with everyone filling envelopes.

In time, even the patient and kind-hearted Dorothy Scott felt that the office should be moved so that she could recover her sitting-room. Ingleborough Estate, which had provided the 'little house' for rent in 1934, now made available for sale

Fellside, Clapham, the first home of The Dalesman. (*Steve Burke*)

some old workshops 'up t'ginnel'. They were extensively altered. The old 'saw pit' was filled in and an old, hand-operated, estate fire-fighting appliance was trundled away.

When Harry Scott died in 1978, his ashes were placed in the rose bed of the garden that had taken shape at the front of the office. I recall that as we gathered for an informal little ceremony, rain began to fall as though from a celestial hose-pipe. An elderly relative of the Scotts talked about him at length, indifferent to the rain. If the human spirit does endure, then Harry's must have been quietly chuckling at our plight!

PROBLEMS, PROBLEMS . . .

When Mrs Scott finally put her foot down and said she wanted her sitting-room, dining room, and cellar back, Mr Scott decided to move his overflowing office. The cardboard boot box, which he boasted in the early days held all the subscribers' addresses, had been engulfed. Some Ingleborough Estate buildings, no longer in use, were converted into offices, and we began the task of transferring books, papers, files, typewriters, desks, etc., to the other side of the village. I borrowed a handcart from the Estate, and Bill Mitchell and I piled it up with too much paper and lighter articles. Down from the gate at Fellside, a strong gust of wind lifted a shower of papers, and dropped most of them in the beck. We retrieved some, but possible masterpieces of literature were wafted under the bridge, over the waterfall, and went to join the Wenning.

Dick Clark, a retired railway signalman, was given the part-time job of cleaning the offices, looking after the coke-fired boiler, making tea, and taking the mail to the post office. Dick, a chubby, friendly, popular man, a competent water-colour painter, was very conscientious. When he brought tea in the afternoon, two cups on a tray, he sometimes said, 'Lets see, one of these is sweetened,' and he took a loud sip. 'It's the other one,' he said, as he handed the tasted cup to me. Then he groped in his jacket pocket and brought out two dingy biscuits, placing one in each saucer. We often wondered how long they had been there.

In 1963 there was a heavy snowfall, starting on Boxing Day and lasting six weeks. The severe frost stopped the water supply to most of Clapham, including the *Dalesman* office. Our house, at the top of the village, the second on the supply from the lake, was free, however, so we became the source of supply. We took large jugs and cans of water for the office coffee and tea, but we couldn't take enough to operate the toilet, so all the staff trooped up to our house every lunchtime to spend a penny. Some of them actually left a penny on the window bottom!

Recollected by Eddie Gower, The Dalesman's *first advertisement manager.*

PIONEER PHOTOGRAPHER . . .

It was in the January 1949 issue of *The Dalesman* that I first had the pleasure of seeing one of my black and white photographs reproduced – a study of an elderly lady leaning on an old gateway with her dog and cat sat in front of her. For this I was paid one guinea – quite a goodly sum in those far off days. This was to be the start of a long and happy association which has lasted forty years during which time I have had many hundred pictures – both black and white and also colour – reproduced in the pages of *The Dalesman*.

It was through my correspondence with the Editor of *The Dalesman* that I eventually met Mr Harry J. Scott who held that office for so long. Despite scores of letters passing between us and an easy familiarity which built up, he always addressed his letters 'Dear Mr Edenbrow' and I in turn wrote to him 'Dear Mr Scott'. Our first meeting was in Clapham, several years after my first letter, when I had acquired my first car and visited the offices of *The Dalesman* with my wife, Marian, and was made more than welcome, given coffee and shown round the various rooms by Mr Scott.

Later I was to arrange a visit to my own home when Mr Scott came to lecture to our Photographic Society. I must confess to feeling a little apprehensive on the night of the lecture when I realised that he had come equipped with only about thirty or so slides when the average needed for a full-scale evening

lecture was a hundred. I had not reckoned with Mr Scott's ability as a storty-teller. With his few slides – used merely as a 'hook' on which to hang his wonderful and comical Yorkshire tales, he had a roomful of members and friends enchanted for over an hour, helpless with laughter and still wanting more after the lecture was over. Mr Scott, a tall, tweed-clad, pipe-smoking genial countryman somewhat after the image of Sherlock Holmes and with a compelling personality to match his stature, could with the aid of a few colour slides bring into the town a breath of the Yorkshire countryside with its down to earth humour and wit, leaving an audience with an unforgettable memory of the occasion.

One incident, which took place many years ago when I was motoring round east Yorkshire in search of pictures, was when I pulled up at a one-pump petrol station attached to the village black-smith's shop. I asked for a 'fill-up' but the owner, on seeing me take out my cheque-book, gruffly said, 'Ah doan't tek cheques – cash only here'. However, he leaned over to have a closer look at the printed name on my cheque-book and said, 'Edenbrow – art tha the chap that has all them photos in't *Dalesman?*' I confirmed, highly flattered, that I was indeed the same fellow. The owner placed the petrol hose into the car's petrol tank and said, 'Na then lad, 'ow many did tha say tha wanted?'

John Edenbrow

2

COUNTY OF CONTRASTS
A Tour of the Broad Acres

Our County

Grimy townships cling to craggy hills,
Soot-stained dwellings in the narrow streets,
Grey smoke belching from the sprawling
    mills,
This dull sight is what the traveller meets
Through industrial Yorkshire.

Misty purples under moorland sky,
Glowing crimson as the sunlight wanes,
Springy turfland and the curlew's cry,
Shaggy cattle on the winding lanes,
This, again, is Yorkshire.

Georgian mansion that 'His Lordship'
    owns,
Rolling parkland with entrancing views,
Lichened farmhouse of enduring stones,
Sturdy farmer with his thoughts on ewes –
All are part of Yorkshire.

Mountain torrent with its rocky bed,
Verdant downland merging with the seas,
Ancient churches where the sleeping dead
Lie with sunlight filt'ring through the trees
In our varied Yorkshire.

Changing county with its Ridings three,
Homely people with a stubborn pride,
Dry-walled acres are a home to me
Once the stranger – now with roots well-
    tied
In this lovely Yorkshire.

D. WHITING
(January 1965)

CLAPHAM – DALES VILLAGE WITH A DIFFERENCE

It seems only right to begin a journey through the Broad Acres at The Dalesman's home-village of Clapham, six miles north-west of Settle. W.R. Mitchell guided readers on a tour of the village to mark the magazine's fortieth anniversary.

THE VILLAGE of Clapham, in which *The Dalesman* has been published for forty years, stands where a beck from the heights of Ingleborough breaks from the confines of Clapdale. It does this in style. After heavy rain, the water thunders down three man-made falls and then makes a mighty leap near the church with such force that the ground appears to tremble. Clapdale retains a sense of mystery. You must traverse it on foot. Follow the unmetalled carriageway to Ingleborough Cave, and you walk largely in shade, with the smell of leaf-mould in your nostrils. Massed trees, groves of rhododendron and bamboo give the appearance of a Himalayan valley.

The beck, which rises high on the fell, spends one-and-a-half miles of its life underground, having plunged into the main chamber of Gaping Gill as a waterfall of over 300 feet. In due course, and after flowing down a ravine, the beck enters Ingleborough Lake. Until six years ago, this acted like a giant settling tank. It was the source of Clapham's water supply. Improvements had been made in the late 1880s, when small settling tanks complete with a bacteriological filter were installed. A water supply that served the village was extended to the farms of Eldroth in the 1930s, and in the 1970s a fresh source, in gritstone across the valley, was provided.

Clapham was the first village in the North-West to have electrical street light-ing; it was derived from the powerful flow of Clapdale water. A turbine was installed at the sawmill to assist with estate work, and at night-time power conserved in batteries was used to light up the village. At Clapham, the beck makes the strongest visual impact. Where the village now stands was a glacial lake – its moraine still evident near the modern cemetery. The beck divides the village into two and made it necessary for many bridges to be constructed. Confined by hills, its development inhibited by the beck, the village spreads from either side, rather than along, the main road through the district.

As a settlement, Clapham is old, being of Anglian foundation. The Claphams were succeeded by the Ingilbys, who in turn gave way gracefully to the Farrers. The Clapham we see today is essentially their creation, many of the buildings dating from around 1840. When Dr J.A. Farrer inherited the estate twenty-five years ago, Clapham had fifty-two houses, fifty-one of which belonged to Ingleborough estate and were rented. The exception was the vicarage. Farrer enterprise created the Hall which, during the days when the main family home was in London, was little more than a shooting lodge, to be occupied during the season. It was extended at various times. An old trackway was bridged so that the grounds could be expanded without interruption, and The Tunnels are now a familiar feature to those whose walk to the fells begins near the church. Ingleborough Lake, created by embankment, was at first a fashionable status symbol. The water is some 40 feet deep near a bank dominated by cliffs. A boathouse was constructed.

In due course, a new drive was cut from the main road to the house; the drive is no longer used, but the copper beeches planted beside it bring a glow of rich colour to the area. The body of the church was re-built, and a building boom developed as many new dwellings were constructed. The Farrers provided a sewage system by 1893. They ensured that Clapham continued to have a well-wooded appearance. Among the more unusual species seen today are

Clapham church, drawn by Godfrey Wilson who contributed much of *The Dalesman*'s earliest artwork.

Norway maple, sugar maple and whitebeam. An almond – here at the northern limit of its natural range – could not be kept alive, alas, and was removed.

Clapham was for years the centre of a sporting estate, and by 1890 the rents from shooting were much larger than were those from the farms. Farming and forestry dominate the estate activity today. Ingleborough Estate has 3,200 acres of farmland and its woods, some of them high-lying, cover 210 acres. Manorial rights held by the Farrers extend over 7,000 acres, including half of Ingleborough, a noble fell which within living memory was outstanding for red grouse, being bountifully covered by heather. The heather declined as the number of grazing sheep rose.

Walk up the village from the Fountain, ideally on a sunny afternoon in autumn,

GODFREY WILSON.

and no great changes are apparent. The buildings seen are venerable. Across the beck lies the market cross, and beyond it is a manor house that became a Reading Room. This building appeared in the days of the Ingilbys, and is used as an information centre by the Dales National Park. Last summer it was visited by 42,000 people. An adjacent car park has space for sixty cars and eight buses. A packhorse-type bridge extends across the beck in a single graceful span. It is known as T'Brocken Bridge, a notion that must go back to the early part of last century when it was built, replacing a wooden structure washed away by a flood. I shall always associate that bridge with the dipper, a distinctive bird of Clapham. I have often watched the bird perched on a stone or moving through gin-clear water, using its wings for propulsion against the current. In this area, too, is the start of a waterside path leading into the tangle of The Park which, before the Farrers re-styled Clapham, was part of a tract known as the Arch-deacon's Croft. Could it have been glebe land?

Ingleborough Hall is not seen from the village; it lies beyond earthen banks and trees. Today it is used as an outdoor centre, being owned by the county council. It had previously catered for West Riding children who might benefit from the fresh air and healthy exercise, which they did. Through the sawmill yard tramp thousands of visitors intent on walking through Clapdale and on to Ingleborough Cave and Trow Gill. The more athletic scramble on to the open moor and follow a much eroded footpath to Gaping Gill.

Since 1963, the Cave Rescue Organisation has had its headquarters at Clapham. The CRO was formed in 1935. During the first twenty years, there was an average of a call a year. Now there is a call-out every week. One day the team impressed an elderly woman by their efficiency. She broke an ankle, just as cave rescuers, complete with stretcher, were hurrying to another emergency call. She thought that they were seeking her and thankfully occupied the stretcher.

An alternative route back to the village runs close to Clapdale Farm, which was described as a 'castle large and strong . . . on ye outskirts of the high hill Ingleborough.' I used to hear a story of a secret passage. Could there be an unexplored cave system in that area? This is a countryside abounding in mysteries. Is the ancient cut, high on Ingleborough, really of monastic origin? Were the human bones recovered from a cave in 1947 really those of a German agent who was parachuted into Yorkshire during the 1939–45 war? There was something eerie about Ingleborough Cave in the days when Arnold Brown guided visitors into the further reaches, for he handed each member of the party a three-pronged holder on which candles were placed. When the explorers were deep underground, Arnold would play a series of notes, rapping the key of the cave against stalactites.

To devout rock-gardeners, Clapham is well-known as the birthplace of Reginald Farrer, who established in the grounds of Ingleborough Hall a rock garden incorporating his ideas about how alpines should be displayed – in pockets of earth between stones set as though to represent a natural run of strata. He first outlined his ideas in *My Rock Garden*, published in 1907. Over twenty-five years ago I made my own humble contribution to the well-being of his garden by helping Jack Winton, the gardener at Ingleborough Hall, rid the rock garden of an invasion of mare's-tail. As a member of the Clapham Art Group I had the pleasure of meetings held in the building which Farrer had used as a potting shed. Clapham now has its Reginald Farrer trail, of some one-and-a-half miles, based on the old carriageway through the woods. A stone bridge, deep-sunk in the luxurious growth of rhododendrons and bamboos somewhere in the ravine below Ingleborough Cave was associated with Farrer and called the Chinese Bridge.

When I first knew Clapham, during the 1939–45 war, it was basically the Clapham of the previous century. The *New Inn* was really quite old. The painted sign of the older hostelry, the *Bull and Cave*, was stowed away in an estate workshop: the place is now a farm. So many people turned up for dances in the village hall that one had almost to fight one's way out of the area, constricted by the necessity to find a stage for the band. All the villagers were well known to each other. Swans, disillusioned with life in the chilly, gloomy Ingleborough Lake, plodded through the village seeking food, and in the depth of winter, hill sheep wandered down to the Clapham gardens to feast on wallflowers. Traffic was negligible. We remember occasions on which vehicles failed to negotiate the blind bends or the hump-backed bridge and came to grief lying smashed on the bed of the beck. A lorry full of tinned food left the road. It was at a time when food was rationed! A lorry driver from Leeds ran over a swan, tossed the corpse of the regal bird over the bridge parapet, and blithely told an enquirer: 'It was nobbut a duck.'

(March 1979)

TWO SMALL CORNERS

Geoffrey Smith took time off from the world of gardening to visit his favourite places in the Dales.

NO SINGLE person can gain more than a casual acquaintance with all the Dales, no matter how determinedly they pursue intimacy. What can happen, as it has in my case, is that small corners – sometimes only a few acres in extent – develop a special significance. Occasionally the rapport is immediate, in most instances the relationship grows out of familiarity. Over the years repeated visits, at all seasons, develop an understanding which is more spiritual than actual. I believe that such places are an essential part of maintaining a whole mind. Corners of wilderness provide a contrast which enables modern man to keep a proper perspective on what is important or trivial in a world becoming increasingly insulated from, and unaware of, natural things.

One such place – what Richard Jefferies describes so vividly as 'a rocky cell in concentrated silence of green things' – is close enough to where I live to be visited frequently, yet so small as not to warrant a name on the Ordnance Survey map. The sense of lived-in quiet pervading the place

is accentuated rather than depleted by the sound of the beck as it cascades down a steep rock slide. In winter the tone increases in proportion to the volume of peat-stained water rushing down from the moor above. In summer the tenor is merely a suggestion, a murmurous undertone which serves only to increase the mood of reflective consciousness essential for properly appreciating the unspoiled beauty of the location. The descent into the ghyll is steep, almost precipitous, in the upper part; lower down the slope is easier with silver birch and rowan able to gain root hold. Bordering the stream, ancient, many-branched oaks, with a sprinkling of holly increase the feeling of secure isolation. A carpet of moss of a particularly vivid shade of emerald green carpets a part of the ghyll kept continuously moist by the cascade.

Being so close to the heather-covered moors the variety of bird life is limited by the amount of food provided in the ghyll itself. Dippers haunt the stream, blackbirds gain full appreciation, for each note of song is heard full-rounded and free from competition. Long-tailed tits engage in endless chit-chat practising their trapeze artist foraging for food in the trees above. In May curlews and plovers persuade spring to spread a flush of delicate green over the intakes. Of all seasons it is in autumn that I enjoy my visits most as the leaves on birch and rowan change colour. Sunlight forming a lazy pattern through the tree branches across a leaf-dusted, moss-carpeted, floor serves to emphasise the natural completeness of the seasonal pattern.

One must be careful in conserving place-induced moods or, like water lifted in cupped hands, they can quickly be lost. And so it is with another corner which I visit at intervals. It is impossible to com-

Geoffrey Smith.

pare the fragile beauty of the first with the awe-inspiring, at times violent splendour of Ravens Ghyll. Here the stream drops almost a thousand feet in a series of jagged falls. Even in summer drought when the water level is no more than a trickle, flecks of foam betray a violence restrained. Beech trees growing tall and straight in the deep, sheltered ghyll offer shade in summer, red gold of leaf in autumn and symmetry of outline all year round.

I visit the wooded ravine most frequently during the winter months. The silver and lime-green boles of the beech add to the sense of cathedral quiet, particularly when the stream is for a brief time hushed under a casing of ice. The forest floor is carpeted in moss and nowhere else have I ever found such a variety of shades and textures of green. Moss covers the stones, fallen trees and the bare earth in a deep carpet and leaves no tracks to betray my passing. It is a wild, lonely site with a wanton, violent beauty which finds complete expression in strength, for even in spring the steep boulder-studded grandeur rarely softens to gentleness. During all my visits I am aware that Ravens Ghyll owes all of its beauty to natural events, nothing to man. Had humankind never walked on this earth the knife gash cut in the steeply sloping hillside would be as it is. Should man succeed, as seems more than likely, in self-destruction, Ravens Ghyll will remain, of that I am sure, aloof, uncompromising, inviolate. That is why the place restores me.

I find that watching the sun rise on a dawn-fresh morning in spring more than compensates for being out of bed early. From a knoll on the wood edge there is a prime view to the east as the sun's rays reveal points of green on the tallest trees. A dunnock or possibly a robin tries a few night-cooled notes of song. A thrush just below in the still, shadowed ghyll takes and embellishes the first, almost apologetic piping and suddenly like a tidal wave light and bird song fill the dale. To watch a spring dawn in the Dales is, so far as I am concerned, like witnessing the miracle of creation all over again.

(August 1988)

SHODDY KINGDOM

Batley, a town built on shoddy, was thinly disguised as Barfield in the humorous Yorkshire novel Value for Money *– in 1955 made into a film starring John Gregson and Diana Dors. Its author was Derrick Boothroyd, who in 1978 described his home town.*

BATLEY'S scenic charm is not the chief claim to fame of this West Yorkshire industrial town, which a film director once viewed from the commanding heights of Hanging Heaton and pronounced to be the nearest approach to hell he had ever seen. When Batley was my home town in the 1920s and 1930s, however, it was famous for two things – its rugby league football team which, way back in antiquity, had won the cup, and, of course, shoddy, which was discovered in the town in 1813.

For the enlightenment of non-Yorkshiremen who have never heard of shoddy in any other connotation than what the Oxford dictionary unflatteringly defines as 'counterfeit, pretentious, trashy – anything of worse quality than it claims or seems to have' – shoddy is a valuable textile raw material which brought about a sartorial revolution in the 19th century. The use of it dramatically reduced the price of woollen clothing and brought it within the means of the working man and woman for the first time in history. The attire of

the workman became indistinguishable from that of his master – a social change of great significance.

Batley in 1813 was a completely rural area dotted with the cottages of the hand-loom weavers. The discoverer of shoddy was a man called Benjamin Law. He found that if old clothes made of wool were ground into a fibrous mass (shoddy) they could be mixed with virgin wool and rema-nufactured into new cloth. From 1813 onwards, assisted by the development of the power loom, shoddy mills sprang up all over the town and by 1850 there were over thirty, most of them substantial three or four-storey buildings, each accommodating several hundred workpeople. It took a couple of wars – the Crimean and the Franco-Prussian – to bring Batley's indus-trial expansion to its peak, and Batley in the 70s was a microcosm of Victorian England – a town of great industry and enterprise but also of great extremes of wealth and poverty.

The manufacturers owned carriages and pairs and lived in great luxury in the select residential area known as Upper Batley and the workers lived in grim, back-to-back terrace houses in the town, with twenty or more people sharing one outside privy. This first generation of manufacturers was largely uneducated and some had to sign their cheques with a cross because they could neither read nor write. The manu-facturers competed with each other in their display of wealth, just as they competed in business, and every house that was built in Upper Batley was a little bigger and more grandiose than the last.

The story is told of one illiterate *nouveau riche* whose sole instruction to the local architect was to build him 't'biggest house in t'district'. The architect asked him what aspect he would like. The manufacturer looked at him perplexed and asked if the last manufacturer's mansion to be built had an aspect. The architect said all houses must have an aspect.

'Aye, well, then,' came the reply, 'tha mun gi' me three.' It was said that when his house had been built – complete with legions of reception rooms and bedrooms – he spent most of his time in his shirt sleeves in the kitchen.

Some of the big manufacturing families, now public school educated, still survived in Batley in the 1930s – the Taylors, Stubleys, Robinsons, Blackburns – and the doyen was Theodore C. Taylor, head of the famous profit-sharing firm, J. T. & J. Taylor Ltd., and undoubtedly Batley's most famous son. He was a Member of Parlia-ment for many years and lived to the remarkable age of 102. Theodore Taylor represented the triology of Victorian causes which dominated the social environment in Batley – Liberalism, non-conformity and teetotalism – and although a great bene-factor to his employees through his profit-sharing scheme he was an autocrat to his bootlaces and ruled his workpeople with a rod of iron almost until the day of his death. He celebrated his 100th birthday by doing the palais glide with some of the mill girls on a trip to Blackpool!

Two other institutions in Batley in that era were the two local newspapers, the *Batley News* and the *Batley Reporter*. The *Batley News*, edited by Rayner Roberts, was Conservative and Church of England and had a mania for Freemasonry. The *Reporter* was Liberal and non-conformist with a

OPPOSITE
Much of the old West Riding of Yorkshire is a blend of mills, terraced housing and open countryside – as epitomised at Hebden Bridge in the Calder Valley. (*Clifford Robinson*)

mania for temperance – characteristics attributable not so much to its editor, Oswald Jones, as to the chairman of the board of directors, the redoubtable Theodore C. Taylor.

While the *News* churned out column after column about the Freemasons (which presumably no-one read except Rayner Roberts) the *Reporter* churned out column after column about the battle with the brewers, which was run by a formidable woman known as Mrs Herbert North, who was reputed to throw people out of her house if they had as much as a cork in their pockets.

Another mania which the two papers shared – and which presumably kept them in business – was a mania for funerals, another example of the rather lugubrious flavour of Batley life at that time. Both papers carried dozens of funeral reports every week containing long lists of family mourners and others present, and long lists of 'floral tributes' complete with their inscriptions. The reports usually concluded with a reference to the undertakers who were described as carrying out the arrangements with reverence and dignity. Sometimes, however, the name of the undertaker was omitted altogether. This was when he did not advertise.

Unlike the Freemasonry and the Temperance reports the funeral reports were read avidly by everyone, as I soon discovered when I joined the editorial staff of the *Batley Reporter* in 1938 as an articled pupil in journalism at a salary of 7s.6d. a week. Initially my work consisted almost entirely of covering funerals and if I got an initial wrong or failed to give the name of the firm which a particular mourner was representing I was in immediate trouble. The importance of putting the name of the firm in the paper was not apparent to me

until a mourner explained one day that the deceased was one of his best customers. 'If tha' doesn't put t' name of t' firm in there'll be no more bloody business for me,' he explained.

This commercial aspect of funerals underlined the mercenary preoccupation of many Batley businessmen. It was not uncommon, for instance, for mourners at a manufacturer's funeral to gather at the foot of the steps of Zion Methodist chapel (known locally as Shoddy Temple because of its strong commercial links) after the cortege had departed for the cemetery and do a bit of business before returning to their mills. Nor was it unusual for speculation to take place on the amount the deceased's will would be proved for. 'Thirty thousand at least,' one mourner would suggest. 'I'd put it at nearer fifty,' another would observe. 'He'd never spend a shilling if sixpence would do. And he always diddled t'tax a bit.'

Since those days the appearance and activities of Batley have changed a lot. The soot-blackened town hall and public library which stood at opposite ends of the cobbled market square as appropriate monuments to Batley's industrial history have been sand-blasted by the environmentalists and are now so disgustingly clean that they could belong to a spa or a seaside resort rather than to shoddyopolis. The dark satanic mills which Blake must have had in mind when he wrote *Jerusalem* have also either been pulled down and replaced by modern housing estates or converted into streamlined factories no longer producing shoddy but kitchen furniture, electronic equipment, birthday cards and, of all things, ladies' panties. Even the name shoddy has been euphemised out of existence, and what remains of the local industry following the traumatic contractions of the whole wool textile industry during the past twenty years rejoices in the name of the waste reclamation industry. It must make the old shoddy manufacturers turn over in their graves in Batley cemetery.

(May 1978)

Yorkshire is an amazing county of contrasts. Both the rolling Wolds and the heather-covered North York Moors are utterly different to the Dale country of the west.

DALES OF THE EAST RIDING

I SUPPOSE that if I claim to be a Dalesman from the East Riding of Yorkshire I shall be rejected as an upstart by that *bona fide* clan of Dalesmen from the West and North Ridings. But I shall persist even in company of the élite. Without attempting to conceal the vast acreage of flat, low-level farmland that makes up the greater area of our East Riding, we can produce an idyllic nest of dales that every cartographer with a reputation to maintain will accept without quibble. Our sense of realism will not allow us to challenge a cluster of great names like Teesdale, Swaledale, Garsdale, Wensleydale, Nidderdale, Wharfedale, Airedale and Ribblesdale, of which some readers may have heard. But while conceding the reputation of those giants, even beyond the borders of Yorkshire, we East Riding Dalesmen would not exchange them for our small nest of four.

For centuries we have been justifiably proud of our Brantingham dale, Elloughton dale, Welton dale and Swanland dale; all genuine dales, not village streets or cart tracks with fancy names. Possibly such euphonious names have never hitherto struck a chord in the ears of Dalesmen outside the Riding; and, if references are required, we give you the massive Bartholomew, whose survey atlas of the county, old or new edition, is as good as a banker's chit for our reputation.

Where exactly are these dales that this fellow is so het up about? Why have they not crept out of the atlas before now? We cannot understand the omission ourselves, except, of course, for the possible reason that East Riding Dalesmen are as modest as violets. Then, too, this Riding has always been the Cinderella of the County, the forgotten corner of England . . .

Our four dales spread up to the Wolds like the Prince of Wales' feathers, all converging from the flat land above the Humber in the direction of the big village of Brough. Whereas the more famous dales of the other Ridings mostly derive their names from the rivers that scour them, our dales are identified by the very old East Riding villages of Brantingham, Elloughton, Welton and Swanland. The first three lie at the very entrance to their dales, while Swanland is at the summit. Within

this cluster Bartholomew also clearly shows a Brookdale, but that is a farm at the foot of Elloughton dale.

In the East Riding we do not divide our countryside with a hard outline of stone walls as they do in the west, and so the pathway through the dales is an avenue of wooded slopes and soft banks, a natural setting in the land, not comparable in magnitude with the climbs up famous dales, but more seclusive, more rural – and less exhaustive.

Elloughton and Brantingham cut deeper into the Wolds than do Welton and Swanland, and one invariably walks or drives up them in silent possession. Brantingham is the longest, stretching for nearly three miles. In summer heat it has a lush tropical

Middleton-on-the-Wolds. (*Richard H. Pearson*)

setting. It is the most beautiful of the four as well as the most remote. One of its attractions is the old village church half a mile from the village and in the dale itself. It stands alone on the straight stretch of road, its ancient grey walls embedded in the foliage of the sloping bank of the dale. That slow promenade of the villagers to and from church on Sundays in that peaceful rural setting is touching to behold. It is a perfect path for its purpose.

Elloughton dale, also leading straight from its village with a level stretch, is about two miles closer to the Humber. It is shorter, about one-and-a-half to two miles, and there are few inhabitants in its lower

OPPOSITE
Daffodil time at Warter in East Yorkshire.
(*Ivan E. Broadhead*)

reaches. There are steep sides to the dale, which are considerably wooded, but in the upper reaches leading into the Wolds it is all farmed, arable and cattle, particularly sheep.

Welton dale and its village are about a mile further south, and it differs from the other three in that it does not offer itself as a road to anywhere. It is part of a large estate that in its heyday was thought to reach from the Humber bank below the village to Scarborough. It is a natural dale in that no road has been cut through it; of woodland and grassland, and once a favourite scene for picnics. But the changes that have befallen so many of the country's large estates in the last decade are in evidence in Welton, and it has a wild and rather forlorn air in these days.

A stranger wandering from the old village might only discover the rough route to the dale by chance, and then wonder if he were trespassing by struggling through the heavy gate to the wood. If he then bears on through the wood instead of entering the open dale lower down, he will suddenly feel a shock of morbid curiosity by emerging into a dark clearing amongst the trees in which stands a decaying, dome-shaped mausoleum. It is the burial place of an old local family, a melancholy monument in an eerie, sunless vacuum in the woods. On a higher level and parallel to the Welton dale is a good road, leading out of the village to the Wolds and eventually converging on to the continuation of Elloughton dale.

Swanland dale also rises out of the village of Welton from another end, and from the base here one catches a glimpse of a section of white road curving against a fringe of tall trees to the top of the Wolds. It leads to Swanland, the nearest of the dale villages to Hull, a pretty, neat and spruce place in contrast to the rural antiquity of Brantingham, Elloughton and Welton . . .

These then are our dales, overlooking the wide plain of Howdenshire to the west, the broad gleaming sweep of the Humber to the south and its confluence with the Ouse and Trent.

Charles Dixon
(August 1956)

MOORLAND DAYS

A STEEP moorside, bracken-covered and boulder-studded, with sheep tracks covered with short, springy grass; a small copse of fir trees near an old track, and beyond the greenery of the valley a river winding like a blue ribbon between clean, stony banks. A hundred gem-like pictures like these are still jumbled in my mind after some days I have spent on the high moors of North-east Yorkshire. They have been memorable days perhaps because of the change of scene and perhaps because I saw them under ideal conditions.

The sun shone undisturbed by cloud on the whole countryside, but there was a light refreshing breeze; a heat haze hung over the ground, and through it the dry-stone walls and the hedges appeared to be shivering. The hum of insect life mingled with the reedy song of a yellow hammer, but otherwise the country was still and quiet. Along a well-worn sheep track I came across an old man rummaging among moorland growth on hands and knees, with a brown paper bag near at hand. He was gathering crowberries, the fruit of a rather insignificant little plant quite common on many northern moors. Crowberries are not unlike bilberries, which grow in much the same conditions, but they are smaller and not as rich in colour. They are still made into pies and served piping hot, although a

good crowberry pie demands a little more sugar than one made with bilberries. Or so he told me.

Further along the track I flushed a cock ring ouzel. This summer visitor looks very much like a blackbird, but haunts open country and has a beautiful white crescent on its breast and whitish edgings to its feathers. The way the bird remained poised on a large boulder, stonily alert, before disappearing mysteriously into a stretch of bracken after a short flight also reminded me of the blackbird. I flushed the bird again, and this time it flew swiftly to the copse and was soon lost to sight among the trees.

A curlew rose from the ground higher up the moorside, uttering its lively rippling call, but instead of flying off it flew down

Hasty Bank, North York Moors. (*Alec Wright*)

Hasty Bank.

towards me. Jerky harsh cries came from its long curved bill as it flew low over the bracken, barely cleared an old stone wall and alighted in a field of rough pastureland on the other side, its wings held up for a few moments before they were folded away. This was repeated a number of times until I reached the moor top, when it alighted on a boulder. I put down its strange behaviour to family matters, for at this time of the year the large waders are busily engaged in teaching their offspring the ins and outs of existence. Soon the families will fly to their winter quarters at the coast, where they will dine on sea creatures until next year.

A pall of smoke attracted me further on to the moors, where a stretch of heather was blazing furiously. Much ground had been bared by flame when I arrived, but the breeze was gradually driving the fire to a junction of walls where it would burn itself out. The annual burning of strips of heather to make way for fresh growth has been practised in moorland parts of the country for a number of years, but this fire may have been accidental as there appeared to be no one about to control its spread.

There were a number of house martins in the air. One swept low over the lane and rather surprised me by alighting on the ground near a muddy puddle. I understood its action, however, when it scooped up a pellet of mud with its beak and flew off to one of the farm buildings. Housing problems were in the air and, unlike the situation in the world of men and women today, the bird had plenty of materials and ample sites with which to tackle them.

It is curious how those moorlands of the North East can offer things rarely seen in

(Fred Lawson)

the Western dale country; foxgloves, which do not thrive on limestone, sundews, and a great many orchids. There were vast seas of heather, too, which was just beginning to take on its autumn purple, and acres of bracken, an evil plant in many ways but a delight to the eye whether in its spring colour of green or its autumnal brown. The soil has a reddish tinge which matches the red-tiled roofs of these parts. Beyond all this were glimpses of the sea far below, a lovely blue on these cloudless days and a glorious background to the rich colouring of the moorlands. Yorkshire is a wonderful county for contrasts and there are few things more striking than an exchange like this of limestone fell land for the colourful sweeping moorlands. Each has a beauty of its own.

OPPOSITE
Rievaulx Abbey, tucked in a hollow of the North York Moors west of Helmsley. (*Kenneth Scowen*)

Dalesman's Diary
(*August 1951*)

ROMANCE OF BAYTOWN

In 1966 Barrie Farnill told the remarkable story of Robin Hood's Bay in a Dalesman book. Eleven years later he took another look at the holiday township which has retained its salty character.

THAT magical crescent of cliff, sand and rock, sweeping from Ness Point to towering Ravenscar, a few miles south of Whitby, is known as Robin Hood's Bay. So is the red-roofed village clinging to both sides of a ravine carved centuries ago by King's Beck.

Fylingdales abounds in Norse names, yet its largest settlement carries a romantic reminder of a legendary, 13th-century folk hero, and it first bore this name, in records at least, in 1536. Why? Nobody knows. There are many theories, some more improbable than others. My own choice is the possible connection with the Bronze Age burial mounds overlooking the bay on the high moors to the south. Known as Robin Hood's Butts, they are associated with the mythical Robin Goodfellow, a woodland sprite of medieval folk mythology.

Too much academic discussion cannot improve the enormous natural charm of this place; in fact one more mystery to add to the rest even improves it. The fishing village atmosphere is still authentic, and mercifully ineradicable, as most of old Baytown is under a protection order as a historic centre. There can be very few holiday townships which retain such salty character. The very names of its tightly packed alleys, Tommy Baxter Street, Jim Bell's Stile, Fisherhead, and The Bolts – to name but a few – evoke haunting chords of times past, as do those of the natural features nearby, such as Boggle Hole, Stoupe Beck, Millers Nab, Home Haven,

and also the names of the scaurs, those long fingers of 140-million-year-old rock stretching seawards – Landing Scar, East Scar.

Thus the romance and generally unique qualities of 'Bay' have attracted many generations of holidaymakers over the past century and more. For many hundreds of years a fishing community, then a hide-out and depot for 18th-century smugglers, it has become a haven for those weary of cities. In 1817 there were five 60-ton fishing boats here, each manned by five men. These large craft fished between the coast and the Dogger Bank until November, their crews then turning to the smaller inshore cobles. And in 1867 the village owned a total of 174 ocean-going ships, many registered at Whitby. By 1914 there were but two families, the Storms and the Dukes, fishing out of the Bay. Old Baytown had thirteen pubs; now there are three, but each has its own delightful personality. Of the few hundred cottages few are lived in all the year, but their roofs are secure, their fabric lovingly cherished. The holiday trade and the weekend cottagers have, in fact, preserved this village, which in the early 1930s might have been bought almost entirely for the price of a handful of its restored homes today.

Wild smugglers, villains who were not romantic but often mercilessly cruel, trod

OPPOSITE
The Openings, Robin Hood's Bay.
(*D. Mark Thompson*)

[30]

The Openings, Robin Hood's Bay. © D. Mark Thompson.

the passageways here for most of a century; their luggers were moored off the scaurs with a load of Dutch gin, and tea, and French brandy. Smugglers and donkey trains trod up the moorland track to Saltersgate and beyond. Fishermen, the bravest of harvesters, struggled against the North Sea for perhaps eight or nine centuries, their graceful cobles supposedly derived from the Norse longship. Now one or two light boats will ply the ancient trade for an hour or two a week. The red brick coastguard houses were sold; the lookout is opened up only in emergency. The lifeboat station, which saved 91 lives until it was closed in 1931, is now a shelter. The Bay Hotel at Wayfoot, where once a ship's bowsprit entered the bar window in a storm, is still open; its windows frame one of the finest views in England.

There is no happier summer community than this. My own second baptism, so to speak, came at the age of four, and this is about right for an introduction to one of the most delightful places in Britain, as thousands of families testify. Bay, as you grow to love it, soon becomes your home town.

Beauties and mysteries abound. There is the mystery of the early spring flowers which always bloom in the cliff gardens, however blustery and cold. There is the beauty of nearby Ravensdale Woods in autumn when the sun lights up the leaves like a million copper mirrors. There is the beauty of the bluff cottage stonework, mute witness to the strength and simplicity of a race of men long gone, and the sombre magic of giant Ravenscar lost in summer cloud cap or purple rainstorm. There are the miles of loneliness of the sands at low tide.

Why am I not planning to live there one day? Ah, that is a very different thing. Bay is a place that likes to be visited, like J. M. Barrie's island. To live here one would have to face the winter, the north-east wind boring your cheekbone like a hot wire, the endless thud of millions of tons of threshing water against the newish sea wall, the ghostliness of deserted alleys. You cannot live too long with ghosts for company. You would soon stop visiting the old church graveyard on the hill with its sleeping mariners at peace, and cease to watch every dark January corner for the echo of the Elizabethan seamen.

Leo Walmsley, who immortalised the fishing families of the 1930s with his beautifully characterised novels, was perhaps the last writer to actually witness the community at its natural best. Those days are gone and, though something of their spirit lingers, they cannot be easily recreated. The Bay's attraction lies in the remoteness of urban life, and the relaxation it offers through its refusal to become commercialised. Its quaintness is peopled now, when the tide of day-visitors has receded, into far-off hinterlands, by those of like mind, from all walks of life, but seeking a rich and warm community. The visitor may take his choice then, and dream on cliff walks and lonely beach; or join the village life.

The Congregational chapel in the old town offers a lively Sunday service, just as the old fisherfolk knew it. Beyond Bank Top, the parish church with its elegant tower stands like a small cathedral. There are Methodist and Roman Catholic churches. On Bank Top, a number of small hotels offer sophisticated pleasures. The three ancient taverns in the old village

OPPOSITE
Flamborough North Landing – one of the more spectacular pieces of the Yorkshire coastline, photographed in the late 1940s. (*Charles Haines*)

below, once depots for contraband goods, and linked to the stream tunnel that carries King's Beck, offer a warm, but well regulated evening. The old Men's Institute has developed a remarkably lively new lease of life, and the village notice-board carries news of all manner of social events, from local history lectures to coffee mornings.

The maze of alleys, with each corner turned, offering intriguing and often splendid views and every cottage with a story to tell if you can find the owner, is entertainment enough for a whole day's wandering within a radius of a mere 150 yards. Of course, TV screens flicker through the cottage windows but, if you seek the right places, the talk is still of lobstering and salmoning, of far-off places (the Merchant Navy tradition is still strong), of storm and tempest, and of local affairs with a flavour of their own.

If anyone were to ask me what I personally enjoyed most about Bay, I would, despite our long years together, so to speak, have to answer somewhat vaguely, 'Just being there.' Many will know what I mean. As Leo Walmsley once put it so succinctly and yet so eloquently: 'Intrinsically, its beauty and fascination remain.' One hopes they remain for ever.

(July 1977)

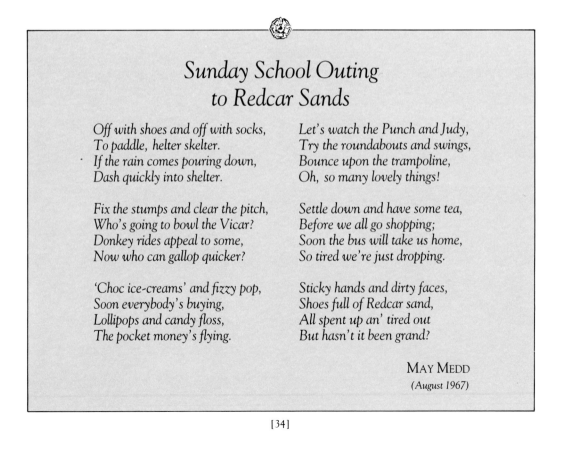

Sunday School Outing to Redcar Sands

Off with shoes and off with socks,
To paddle, helter skelter.
If the rain comes pouring down,
Dash quickly into shelter.

Fix the stumps and clear the pitch,
Who's going to bowl the Vicar?
Donkey rides appeal to some,
Now who can gallop quicker?

'Choc ice-creams' and fizzy pop,
Soon everybody's buying,
Lollipops and candy floss,
The pocket money's flying.

Let's watch the Punch and Judy,
Try the roundabouts and swings,
Bounce upon the trampoline,
Oh, so many lovely things!

Settle down and have some tea,
Before we all go shopping;
Soon the bus will take us home,
So tired we're just dropping.

Sticky hands and dirty faces,
Shoes full of Redcar sand,
All spent up an' tired out
But hasn't it been grand?

MAY MEDD
(August 1967)

3

A YEAR IN YORKSHIRE

FIVE SEASONS IN NORTH RIBBLESDALE

E.I. Myers succinctly observed that the Dales do not have spring, summer, autumn and winter. Instead there is lambing-time, cuckoo-time, hay-time, back-end and winter!

THE TERMS 'Spring, Summer, Autumn, Winter', are usually accepted as bearing some relation to the four seasons as experienced in most parts of the country, even in most parts of Yorkshire; but such nomenclature is useless in attempting to divide the weather of North Ribblesdale into sufficiently homogeneous groups to be classed as seasons. The months may vary in themselves enormously from one year to another; but no month except perhaps July is sure to be free from night frosts; flooded roads occur as regularly in June and in February; fogs and mists are as frequent in August as in November; a week in March may be more sunny and warm than any week in June; snow covers roses in November; leaves may decay and fall in August; there can be drought and withered grass in May; a snow-storm in mid-May is not a great rarity and I have heard the remark 'It blows back-endish' also in mid-May. How can one classify such weather into seasons?

The year in this Dale falls into five seasons. The first is Lambing-time, which begins at Horton the third week in March and continues into May. At the Settle end of the Dale, lambs are arriving from early March onwards, though at Selside the season does not really open until the first week in April, and continues longer correspondingly. The weather may be stormy or mild; there may be deep drifts of snow behind the walls, or there may be sunny skies with occasional scurries of snowflakes, or driving hailstorms; there may be rich emerald grass or there may be parched dry wisps in place of it; but every field is full of staid grey horned ewes and hordes of racing, leaping, chasing, white lambs with little black knees and noses. As the lambing season proceeds, the older lambs and their dams are moved to slightly higher ground, and the home pastures are replenished with fresh crops of frail-looking, though really hardy lambs. Then one day in May all the lower fields are empty; there has been a melodious medley of high pitched 'maas' and contralto 'baas', as the lambs were gathered for marking with the owner's mark, later to be shepherded up the moorland lanes to the higher pastures so that their first feeding-grounds may settle down to grow meadow grass. And the first season has merged into the second.

This is Cuckoo-time, and varies from two to six weeks in length. Now primroses crowd all the sheltered banks, powdering them thickly as if with pale yellow pollen-dust; cowslips cover the railway embankments, wild lilies of the valley lurk in certain of the woods, kingcups gild the marshy banks of streams, and the cuckoo calls from every clump of trees, his two-fold

note echoing across the valley from cock-crow till dusk. Now we Dale-dwellers agree that we are fortunate indeed to live in such lovely surroundings, for at this time all is fair. My advice to prospective visitors who have not yet become all-the-year-round devotees of our Dale is to come with the cuckoo and leave with him, for should the weather become cold and grey, cuckoo leaves us, for he is a fair-weather friend.

Cuckoo-time lasts normally until the third week in June, when most weather-wise farmers try to 'snatch' a field of hay, only a small one near to home, but nevertheless marking the beginning of the third season, haytime. Significantly we never speak in these parts of 'hay-making', but only of 'hay-timing', and the difference, although subtle, is very real. Farmers may hopefully hire their hay-time men for a month early in July, but it often happens that at the end of the agreed period not one quarter of the crop has been won, and the hay-timers have spent most of their time liming shippons, etc. Concurrent with or immediately preceding hay-time is clipping time, for the wool must be shorn just when it 'rises' on the sheep's backs, and hay must wait even though the weather be good. Clipping-time does not form a separate season, as those with large flocks of sheep are still coping with it when others have already got hay-time well under way.

Even when perhaps only a small proportion of the haycrop has been gathered, some chilly, misty morning in early August, someone will spy a tree with yellowing leaves and remark, 'It's a bit back-endish,' and the fourth season, 'Back-end' may be said to have commenced. Root crops, oat harvest, potatoes are gathered if and when weather permits, but even though floods should rise and playfully lift the relic of the haycrop over a wall and deposit it on the blackened ungarnered oats, the Back-end may equally well give us mellow sunny days in any month up to the close of December. But the Back-end is not to be relied on for fair weather. I have known more than twenty wet week-ends in succession at this time of year, really wet, not just damp! When a mere drizzle may be falling Skipton way, the deluges fill up the becks, the river rises and floods the fields, and the stemmed becks then discharge their contents on to the main road, swelling the tide swirled from the river under the gates, until it is dangerous for the local bus even to venture through.

About Boxing Day sees the onset of the fifth season, Winter. Winter really *is* winter, and we consider ourselves lucky if the roads are only snow-blocked two or three times up to the end of March. Severe frosts are invariably brought by January, even in a mild open winter. One rule it is fairly safe to make: if the weather be mild it will be wet; if dry, then cold. We have a special brand of winter wind, the Face-freezer, that sets the mouth as if paralysed while pitting the brows with tiny particles of blizzard-borne ice. The temperature is too low for these minute crystals to cohere into flakes of snow; and they find their way through doorcracks, keyholes and window crevices, and under the roof slates; yet they are individually beautiful, each one forming a perfect six-pointed star, visible to the naked eye. Of course, we do have snow, lots of it; but February can be a delightful month, clear and fresh with blue calm skies, though cold, and with winter aconites and snowdrops blooming bountifully; or February can be true to tradition, filling the dikes with both black and white.

OPPOSITE
Winter in the Dales. (*David K. Harris*)

DAVID K. HARRIS

Yet, taken all the year round, the fair days more than compensate for the foul; nowhere else can you breathe more intoxicating wine-like air than on our fells, nowhere else have the outlines of the hills such a clear-cut clean edge to them, nowhere else do the earth's dimples have softer shadows; even if three fine days do breed thunder and break the weather, the experience of those fine days is one to be treasured for ever in the memory. Our weather is like the little girl with the curl on her for'head; when its good it's very good; when it's bad, it's HORRID!

(August 1944)

As The Dalesman *started in April 1939, so our year has always begun in April. The following twelve extracts look at contrasting facets of a year in Yorkshire.*

APRIL

Plants on the Peak

IT WAS an unexpectedly bitter day in April – we had gone North so that my son and his friend could inspect every sleeper and piece of ballast on the Settle–Carlisle line but, secretly, if the opportunity should arise, I had another idea.

Settle was nice but full of lorries. An old lady and I cowered on a corner of the pavement near the traffic lights and agreed that it was a freezing day for April and that the lorries did not improve it. We, the boys and I, not the old lady, hired bicycles to carry us out to Horton-in-Ribblesdale, and beyond. The boys were going beyond, to Ribblehead Viaduct, they hoped. I? Well, maybe, I thought perhaps . . .

It was astonishingly cold. The sleet spun round us, blowing in our frozen faces. We gritted our teeth and battled on. Lorries overtook us every half minute. What should have been idyllic was rendered appalling, but the boys were not discouraged. We passed Stainforth Youth Hostel, where we had spent the previous night.

The road ran up and down and up again. Helwith Bridge and a quick glimpse of a train trundling along the railway line. A hopeless photograph was taken and I suggested turning back, but Ribblehead Viaduct was what they had come to see and if it meant fighting against an icy wind for twelve miles, well, too bad. I abandoned the struggle at Horton-in-Ribblesdale and was left with the afternoon to myself. The idea at the back of my mind became more than a hope. I shed my rucksack, left the bicycle against a stone wall and set out.

Immediately, away from the B6479, the country re-asserted itself. It was bleak and rolling and harsh. At other times of the year perhaps gracious, rolling and lush? Half a mile up the stony lane a group of farmers were, I think, castrating lambs. I edged round them all and the path stretched away into the shadowy afternoon with flurries of snow obliterating it from time to time. It was not a difficult path. I could hear streams running, sheep baa-ing and an occasional intrepid bird. I passed two giant craters in the earth, Hunt Pot and Hull Pot. Safely on the right side of the fence from it Hunt Pot was still frightening. Water dripped off the rocks into deep cavernous darkness. According to Wainwright, Hunt Pot is 200 feet deep. I was grateful for the fence.

The sleet had turned to snow. I struggled on, ignoring all the instructions I had ever received about not walking on my own. The path became peaty and boggy. Some kind souls had laid down wattle fencing, this path being part of the Pennine Way and getting a lot of feet along it. The

Snow makes the 2,273 ft bulk of Penyghent seem even higher, when viewed from near Ings Farm. (*Bertram Unne*)

ground around resembled uneven lumps of ginger cake. Cracks and chasms filled with snow as I walked past. My eyelashes silted up. Turn back, said my mind, abandon it, you fool, before you become a statistic. But the path was obvious under my feet even if most of the time, because of the mist and snow, I could only see three yards ahead.

It must be late now. I had no watch and I could not see the top of Penyghent even in the clearer moments. I couldn't even see as far as the next cairn. And then, suddenly, the swirling snow cleared, just for a moment. And in that moment I just happened to be having another try with my binoculars. Right in front of me, perhaps thirty yards away, in the middle of a cliff of rock, there was a small purple patch. Had I imagined it? Chance, surely, could not

have placed it there, right in the centre of the only gap in the mist. It was supposed to be rare, elusive, difficult to find. Was it, wasn't it? I stared and stared and my eyes watered.

The curtain of cloud blew across in thick white swags, obscuring the rocks entirely. I knew where to look now, though, and I clambered over the fallen stones and boulders, breathless with excitement and careless of the intensifying snow. Behold! Eureka! And not just one patch either! There were half a dozen. *Saxifraga oppositifolia*. Purple Saxifrage. Two stars in Collins! It was flowering in little clusters all over the rock face, oblivious to snow, wind or weather. I had not had to scour the area,

I had hardly had to search. It was right there, waiting for me. I was cold, exhausted, and over the moon! The way back when I turned round was almost blotted out but I ran down it, jumping, leaping and occasionally falling over. Two and a half hours up, half an hour down.

The next day the sun shone. I hired a car and we went to Ribblehead Viaduct, Aisgill, Dent station, Garsdale . . . then took photographs of the Settle–Carlisle line from everywhere. In the circumstances, hugging the memory of those amazing splashes of purple appearing out of the mist for me, I felt it was the least I could do.

Jill Chaney (1984)

MAY

Whit Monday Walk

SOME OF the youngsters thought it marvellous – all that marching, shouting, and showing off round the village streets – but the Whit Monday Walk in our little Yorkshire village was an event that warranted no eager anticipation from me. Forty odd years ago I used even to pray that it would rain 'cats and dogs' so that 'they' would call it off. But 'they' were a hardy lot, and the sun, in the days of my youth, always seemed to blaze down on the Whit Monday marchers.

I lived with my parents and grandparents at a grocer's shop in the main street of a West Riding village. Grandad was an enthusiastic 'Chapeller', and I suspect that he had something to do with The Walk. He was so insistent that I join in. How I hated it! The buns were invariably supplied by Grandad from our shop, which added to

the boredom of the affair. There were plain Queen cakes in neat bun papers, done up with white icing and quarter of a cherry on top, or white icing tops sprinkled none too liberally with coconut. (Grandma, to give herself a treat, used to slice the icing top off her bun, and lay it at the side of her plate as a titbit for when the plain bit was eaten.) Whit Monday after Whit Monday buns of that type appeared on the long, scrubbed Sunday School tables, and just as regularly the Sunday School superintendent, and attendant cronies, appeared to do justice to them . . .

Down at the school, Big Girls and teachers busied themselves in forming children into lines. They then placed themselves at strategic intervals on the outsides. With a terrific clash, the band would strike up and my feet would shuffle unwillingly into the varying tempos. Frequent halts were made at important places along the route, our shop being one of them. How my heart would thump as we thundered ponderously down the hill, nearer and nearer to The Great Stare.

The shop doorway was always jammed with people calling out to individuals in the moving mass, with weary marchers who had run into the dark interior of the shop for a quick 'sup' from the glasses already filled with pop for quick consumption. Grandma set out stools and shop chairs – those bentwood ones, with holes punched in the seat – outside the shop. It was a bit like a garden party, without the flowers and the top hats. Grandma and Grandad wore freshly starched white aprons down to their ankles for the occasion. Dad, grinning from ear to ear beneath his inevitable bowler hat, bawled indistinguishable remarks, while Mother made ducks' eyes at the bandsmen.

Many were the pointing fingers and craning necks, while desperately I attempted to slink by unnoticed, with knees bent to bring me lower than the Gollywog who marched in front of me. Or I would try to get by, shrinking behind a Red Indian's feathers. I felt so silly marching all that way for a cup of weak, sugary tea, a couple of fish paste sandwiches, and a bun from our shop. During the pause outside our shop the band thundered through a couple of rousing hymns. It was maybe *Onward Christian Soldiers*, followed by the one that goes *Hark! hark! hark! While infant voices sing*.

I could not help feeling more like a dutiful rat following the Pied Piper than a devout Christian child, as the throng continued its noisy way to the Sunday School for tea. Here all and sundry were greeted with exclamations of admiration from the refreshment ladies; they were local women who attended the Bright Hour every Tuesday afternoon. Without exception they kept their hats firmly on their heads throughout the proceedings. Indeed, one hardly ever did see a Bright Hour woman without her hat.

After tea, it was off to the field for races for those whose feet could stand up to it after the afternoon's march. There was all the tenseness of the Fancy Dress judging, more communal singing, a prayer and then, about nine – as the sun dipped below the horizon – the last stragglers drifted home. Scholars had been treated to drinks of free lemonade and another bun each. Another Whit Walk had passed into memory. I would not be on view, publicly, until another Whit Monday afternoon came round. Wasn't I glad!

Hazel Wheeler (1980)

JUNE

On the Scent

FOUR was just striking one June morning as we turned our bicycles into the A659. In another few hours this road that follows the river from Burley-in-Wharfedale almost to the East Riding would be full of the din and stink of traffic. Now it was all ours – two cyclists and a wide ribbon of tarmac as smooth and silent

as the river itself. With the moon setting, a pale Chinese lantern behind the Chevin, and white mist from the water meadows wreathed about as we rode through a world in which both sight and sound were eclipsed. So as our whispering tyres sped on we began to recognise places, not by sight but by scent.

First the cool mushroomy smell of pasture and the vanilla tang of hawthorn hedges by the road. At bends the angler's lure – a faint hint of mud, weed and peat-tinged water. Then a stronger, a characteristic West Riding smell, sour-sweet, oil, heady, and we knew that Otley's woollen mills were at hand. On still night air you can feel the presence of wool exhaled like a warm breath. The next scent to signpost our way was an acrid, sizy odour – the paper mill at Pool, and across it drifted a waft of fertiliser and weed-killer from the market gardens. For a minute we rose out of the mist and half saw across the valley, like some extinct volcano, the dim mass of Almscliffe Crag. The most nostalgic of scents followed – not one really, but a compound of many. It marked Arthington Nunnery and a garden of dewy grass, clove pinks, hollyhocks and stocks, redolent like the building of Elizabethan England.

Harewood's famous avenue was to us a long, pine-scented tunnel. Then came a breath of potato fields and new hay for the run down to Collingham. At first light we surprised a pair of buck hares shadow-boxing near a gate. As we watched, a snail on a thorn cautiously extended its 'horns' to the faint fragrance of a wild white rose. Dawn and the cottage garden scent of

herbs, vegetables and lilac focussed our attention on the bow-windows, pillared porches and fresh blue paint of Boston Spa's delightful Georgian houses. By contrast, long before we reached it, a powerfully sweet, but slightly sickly odour of brewer's malt advertised the town of Tadcaster.

Now, as the mist dispersed, there was no need to ride 'on the scent'. But the habit is rewarding, for nothing is so memorable as scent – a fact that all women know. So I remember the next village, Ulleskelf, not only for the brassy, antediluvian monster of a steam traction engine parked on the tiny green, but for the pungent breath of purple-flowering comfrey in great drifts by the waterside. So, too, Cawood, where Wharfe becomes Ouse and divides West from East Riding, means to me yellow clumps of wild iris yielding their honeyed savour to the risen sun – but to others it may mean the ancient gatehouse of an archbishop's castle still standing among a huddle of brick cottages and Dutch gable ends. Of one last smell, though I'm sure all will agree that there is nothing to surpass it: at our breakfast time in Selby, when the morning ride was over, the irresistible smell of a vast dish of fried bacon and eggs.

OPPOSITE
Summer scents waft through a Dales window.
(*Geoffrey N. Wright*)

Alan Walbank (1960)

JULY

To Rosedale by Carrier

YEAR after year, when we were children, my sisters and I used to alight from a certain train at Pickering on the last Monday in July and then look for the old carrier and his cart just outside the station. For we were going to Rosedale for a holiday, and the only means of transport (unless you were fortunate enough to own a trap) in those days, was the carrier's cart on market day and, if you missed it, you had to wait another week.

This particular Monday we found old Tommy Johnson waiting for us, and when our luggage was hoisted aboard, we three girls climbed up on to the cart and off we started on our eight-mile drive. Passing

Carrier's cart of old, photographed near Whitby.

through Middleton and Wrelton did not cause much excitement for we never really felt on our way until we reached Cropton. We knew from experience that there were many calls to make – at some houses leaving parcels, at others messages, and that was why it took us about two hours to complete the journey.

Cropton Bank was always a great thrill, and it seemed that there the real adventure began. After the slow descent we ambled along, taking in the moorland scene until we came to the bottom of Hartoft Bank. We children approached this spot with mixed feelings, for we knew that on reaching it our progress would slow up, because for one thing we had to get out of the cart and trudge up the hill (a thing all children hate

doing) and for another, old Polly had to stop here and have a rest and a drink of the lovely cool spring water from the rough stone trough – no doubt put there many years ago by some kind farmer, but enjoyed by humans and animals alike, until this day.

These rituals concluded, there was still one more to fulfil when we reached the top, and this was the visit old Tommy made to the inn (whether for his own comfort or the landlord's benefit I'll leave you to guess). All this seemed a sheer waste of time to us children and very irksome, as we wanted to be moving on as quickly as possible. We then took our places again in the cart and waited as patiently as we could for Tommy. A thrill of excitement went round when the old man emerged at last, climbed into his seat, and said, 'Gee up, lass.' And off we started on the last lap.

No more stops, thank goodness, we used to say. And, as if Polly knew too, she would jog along at quite a good pace. As we passed on, the moors began to take on a more familiar aspect, as we considered them our moors, and in their purple majesty they seemed to give us a royal welcome. As we went we would exclaim when the old chimney came into view (it was a real landmark, we could even see it on the horizon from roads at home on a clear day). Then as we passed farmhouses

we knew we'd look eagerly for old friends, so that we could wave to let them know we were back again. At this distance, Polly would almost trot, knowing, or scenting that she was nearly home.

Approaching the Abbey we'd espy the doctor's house away on the left and some-one would wonder if he still had those lovely borzois, and so we'd talk until we came to the avenue of glorious beech trees at the entrance to Rosedale, looking so green and welcoming. At last we reached the Abbey, but as our destination was up in the dales, Tommy again obliged by driving us there, and so passing the church and on round the corner, we came into full view of the hillock crowned by a spinny, as if it were standing sentinel to the dales. On past Redfirn's Farm with Duker Woods opposite, all these familiar landmarks con-veying some message to us as we passed. Bell End topped the rise, and we dipped down towards the Plain Trees where our friend was on the look-out for us. As we approached she would leave her door and come out into the road to welcome 'her bairns'. We would pay off old Tommy, with many thanks, then laughing and chattering we'd enter the wee cottage and shut the door. Our holiday had begun.

E. Nicholson (1948)

AUGUST

Sheep-Dipping Day

IT WAS early August, and as a youngster of thirteen I was spending one of many, many happy holidays with those great people, Dalesfolk, at my uncle's farm at Burtersett. Today was a monumental day

in my holidays – sheep-dipping day; hay-timing, sheep and cattle sales, shows, all took second place in my youthful mind on this day.

My cousin and I, armed with stout

sticks, went out into the cold morning air from the kindly warmth of the shippon, picking up Lady and Spring, the dogs, on the way. A grey glimmer of dawn was breaking the sky as I stumbled after him on the grass-covered cobblestones outside Chapel House. A sharp call subdued the excited barking of the dogs, bringing them to heel. The heavy dew made me thankful for my strong country boots as we started to climb Yorba. Gradually the sky lightened and then I felt that glorious warmth of the early morning sun on my face. A curlew's cry broke the early morning stillness. My cousin paused a moment and, looking down the dale towards Bainbridge and Askrigg, I saw smoke curling lazily up from early-lit fires. A sharp bark from the dogs caused us to turn our heads to watch them chasing a rabbit; it twisted and turned trying all ways to get to the sanctuary of a grey stone wall, but to no avail. Dick shouted and hurried across the pasture to take a twitching rabbit from Lady's mouth. A sharp blow behind its ears stilled its struggling. 'Rabbit pie for supper tonight, lad,' he laconically remarked as he strung the rabbit's body through his belt.

At the Cow Pasture gateway we parted company, Dick to go with old Spring to the top of Wetherfell and beyond, gleaning sheep from high pasture, while Lady and I combed the lower pasture. My inexperience and youth were saved by Lady's instinct, and afterwards I wondered who had run the furthest, Lady or I. But we had

Sheep in Wensleydale.
(*Sonia Lawson*)

gathered some eighty 'yows and lambs' and bunched them together awaiting Dick's return. Soon be came with three hundred ewes and lambs, bleating and milling their way down.

Breakfast over – home-cured bacon and dark-yoked eggs, a memory that has served me well in these rationed days – the real business commenced. Pail after pail of hot water was put in the sheep trough, sheep-dip added and we were ready to start. My job was to catch the sheep and drag them to my cousins who dumped them bodily in the trough. Soon I was 'clarted up' with water and sheep-dirt. But how gloriously happy! It was a constant source of wonder to me how my cousins unerringly picked out a neighbour's sheep to put on one side – and how often had I to appeal to them to ask them to point out to me once again which 'yow' they wanted. A momentary pause to watch the sheep swimming in the trough made me envy their confident reaction to water, but how hurriedly I jumped aside to avoid their vigorous shaking of water from their wool as they clambered up the sides of the trough! As the sun grew stronger, tempers became a little shorter and the imprecations thrown out at random by the dippers became more varied, but none the less poignant as an old ewe struggled and kicked to avoid its dipping.

About mid-day the local constable arrived to give official blessing to the event; a careful scrutiny of both contents and dipped sheep was followed by an adjournment by my uncle and the pillar of the law, no doubt to seal the legal formalities over a glass of the 'White Hart's' best brew. Dinner-time gave a welcome respite to my tired and chaffed hands, and in the afternoon a more leisurely gait was followed in finishing the dipping of the remaining sheep and the branding with hot pitch those few sheep which had missed being marked after shearing. Finally the trail back to the tops with that brown-coated, damp-smelling flock, and a return home for milking in time to catch the evening train out of Hawes. A happy full day whose memory remains warm with me throughout the year.

E.E.M. (1948)

SEPTEMBER

Redmire Feast

ONE OF the big events in Wensleydale's calendar of the year was Redmire Feast with its attendant ceremony of cheese-cake gathering. Feast Sunday was the first Sunday after 19 September, but it was on Monday that the event got into its stride. For that and the two following days the district gave itself up entirely to having a good time, when relatives and friends came from miles around. Many came from Lancashire where numbers of local families had gone to live after the closing of the lead mines, and where they had found a strangely new occupation in the cotton mills. These exiles looked forward to 't'Feast' as much as anyone, as it was an occasion to return home. (I once saw a bus-load coming to Muker Show with a big notice on the front – WELCOME TO OUR NATIVE LAND.)

At Feast time every house was filled with visitors and the population was at least doubled. The butcher who came round weekly with his trap always brought two traps at Feast weekend – Feast beef was a good foundation. A gay gathering of caravans, roundabouts, and stalls would crowd the Redmire Green, and there would be enthusiastic contests at quoits, 'wallops', and foot-races, with several trotting matches during the three days. There was, of course, a dance every evening.

A copper kettle was the recognised prize for quoits competitions, except on the Wednesday, when it would be a metal teapot. I know a man who won over fourteen copper kettles at various times, and I have seen in a cottage parlour three highly-polished copper kettles standing on wool mats on the top of the piano! Local inns put up every sort of attraction they could in the way of singers, dancers, and comedians, and did a wonderful business. One much-favoured comedian, known as 'Weary Willie', had been first spotted on Redcar sands and persuaded to come to Redmire Feast.

The cheese-cake gathering was the highlight of the Feast. I think this came to an end about 1910, and I think I saw – and heard – the last. I was in the pastures about half a mile above Redmire when I heard so much noise that I thought the place had gone mad. I was told it was the cheese-cake gatherers setting out. Anyone and everyone joined in, so long as they were dressed

in an absurd rig-out and – for preference – had blackened their faces. The whole body went in procession through the village.

One or two would call at each house, often on the pretence of oiling the clock, and they would only come away when they had been given something to put in the baskets they carried with them. When the whole village had been visited the proces-sion moved back to the local inn where the cheese-cakes were eaten. These cheese-cakes were a kind of tart, sometimes made in a saucer, sometimes smaller. But instead of a jam filling there was a mixture made of cheese-curds, eggs, sugar, butter, and a little nutmeg. They were very good.

Fred Lawson (1948)

(This was Fred Lawson's first written contribution to the magazine. For more about this unique Dalesman and artist, see page 106.)

OCTOBER

Cleveland Revisited

SUNDAY MORNING, late October. Fine, calm, bright and warm – much warmer than most October mornings that I remember on the Cleveland coast. I sit on the grassy ramparts of all that is left of the Roman coastguard station at Huntcliff . . . Now I can look down on Skinningrove, the iron works smoking only thinly on Sunday, perched above the beach where the North Sea perpetually washes away the industrial odour of its slag heaps. It does wash remarkably clean, and Cattersty Sand looks as pristine as in the days before smelting began, perhaps as in the days when Cattersty – 'the steep path of the wild cats' – really meant what it said.

Now I walk down the gentle slope, still close-cropped by sheep as in old times, to the cliff edge itself. I peer over into Seal Goit where the scar, the smooth pavement of shale rock, begins again after the sand. No man in my time has seen a seal in the goit, or anywhere nearer to it than Redcar – or remembers such a thing related by his elders – but there is nothing remarkable in this because recent experience on the coast of Britain shows that seal colonies can be established and decline remarkably quickly.

A little further round, between the cliff edge and the railway, devoid now of Sunday traffic, for it is only open for mineral trains to Skinningrove, is the lip of the cliff and I peer down into Birdfleet Goit, where the tide crawls slowly and almost unruffled over the tang-grown scar. Although the state of the tide is such that there will have been time for people to walk round the point and into this inlet from either end, there is no-one there – no gatherers of bait, no setters of night lines, no-one groping after crab and lobster under the rock ledges. Only the gulls and the

OPPOSITE
The Cleveland Plain, as seen from Clay Bank on the edge of the North York Moors. (*Geoffrey N. Wright*)

cormorants and the jackdaws are wheeling above it.

I walk back to the Roman station, and a very suitable perch for cogitation on past and present. It is now thirty years since I left this place to go to work, and nearly twenty years since I last came back to it . . . Down in the encircling valleys where the leaves are only just beginning to turn to autumn auburn, little has changed except the most important thing, only revealed gradually to me as I pass through Riftswood with an occasional glimpse down into the ghyll. Out at the far end of the woods is the viaduct which is surely one of the very few really distinguished red-brick structures of the Railway Age. I walk down the rocky road to Marske Mill, and along the gangway between its now dry millrace and the steep gorge of Skelton Beck.

Now it impinges. Now the penny drops. The beck is clean, the beck is clear, the beck is the colour of water again! Previously it was of a poisonous chemical ochre colour, thick, even in times of drought, with a ferrous silt that would permit no life in the water, piscine nor insect nor even vegetal. And that was it. That was why neither I nor anyone else fished in that beck, but ground our way over the hills past the watershed, on ancient bicycles festooned with rods and bags of gear.

Anthony Dent (1968)

NOVEMBER

Guy Fawkes Night at Harpot Green

THE ANNUAL event of 'Beckermonds bonfire', held on each Guy Fawkes Night on Harpot Green, was enjoyed by all the adult population of Upper Langstrothdale, just as much as it was by the children. First came the ceremony of lighting the huge pyre of sticks, dead trees, and tar-barrels. Some of these tar-barrels were given by the local farmers, others were collected by the young men of the dale on dark nights. They had great fun in 'pinching' them, and took especial pride in getting hold of a tar-barrel by 'french leave' from some farmer who had refused to give one when asked openly. These farmers, knowing the pranks of the Dales youths, would try to hide their barrels as 5 November drew near, but some young man would invariably find out their whereabouts, and he and his friends would then quietly remove a barrel and hide it away somewhere until the great night came. It was then proudly produced as a trophy to add to the fire.

These barrels had nearly always contained sheep-dip or tar used for marking the sheep after clipping (or shearing, as it is called elsewhere). A great tongue of flame would shoot up high into the sky as each tar-barrel caught fire, lighting up the stone arch of the old bridge and sending a hissing shower of sparks into the peaceful Wharfe.

Next came the fireworks, always referred to as 'crackers'. By this time all the natives of Upper Langstrothdale capable of walking had assembled, and each brought his or her own supply of fireworks. Hence there was a grand display and much fun and merriment. The Guy, made of sacks well stuffed with dead leaves, would be duly thrown to the flames, possibly with a few crackers hidden about his person by some mischievous Dalesman. Then came the music, one of the chief features at any celebration in Langstrothdale.

My father always took his own concertina with him to the bonfire, or one of the children was sent to bring it, should it have been left behind. He played this very well by ear (like so many of the Beresfords) and he could also play a mouth-organ and fiddle in the same way, but excelled on the concertina. Pete, Tom and Alan Beresford would turn up too, with concertina or fiddle. Somehow Bonfire Night remains in my mind as a concertina night so far as the music went. Maybe these were easier to carry about, or their music more suitable for an outdoor gathering. There was always someone with a mouth organ to produce, in addition, from a pocket. Even a clarinet would be heard at times. My father had two of these instruments but was never able to play them so well as the concertina.

Never have I heard this instrument – the concertina – played with such zest, zeal and skill as by the men of Upper Langstrothdale. Alan Beresford could dance a reel, which he called a clog dance, at a furious pace, and accompany himself at the same time with his own concertina, waving his arms up and down to keep time with the wild rhythm of the dance. This gift of concertina-playing in the dale runs almost exclusively in the Beresford family. 'Tot' Middleton could play both a mouth-organ and a concertina at the same time. His mother before her marriage was a Beresford.

Once the music had started someone would sing an old song, or dancing round the bonfire would start spontaneously, according to the tune set by the player. There is an old dance where the lady runs away to hide, and has to be found by her partner. This went very well on Bonfire Night. Finally came the roasting of potatoes in the embers, and after these had been eaten all would disperse to their homes, some few miles away. Walking in those days was not considered the hardship it is today.

Florence Foster (1948)

DECEMBER

Christmas in York

SNOW is not a major factor in York's thinking. Blizzards are almost unknown; occasionally white flakes gently tumble from heavy skies and, with the aid of spasmodic flurries, settle on the pavements to a depth that is invariably measured in fractions of an inch. They stay white for a few precious moments and then quickly turn into a dirty, slushy mess. A white Christmas in the traditional sense simply does not happen in the centre of York. Coloured lights reflected in wet streets are really the city's seasonal symbol. Also symbolic in a more frigid sense is the damp and biting cold that often percolates in a sinewy fashion through every street and alley, and has as its lair the murky depths of the River Ouse which cuts through the city like some super highway. Around Christmas the river is prone to breathe out obnoxious fogs like a stream of cooling lava.

Stonegate, York. (A. Walker)

STONEGATE, YORK

A. WALKER 1946

York is a place where even Jack Frost could catch cold. I have stood on top of the Pennines in a howling blizzard and felt coats warmer than when miserably tramping inside the City Walls looking for that last minute Christmas present. The citizens, though, seem to be at one with their climate and even in the harshest winter neither wither nor wane. As the number of shopping days before Christmas grow perilously short they pack the narrow city centre streets and drive the motorist almost to despair.

Coney Street and Goodramgate seethe with humanity to a greater degree than most of the other thoroughfares. Traders in these two streets have formed associations, each of which has as one of its prime objectives the provision of Christmas lights and decorations. Their efforts would probably be scoffed at by Londoners used to Piccadilly Circus, but they are brave attempts for a city with a population of little over 100,000. York is more crowded than other cities at Christmas shopping time because of a simple arithmetical fact. In Leeds, for instance, there is room for four lanes of traffic in the main shopping streets; in York there is only room for one or, with confusion, two.

If people are not bustling they are queueing – for pork pies, for chickens, or for buses that seem to take hours to come, and then are full. The restaurants are jammed; the multiple stores are unbearable; Whipma-whop-ma-gate is bulging at the hyphens. A haven of peace in a city gone mad is the market, now moved from Parliament Street to the more secluded Newgate in one of the almost monthly attempts to solve the car parking problem. Here turkeys and ducks, mistletoe and Christmas trees, can be examined and bought under conditions less resembling armed combat.

The hands of time point to 5.30 p.m. on Christmas Eve and shopkeepers and their staff breathe sighs of relief. The pandemonium ceases, and the shop doors are shut. At exactly the same moment the doors of the public houses are opened. Soon the revellers are out, but, alas, it is no longer advisable to join them. Many of York's streets have achieved a nasty reputation for violence in the evening – a reputation that has spread far beyond the city boundaries.

At last, though, the festivities are over. The streets are still. Christmas Day becomes a reality, but the calm remains. It is almost as though gates have been closed at each of the four bars on the City Walls, just as they still are at Jerusalem.

David Joy (1965)

JANUARY

Land Letting at Hubberholme

ON A BITTERLY cold evening, that of the first Monday in January, I drove up Wharfedale from Leeds with some friends. Our destination was Hubberholme, at the start of the valley of Langstrothdale, although we made a short stop to visit some friends in Kettlewell. Someone there asked us where we were heading.

Hearing of our pilgrimage, he suggested that we ought to be early to attend the Poor Letting at Huberham – the ancient name. We were indeed fulfilling a long held desire to see an ancient Dales custom being upheld both in church and at an inn. It seemed odd to join a church congregation and then walk across the stone bridge to the *George Inn* for another ceremony conducted by the Vicar. This historic hostelry was owned by the church until 1965. At one time it was the vicarage.

Our evening began in the candle-lit church of St Michael and all Angels, once a chapel on an old burial site and having associations with Coverham Abbey. It has been in nearly continuous use from about the time of the Norman Conquest. There was a reverent atmosphere in the small church which rapidly filled with muffled people coming from sub-zero temperatures. Everyone seemed to know everyone else. Seasonal greetings were wafting across the aisles. Thin wisps of smoke from the many candles in their iron chandeliers also wafted through the air. In such an atmosphere one would not have been too surprised to see the Viking War Lord, whose name was involved in the hamlet, come through the door and take his place with the rest of the congregation.

We looked around the gathering. Two small boys were silently counting, and pointing out to their parents the tiny mice carved on the pews. Thompson, master wood-carver of Kilburn, was responsible for the young people's diversion. A few adults were clearing their throats for the service of lessons and carols that was soon to start. In this medieval setting, the Vicar changed his cloak for a surplice and the organist rubbed hands together and glanced at the yellow programme that was the order of service. *Once in Royal David's City* rang out

fine and clear, led by resonant voices, some of whom may, a little earlier, have been calling sheep on the Pennine moors. The story of the Nativity was slowly unfolded as our carols and lessons progressed.

The service ended with a rendering of *O come all ye faithful* in the presence of some delightful Christmas decorations and, of course, the candles shining down from above. The faithful heard the Vicar explain the events that were to follow our service in the inn. He told us that it had been the custom of the parish to annually hold the letting by auction of a sixteen-acre field on Kirkgill pasture. Although, he explained, there were now few poor people in the parish, the money raised at the land-letting to follow would be used to give a helping hand to anyone within the parish who entered a period of financial embarrassment.

The Vicar donned his warm black cape and was soon mingling with us at the door of the church. We all walked slowly and pensively over the bridge, where the frost had thickened on the parapets and the stream beneath had frozen. The stars above were twinkling. We thought that there would be plenty of room at the inn that night, but we had not reckoned with the many folk who had not attended the service and who were to be certain of a front seat at the letting ceremony. Soon, all were incredibly squeezed tight in two rooms.

Our custom took place only once a year and was to be conducted by the Vicar, who had now doffed his cape. We settled our-

OPPOSITE
Hubberholme church, for centuries associated with the Land Letting on New Year's Day.
(*F. Leonard Jackson*)

[54]

selves to our tables and drinks and awaited the sound of a bell suspended over the bar counter. This was duly rung by the Vicar, who asked for peace and goodwill for the auction and explained again to the throng assembled the meaning of the ceremony. He asked for generous bids, especially as this year was to be the last for the present tenant of the *George*.

Quiet had descended, apart from the occasional clink of a glass. A candle, some three inches long, was lit and placed upon a saucer, which was then put on to the window-sill. We were told that bids could be accepted as long as this candle remained alight. The Vicar waited. Eventually, he had to cajole the first bid. Eight pounds from a gentleman seated near the bar was not greeted with very much enthusiasm by the Vicar, who said that if there were to be no more bids, he would retire to consult with his churchwardens. He would also partake of a few mince pies, before returning in hope that the bidding would have improved.

Although only a few yards apart, we were in one of the rooms known for this evening as the House of Commons, whereas the Vicar and his associates were in another room known as the House of Lords. The Dales Parliament was, indeed, in session! The people seemed more interested in their drinks, both large and small, and the talk was mainly about the weather, farms and local events. The bell rang again some ten minutes later and the assembled crowd heard the Vicar announce that there was to be an added privilege on the pasture: that of keeping down the moles.

It was 9.45 p.m. now, and the crowd was so thick that the only escape for a comfort call for two young folk was through the small window looking out over the back yard. Another bid followed another ring on the bell. It was £7 better now, but the Vicar and his Lords were all hoping for a higher bid in this special year. Someone pointed out that the candle was burning quickly. All eyes were riveted on that candle and then moved to the Vicar, who was busy asking for bids and silence. Then it almost seemed as if both tongues and minds were a little more loosened for the final run into the last bid and the last flicker of the candle.

The bid of the previous year had been £120 and this now was passed . . . £130 . . . £147. Heads turned to see the bidder, and turned again to see the candle in its final stages. At a bid of £155, the Vicar paused, checked with his Lords and eventually helped the candle on its way out. The Poor Pasture letting was over for another year. The bid was a record, and the amount reminded us that fifty-five years ago the Rev. Lindley of Halton Gill had journeyed over the Horse Head Pass to take this self-same service and auction for a fee of six shillings.

The ceremony dates from the mid-18th century, when the common lands were enclosed and a few acres were placed into the hands of the church to help the poor of this small parish. Times change, but fortunately the actual ceremony has changed very little. The dale has seen a long and often violent history, and it is exactly this type of custom that puts everything into some sort of perspective. We drove carefully back to Leeds that late evening, having not regretted our journey. We carried with us warm memories of a close community of friendly people.

John Gilleghan (1978)

FEBRUARY

Pancake Tuesday

We raced each other home at noon,
 Ignorin' t'rain an' mud.
It meant 'at t'year were drawing near
 To t'bluebell time, in t'wood.

If t'show came back to-morrow
 We'd think it nearly spring,
No matter if we felt half froze,
 We'd hed us pancake fling.

Our Mum hed mixed up t'batter
 An' left us on our own,
An' just popped out to t'neighbour's,
 (You'd 'a thought she would 'a' known!)

We made sich play wi' t'fryin'-pan,
 Deciding we could cook,
Not followin' instructions or
 Deigning to look i' t'book.

Wi' t'raspberry vinegar ready,
 T'butter an' t'orange juice,
We'd cook 'em barely through, and then
 Grab t'pan, and shake 'em loose.

Then up they'd goa, and down they'd flop.
 'First come, first served,' we'd yell.
Then gather 'round the table,
 An' eat 'em for a spell.

Then, back to t'last o' t'batter;
 When, suddenly, Mum returned,
An' said, 'All right! Let's end it.
 It's a wonder you weren't burned!'

'We thought that you weren't comin' back,
 An' we'd be late for class.'
She said 'Ah've heard that tale bafore.
 Be off! Ah'll let it pass.

Ah know just how you've acted,
 Droppin' 'em all around!
You've hed one up in t'air too high
 An' missed it, Ah'll be bound.'

We dashed for t'school. On t'ceiling
 You could see a roundish blot,
Where t'pancake pulled t'wallpaper off
 An' left a cleaner spot!

M. T. WALLER
(1963)

MARCH

The Simple Pleasure of Rolling Eggs

OUR NEIGHBOURS no doubt look at us a little askance when we emerge *en masse* on Easter Sunday morning, heading for the lower slopes of Ilkley Moor clutching our cartons of hard-boiled eggs. With friends from Newcastle who make a point of joining us every Easter, we are going egg-rolling or pace-egging, though

[57]

we seem to be the only family in this part of Yorkshire to keep up this grand old Easter custom.

The traditions of Easter are patchily kept at best. I was surprised to discover that not all families hide their chocolate eggs in the garden and trot out first thing in the morning to find them. In our house Easter wouldn't be Easter without that delightful and sometimes frustrating ritual. It was all very well when the children were small but now they seem to take perverse satisfaction in hiding *my* egg in the most remote and

March winds move scudding clouds over the limestone pavement at the top of Malham Cove. (*Geoffrey N. Wright*)

unlikely place – somewhere like the guttering above the porch were it can't be seen from ground level.

Pace-egging properly refers to the mummers' plays featuring St George, Lord Nelson, Old Tosspot and other peculiar characters. But that, too, is a custom which has dwindled, being preserved only in junior school productions, and perhaps one or two villages. The name seems to have become attached to egg-rolling, a totally different ceremony, which still takes place on the hills around Huddersfield and, of course, on Ilkley Moor.

An essential ingredient is the colouring of the hard-boiled eggs, which we usually carry out the night before. This itself has very respectable antecedents. The ancient

Chinese are credited with starting it. They exchanged good-luck eggs as far back as 900 B.C. The East Europeans make an art of it. It clearly appeals to their colourful sense of design, and their choice of colours often has a religious symbolism. Presumably it is this sense of a link with a rural past which encourages egg-rollers to tint their eggs with natural dyes like onion skins, tied on with elastic bands to give a mottled effect. We have also tried cochineal to give a pleasingly blushing pink and the purple of logwood, purloined, I have to admit, from a child's chemistry set. Last year we cheated somewhat by using on one egg a black felt-tip pen, rubbed in with a piece of rag. The resulting bronze effect was quite striking and most unsophisticated so we forgave the use of modern materials on this occasion.

It always seems a little bit sad that such temporary masterpieces are to be shattered, but this is their fate. When you consider it, it does seem a rather odd custom, hurling hard-boiled eggs down a hillside till they fall apart. But it has some similarity to that other hoary rural game of conkers. I have heard it suggested that egg-rolling is some kind of solar rite. That may be so, but I am sure it has survived because it is fun.

The rules are simple because there aren't any. You simply line up at the top of a suitably steep mound and pitch your vari-coloured eggs to the bottom, bouncing as they go. They can take a surprising amount of punishment before the shells crack and the yoke comes leaping out like a hard yellow-grey marble spraying bits of white in its wake. It is, by the way, advisable to keep well clear of the bottom of the mound. A carefully aimed hard-boiled egg can be enough to crack your own egg-shaped dome. Our entertainment is usually heightened by the presence of our exceptionally lively dog who, given his head, will race up and down the mound gobbling unshelled eggs until he makes himself sick.

When it's all over, it brings an odd glow of satisfaction. It's not just an eccentric little outing. I think we all feel in some measure that we've been in tune, if only for a very few minutes, with a long, long heritage, of a way of looking at life, of enjoying life in simple ways, which has vanished with the cart-horse and the milk-maid's yoke. Perhaps it does us good to be reminded, once a year, of where we originated.

John Hewitt (1982)

4

THE YORKSHIRE CHARACTER

WHAT IS A YORKSHIREMAN?

With the aid of market research, Bryan Waites incisively went straight to the heart of the Yorkshire character.

DO YOU beat your wife? Do you chew rather than suck sweets? Do you prefer darker ales? Tea without milk? Lots of vinegar and pickled onions? An abundance of fish and chips? If you do then you will have at least some of the credentials of the real Yorkshireman – real, that is, according to the latest findings of market researchers. Now, more than ever before, the tastes, preferences and behaviour of individuals are well known. Population censuses enquire more deeply than ever, and market research uncovers regional likes and dislikes as an integral part of the sales campaign. It becomes possible, therefore, to build up from such inquiries an identikit picture of a typical Cornishman, Irishman, Londoner, Yorkshireman, or what you will. What is the market researcher's view of a typical Yorkshireman? Does it shatter our historic illusions?

In appearance he would be heavily built, prone to slipped discs. His wife also would be plump, creating the greatest demand in the country for roll-ons and all-in-one foundation garments. He would be a pugnacious man absolutely self-confident and intolerant of affectations in others. He might even be violent, since Yorkshire has the highest rate in England and Wales for crimes of violence. He would work off much of his energy by his frequent and vociferous visits to numerous sports grounds in the county. His stubborn independence would be reflected in his retirement too. There are more elderly couples and single persons living entirely alone in Yorkshire than elsewhere in England and Wales and much less sharing of homes. Yet, the region is noted for its strong patriarchal family pattern and the typical Yorkshireman would regularly visit his relatives maintaining the firm bonds that silently exist.

Home is a real haven to the typical Yorkshireman, and he does not like to be disturbed once entrenched in it. He decorates the interior more frequently than anyone else in the country. His wife takes an active, even a dominant, part in this. On the whole it would be furnished lavishly, with lots of snugly-fitting, patterned carpets, rugs overlying, tripping everyone up, and rooms almost too full of furniture. The typical Yorkshireman would watch over the house carefully and criticise profusely.

He is the most critical of all British husbands of feminine faults and failings, demanding to be treated as Master, with the woman ministering to his needs. He will go out to buy a car without consulting his wife yet, paradoxically, he allows and encourages her to buy all his clothes even down to his socks, ties, pants and shoes. Such is his apathy about clothes which he regards exclusively as being to wear to last rather than for show. He expects his wife to be an expert in home-cooking. This is a virtue. There is much more bread baked at home in Yorkshire than anywhere else, using the best ingredients. He is anti processed food, anti synthetic products, rejects compound cooking fats for pure lard, and his wife resists cake mixes. All this illustrates his plainly rational but traditional approach, where plainness is significant and new styles are regarded with suspicion. His wife was slow to turn to the use of self-raising flour, and it does not sell well in Yorkshire; supermarkets made slow progress at first and pre-packed vegetables were looked on with distrust; fewer shops offered trading stamps. He will cling to his shaving stick longer than anyone else and will be attached to his cardigan. The umbrella is looked on as decadent.

Solid fuel remains in many Yorkshire homes. The typical Yorkshireman believes in cleanliness. The county has an exceptionally large ownership of washing machines and vacuums. Early toilet training for children is favoured. Yet, oddly, 26% of Yorkshire homes were without a fixed bath a few years ago and 15% without a WC. Life is often lived more rigorously and without frills as a sort of Puritanical self-punishment or personal martyrdom. It is sometimes a virtue to be deprived, the typical Yorkshireman may feel.

His typical diet consists of space-filling carbohydrates; brown bread, fish cakes, faggots, rice, sweet puddings, buns and cakes figure prominently. Even the sacred Yorkshire pudding, as a separate course, may be designed to curtail profuse meat-eating at the same meal and so economise. There seems to be a low consumption of milk and cheese despite the Yorkshireman's love of apple pie with cheese and his delight in milk puddings. Strong tea is preferred and it must *mash* long enough, usually in a metal teapot. He does not like breakfast cereals or blancmanges. He must have harsh sauces, more vinegar, pickled onions, liquorice and aniseed than anyone else, and he has the heaviest indulgence for fish and chips, especially chips, in the

Yorkshire folk. (*Mary I'Anson*)

[61]

world. He is always looking for nourishment. Food is not eaten because it is attractive, well-presented or exotic but 'to do you good'. He thinks, therefore, that the darker it is the more nourishing it must be. Thus, dark beer is best; brown sherry rather than pale; Demerara rum above all; darker icing sugar; browner bread. Even so, he believes that he needs supplementary vitamin pills more often than most other people.

By the way, the typical Yorkshireman drinks almost as much as the Midlander, 8.4 pints of draught per week per man. The profusion of corner off-licences (now vanishing due to the interference of planners) points to a great deal of home drinking. He is also amongst the heaviest smokers in Britain, especially of pipe tobacco. But to

'It beats me what men find to talk about.' (Varley)

get back to the diet. It is not so much the food as the eating of it which is notable. There is a modest breakfast of one cooked course without toast or marmalade; dinner as opposed to lunch; a high tea which is so substantial as to daunt a stranger. One in five Yorkshiremen has a late supper at about 10 p.m. which is another hot meal, usually fish and chips. In between all these meals he will carry on eating fruit or any other snacks to hand. Meals, then, are more numerous and sizeable than elsewhere.

When our Yorkshireman marries, he is less likely to marry a stranger from 'foreign parts'. His wedding is a more important event than in many other areas. The couple get more presents, more photos are taken (thirty per wedding compared to twenty-five elsewhere) and bills for car hire are higher. His funeral, too, may be expected to be a lengthy and sustaining celebration with all relatives present, even those previously cut off family photos. He will be cremated, since the typical Yorkshireman fears that otherwise 'worms will come and eat thee up'. When alive, he had a warm and generous heart but was cold and unrelenting in pursuit of his immediate goals. He was a staunch friend and a dangerous enemy.

Here then is your typical Yorkshireman as seen by the market researcher. If you are from Yorkshire, does he resemble you? Dare you admit it? Perhaps he is like your Yorkshire friend? Next time you meet him you can measure him against this formula. One thing about market research – it is discovering that there are still strong regional differences in Britain despite bureaucratic attempts to make us all the same.

(June 1983)

YORKSHIRE SPEYKS

James R. Gregson – playwright, broadcaster and former journalist – recalled gems of Yorkshire folk-speech.

As fair an' false as a new gravestooan! If Shakespeare had heard that, he would have licked his lips and promptly 'set it down in his tablets' just as I did when I heard it – except that I put it into my notebook as soon as I got home from the cotton mill. It was the comment – epitaph, if you'll forgive such an oblique pun – uttered by a disgruntled spinner, retailing an abortive love-affair with a wench who was very much alive and, in the words of another minder, 'a bit of a powse'.

Whenever I recall that gem of our Yorkshire folk-speech – so typical in its pith, point and poetry – I can smell the warm, oily floor on which we were squatting over our breakfasts. It was not the first – and by no means the last – of such jewels that I've snapped up, gloated over, hoarded and finally used in my plays. Here are a few of them – all taken at random from one play:

Ah can read him better nor big print!

If Ah sed 'Traycle!' shoo'd say 'Lick!'

As fluttered as a hen that wants to sit.

He'll simmer quietly now he's letten t'lid off!

Talk o' t'Devil an' yer'll hear his clogs clattering!

He's as much life in him as a bit o' burnt leather.

As uneasy as a dog wi' too monny fleas.

He's a neck like a plucked hen.

If tha wants to play hell, it's no use having a referee!

I cannot remember where I heard those, but here is a couple which came in one lively sermon from a vigorous local preacher: 'As narrer as a hen between t'eyes,' and 'Like t'man wi' t'muckrake, shortsighted wi' lookin' after rubbish.' As I type them I can see the robust lay-evangelist darting out of the vestry, bounding up the steps to the pulpit and announcing the first hymn before he got there.

James R. Gregson, near his Grassington home in 1960. (*Yorkshire Post Newspapers*)

Oddly enough, I gave these two gems to my *Ezra Marsden*, who describes himself as a 'scientific agnostic'!

One of the earliest entries in my note-book is a comment by my father on an Aunt's pastry: 'Tha could shoe hosses wi' it!' And at about the same pre-factory period there is an entry which earns its place, not because it is witty or profound or particularly amusing, but because, pho-netically and idiomatically, it is so York-shire. I heard it while following the coal carts from the railway sidings, picking up the bits that fell from the jolting vehicles. A burly carter was at his horse's head, bawling enquiries about the condition of an ailing acquaintance and finally asking: 'Has he gotten agate o' gettin' aht o' bed yet?' There is a lovely gaggle of Gs.

I remember picking up one little master-piece of natural descriptive genius while on the staff of the *Leeds Mercury* between the wars. I was sent to interview an ancient matriarch at Scapegoat Hill, not far from where the B.B.C. was to build the tower-ing masts of Moorside Edge. The story I was after doesn't matter, for I never got it. The old dame was too full of the local gossip, particularly of a 'set-to' she'd just had with a 'Lady Jane Tape wi' edging on' who she 'couldn't abide', and who was 'jumped-up an' too nice to skin onions'. The old dame ended her description of this 'mimsy-finicky' creature with: 'Ay, shoo's one o' that soort that gooas lookin' for lice i' bald heeads!'

A similar assignment, this time with a male centenarian in York, threatened at first to be just as frustrating, for I found him obsessed with the case of an old friend and I'd to let him 'get it out of his system'. This old friend had had a very hard life, dogged by ill-health and ill-luck and was now not expected to leave his bed again. He had no sooner been struck down, with no prospect of ever being able to enjoy his good for-tune, than he'd inherited some thousands of pounds from a distant relative. My centenarian summed up this sadly novel situation with this bit of doleful philos-ophy: 'Ay, Mester Gregson, that's life, that is. God takes away yer teeth an' then he gives yer nuts!' You may question that pessimistic conclusion, but you have to admire its picture-evoking phraseology.

This vivid imagery is characteristic of Yorkshire folk-speech, and a fine example which I've heard once or twice is 'Ah've licked a cleean thible (wooden porridge-spoon) monny a tahme!' As a picture of hunger and near-starvation it can hardly be bettered. I first heard it on the lips of a cheerful old inmate of a workhouse at a Christmas party. Her lined face was made more gaunt by the gaudy paper cap she sported. Nearly all these native 'speyks' have a touch of humour about them, from the light and glancing to the mordant and the macabre. And in the ones I think of as typically Yorkshire there's an element of self-mockery, a touch of over-simplemind-edness.

An instance of this deliberate over-simplicity I can't resist. It is perhaps the first example I remember meeting. I was walking around Brighouse one evening with my father and, at what we called 't'George Corner', an elderly news-seller pushed a *Yorkshire Evening Post* under our noses with: 'Paper, Charlie?' My father bought one and we went on our way. We returned along Commercial Street soon afterwards and the news-seller again pushed an *Evening Post* under our noses. 'Paper, Charlie?' 'Nay, tha knows Ah've just bowt one off thee!' 'Ay, but [very wheedlingly] have another. Tha'll soon read that!'

But I'm getting away from my theme and my space is running out. So, from the scores of entries in my notebook, let me finish with what I consider my favourite – a real plum. It has everything, I think – wit, the brevity that's the soul of wit, humour and commonsense, couched in homely imagery. It's from yet another old dame, who I heard giving this bit of advice to a young 'ovver-fond' bride: 'Never put thi husband on a pedestal. He'll nobbut want dusting!'

(February 1971)

James R. Gregson's Favourite Yorkshire Story

Joe and his wife, after an even hotter row than usual, sat sulking, he on one side of the fire, she on the other, with the cat on the rug between them.

When it seemed that the sullen silence would never be broken, Joe slowly uncrossed, then recrossed, his legs, sighed and said: 'Ee, Ah wish one of us three were deead. An' Ah dooan't meean misen.'

Just then the cat looked and mewed. 'Ah doon't meean thee, nawther!' said Joe.

YORKSHIREMEN IN A 'HOIL'

To my knowledge, no student of York-shire dialect has ever accorded full and due recognition to the simple word 'hole'. Pronounced 'hoil' or perhaps better still 'oil' without the aspirate, it is one of the most popular and widely adapted words in the language of the West Riding.

In the mills, the weft room is the 'weft hoil', the piece room is the 'piece hoil' and the place where the jacquard design cards are cut is referred to universally as 't'card hoil'. Where I used to work, continuation boilers made a nice warm place to use as a 'kall-hoil' where we sat and gossiped before starting time. Because of the continuation boilers it was referred to by everyone as the 'conny-hoil'. An old building still used for storage purposes was known as the 'dog hoil', not because animals were ever kept there but because loom ends, or 'dogs',

were stored there. The building is now used by mechanics and it is still called the 'dog hoil'.

Young entrants to industry are warned about the dangers of the lift shaft with 'Mind tha don't fall down t' lift hoil' and an obstruction of a doorway will bring the instruction 'Gerrout o't' door hoil.' West Riding children who misbehave are often threatened with being taken to the 'bobby hoil' – the police station – and if they are seen playing by a stream they are told to 'Come out o' t' beck hoil' or warned 'Mind ye don't fall i' t'hoil.' People going for a handy supper or lunch go to either the 'chip hoil' or the 'fish hoil' for their fried comestibles.

When the forwards of local soccer teams reveal a hesitancy to put the ball into their opponents' net, they are urged by vocifer-

ous supporters to 'Gerrit i' t' hoil'. At Cowling which is so near the Lancashire border that the villagers are infected by Lancashire habits of speech, this exhortation is varied to 'Gerrit i'thoil.' This variation is found vastly amusing by the Yorkshire purists who live only a mile or two from Cowling. They roar with laughter and are inspired to heights of mimicry or reduced to depths of heavy sarcasm, all meant to indicate that Cowling modes of speech lack refinement and belong to an age long past. Verbal competition often becomes as keen as the play on the field and sooner or later someone feels bound to issue the challenge, 'Shut thi cayak hoil or I'll gie tha one ower t' lug hoil.' This means that unless the person addressed closes his mouth, he will be struck on the ear.

An untidy house often brings forth the expression 'By, they hev a muck hoil,' or even a 'pig hoil', or, more simply, just a 'hoil', mouthed with a world of meaning. Fortunately, modern fireplaces are not equipped with an 'ass-hoil' from which pit ashes and cinders had to be shovelled when full. People today are rather unlucky, however, in that 'peigh hoils' no longer exist. Peas and pies for twopence or threepence was a tasty dish for supper, and could be eaten either on or off the premises. Still, today there are different kinds of 'hoils' where one can eat.

Roy Mason
(August 1968)

DALESFOLK

Several well-known Yorkshire writers contributed to the first issue of The Dalesman. *Among them was Ella Pontefract, who teamed up with Marie Hartley (see page 207) to produce a classic series of books on the Dales. She reflected on the highly individual characteristics of Dalesmen and -women.*

'He were nobbut a peeat high,' a Dalesman said of a small boy.

'If there's another Noah's flood, there won't be manny folk left alive i' England when t'watter comes blashin' down oor chimney pots,' said another of his high farm.

'Tha's nivver gaen to lig under yon' lump o' clout,' a Daleswoman said to a camper.

THIS vividness of expression, owing much to dialect, is an attractive Dale characteristic. That there was a hill fair here, that this small town had a market, and this village kept up wedding customs are dead facts until the Dalesfolk, by such phrases in their recollections, give them life, making one see the sheep and cattle on the hill, hear the bargaining in the market, and feel the hot pennies thrown at weddings. We had watched men cutting and setting peat on the fells, but an old lady of eighty made us realise the activity when everybody burnt peat. We saw her as a child setting the blocks, and being taken as a reward to Askrigg Hill Fair. A farmer's wife completed the picture by telling of making stacks on the moor herself because her husband was 'nea' a peeat man'. As our first friend talked on, the room faded, and became a village shop with scholars sitting in one corner watching the door for a customer to bring a break in lessons.

Two men in different dales showed us the wide importance of Middleham Moor Fair by telling, one how he joined with a neighbour to buy a cow there to salt for the winter's meat, and the other of his early morning journey to the fair over two fell passes and another valley. They spoke naturally of what had been a phase in their lives, their interest in it as a thing of the past intensified by their interest in the life of the dale today.

Celts, Anglians, Danes, Norsemen have gone to make up the Pennine Dale character, which varies in the upper Dales according to which predominated, but the country itself has done much of the moulding of it. The narrow cultivated valleys with grazing on the fells support the people chiefly as small sheep farmers who are independent and self-reliant because, whether they are yeomen or tenant farmers, they are their own masters. The farm man is generally a neighbour's son who will presently take a farm of his own. The fells also gave lead to mine, and the becks provided power for corn mills and later small woollen mills, bringing industries which developed alertness and enterprise.

We think of four lead miners, three of them dead within the last three years, who

Dalesman. (*Bertram Unne*)

Daleswoman. (*Bertram Unne*)

between them drew for us a picture of lead mining in the Dales. One described long journeys over the moors in snow, rain, and sunshine, and how as they neared home they could smell the bacon cooking; another told of the network of levels and the molten lead in the smelt mills; another of accidents when roofs of levels fell in; another of the thrill of finding and following a vein; and all of them spoke with love for the 'grooves' and joy in the work. Joy in work reminds us of the Dale mason, proud of his skill, his eyes lighting up as he discusses plans, testing his achievements by those of his predecessors, who built the stone walls thick to keep out the weather,

and in their simplicity produced buildings which harmonised with their surroundings.

This gallery of Dalesfolk are most of them old. Not that individuality is lacking among the young. Up and down the Dale young and energetic men are raising the level of Dale farming, liming and draining neglected land, concentrating on pedigree stock, encouraging the Young Farmers' clubs. But the old have a lifetime's memory behind them; they have known people whose names are worn now on the church-yard stones, and who lived in an era which has sunk into history. They belong to a time when the fells shut the Dales in from the outside world and in a great measure from each other. They are reflections of their Dale. Of necessity the people inter-married, and each valley became, what to a smaller extent it is still, like a large family.

Dales children – a group at Bell Busk.
(*W. Hubert Foster*)

As families are given to quarrels, so there have been bitter feuds in the Dales. They are interested in each other as members of a family. We are sitting now in a farmhouse kitchen whose window looks on to the road. Conversation stops as we hear footsteps or a car approaching, and we gaze out to see who it is, and if there is any doubt we settle between ourselves who it is likely to be.

The influence of the old grammar schools is apparent in the men whose parents scraped the few shillings to send them for a year or two to be taught by the vicar. Here is one, a farmer, offering with simple courtesy the hospitality which comes naturally to Dales folk; or returning from shepherding on the fells, eager to tell of the curlews' and plovers' nests he has seen. Industries have left their mark, but the true Dalesmen are connected with farms. Even when they retire the old life holds them, and they keep up a few hens, and are not content for long between walls. Pictures of them crowd up – two old men standing in a pasture discussing the points of a cow; a farmer prodding the tups at a show; a young man fishing for trout after a storm; a farmer's son mending a dry stone wall; a shepherd with his dog turning sheep and lambs on to the high fells; a group of farmers milking cows on a common pasture; an old man and woman round a farmhouse fire pronouncing a neighbour 'a good sheep body'.

It is such people, the men and women of the Dales, who bring the towns and villages, the hamlets and farms to life.

(April 1939)

YOUNG FRED . . .

Two of the most enduring and endearing characters to feature in The Dalesman *have been Young Fred and Old Amos.*

I' bother

Ah's be late for me teea;
　Ah've some thinkin' ter do.
It could even be dark
　Bi t'time Ah've got through.

Ah wor thrawin' some stoanes
　At a rusty owd tin,
When Ah heeard a gurt crash
　An' a winder went in.

Ah've got ter be certain
　Just what Ah s'll say,
An' ha' Ah s'll manage
　Ter raise t'brass ter pay.

Ah knaw what Ah'll do;
　Ah'll reckon Ah'm flaid:
An' Ah might ger away
　Wi' just gerrin' brayed.

Young Fred, 'a son of the Dales', made his first mischievous appearance in our pages in December 1950. Displaying the elixir of youth, he survived for seventeen years as a lively lad until the death of his creator Will Clemence in 1967. He never grew up, but he never failed to bring a smile or a laugh. The poems which told of his adventures were recited in schools, quoted in books, and were indeed highly regarded by dialect authorities. We sold many thousands of copies of the little book in which many of them were collected.

Tich to market

We've been up ter t'market;
  We road theer in t'bus.
The' gave Tich a ticket
  Just same as all us.

He wouldn't cahr quiet,
  An' all t'way ter tahn
He gor inter bother
  An' wouldn't lig dahn.

He barked at a goslin',
  It stretched aht it' neck
An' flaid poor owd Tich.
  By! He trembled like heck!

He raced a young kitten
  Till Mum said 'Tak' care!'
If he does that ageean
  Ah s'll noan pay his fare!'

. . . AND OLD AMOS

Old Amos is still with us, having dramatically defied the ravages of time for thirty-five years since uttering his first pithy comment in the May 1953 issue. In March 1988, Rowland Lindup finally revealed how he came to create the ancient gentleman with a long beard.

ONE EVENING a gentleman called to see me and told me he belonged to a group called 'Kingstown Artists' and that they had all sorts of artists on their books. He had included me on their list as a cartoonist, so I drew some cartoons. These were passed to Harry Scott, Editor of *The Dalesman*, and he sent me a letter asking for further ideas. The first Old Amos draw-ing wasn't a bit like those I draw of him today. However Harry Scott was so taken up with the idea of a monthly character with a witty saying that he invited me to let him have a series. No one has told me to stop.

The name Old Amos came from an old gentleman I knew who lived quite near us years ago. I thought it was an unusual name, but probably typical of Yorkshire. I could have called him Old Bill or Joe.

Nobody is called Amos today, I picked it as belonging to the old days. If I remember correctly, I did three different 'Amoses' before I settled for one with a long, white beard. This saves me drawing a collar and tie! The coat he wears is a pretty shapeless thing really; you don't see many like it around! His trousers reminded me of my Uncle Harry's trousers which were always wrinkled at the bottom. So I suppose bits of

OLD AMOS says:

'If tha want to live to be owd – chuck smokin'! I did – hundreds o' times.'

Amos are Uncle Harry, although my uncle didn't have a beard. I really added the beard to Amos to give the impression of real old age. He's got the family secret of perpetual old age!

Once I discovered Amos was going to be a regular feature in *The Dalesman* I had to improve on the original drawings. Gradually I've got him as I like to see him now. When I look back at the first ones, they were so badly drawn, I'm amazed that anyone was interested in them!

OLD AMOS says:

'It's no good cryin' oer spilt milk – there's plenty more watter in t' tap.'

POOR OLD CHARLIE!

Another much-loved regular contributor to The Dalesman *was J.S. Varley, whose blend of humour, gentle understanding and inimitable line drawings were in a class of their own.*

SETH BRADLEY was a local boy who made good. He left the village at the age of fourteen, and returned in middle age to be the landlord of the *Rose and Crown*, bringing with him his family.

His daughter, Dozy Doris, was a plump wench, who sat around all day reading *Peg's Papers*, and hoping some sheik would come and carry her off to his tent. The sheik didn't come, but she did marry into

royalty of a sort. He was a fat, bald-headed man, old enough to be her father, who carried her off to his 'Little Palace', as Seth described it. It was in fact two rooms with an indoor loo over his shop, which displayed a sign in bold letters declaring him to be *Alf Todd, The Cowheel King of Bingly.*

Charlie, his son, the apple of his eye, and something of a headache, was away at public school. Seth was no gentleman, but was determined that his son would be one. Money was no object. As the boy grew up, however, he found that the 'fair bit of brass' he'd boasted about was going down fast. Charlie was told to cut down on his 'wine, women and song', and this he appeared to do. In his last year at school, his mother died, and Pater, as he called him, had a stroke. It wasn't due to his wife's death so much as to his finding out that his son was in the hands of money-lenders. Before Charlie could get home, his father had died too. Before he received one penny, all his debts had to be paid off. By the time this was done, Charlie was left with only a few hundred pounds. What on earth was he to do? He couldn't live for long on that bit.

The solicitor suggested he found work of some sort, but Charlie was outraged at the suggestion. Him work! He couldn't do that; he was a gentleman, and besides, he didn't like work. The only thing left, if he wasn't to starve to death, was to marry a girl with money. So getting together his few pounds, he set off on a tour of his public school friends. He soon found a chap was welcome for a week's shooting or fishing, but to marry their sister wasn't the thing, old boy. Not with his background anyway. But in his travels he met up with another orphan with some money, and married her. She was a frail sort of gal, given to bouts of the vapours, but with the

rents from the property her father had left her, they were able to manage.

At the birth of a son, four years later, she went into a decline and died. It was a blow to Charlie, especially when he found that her property was entailed, and all he got was a small sum each week to keep himself and the boy, until he inherited at the age of twenty-one. Doris, his sister, now a widow, was sent for, and she after years of unlimited tripe and cowheel pie was so fat she could hardly walk, but in her slipshod way she looked after the child and Charlie. It wasn't long before he too became slipshod in his ways.

By the time he was fifty he looked like a walking scarecrow. He only shaved once a week, but still wore his old school tie, mostly without a collar. To make ends meet he took up a job rate-collecting. For this work he rode a lady's bike without brakes or mudguards, or went round with a pony and old milk float. The pony was what we called 'a standing still trotter'. Its legs would go up and down without moving forward. This was because the float was made for a big horse. When Charlie stood on the back step to drive, which he always did, his weight lifted the pony almost off its feet. It was a grand sight.

One year, a vacant cottage near the village shop was taken by a well dressed widow of about forty years of age. She was plain but pleasant and, according to the shopkeeper, had plenty of brass. Charlie at once had his hair cut, he shaved every day and cleaned off most of the egg and gravy stains from his waistcoat. It wasn't long before he called at the cottage to explain to her about the rates. In a public school voice, of course. She seemed impressed by his talk, and he then called round bearing baskets of fallen plums and bunches of rhubarb.

All went well until one day when Charlie, while cycling down the street, spotted his lady love coming out of the shop. Wishing to speak to her, he stopped his bike in the usual way by putting his foot on the front tyre. Well, that's what he intended to do, but blinded by love or something his foot went through the front wheel and he took a forward somersault on to the road, breaking his leg and nose, and covering the road with blood and false teeth. It so happened that Fred Nelson, a farmer, arrived on the scene with his thoroughbred pony and trap and, with the widow nursing Charlie's head, they took him to hospital, and left him there.

Now just what happened on the drive back between Fred and the widow, nobody knows. But by the time Charlie came out of hospital Fred and the widow were engaged to be married. That's why they called him 'Poor old Charlie!'

(April 1976)

Courting and funerals figure high on the list of subjects of perennial interest to the true Yorkshire tyke:

ARE YER COURTIN'?

JOHN HARTLEY, the Prince of Yorkshire Dialect Writers, declared, 'Courting is the sweetest thing ever invented.'

There are, of course, all kinds of lovers, and some are very shy, like the Yorkshire lad who surprised his mother one night by gulping down his tea, putting on his best suit and spending a lot of time over his topping. As he was leaving the house his mother asked him where he was going. 'Ah'm bahn courtin' that lass o' Dysons.' But he was back in no time.

'Did you see her?' asked his mother.

'Aye, Ah did, an' she's real champion. Do you know, mother, if Ah hadn't bobbed darn behind a wall, she'd a seen me.'

Some courters, I am sorry to note, cannot thoil to part with the brass like the lad who after a bit of coaxing by his girl bought a quarter of chocolates. He allowed his young lady to have one straight away. After walking about a couple of miles, she hinted that another chocolate would be welcome. This he reluctantly gave her. Another few miles were traversed when she again suggested that another chocolate

would not come amiss. This time he stopped and said, 'Art ta barn to wed us, Betty, some day?'

'I hope so,' said she.

'Well, then, think o' t'bairns,' he replied.

It may have been a relative of his who before going into the cinema with his lass bought some sweets at a nearby shop. During the screening of the picture she could hear him champing away, but none ever came to her. So she thought it was time to give him a hint.

'Are them spice nice?' she queried.

'Yes,' said her boy. 'Ther grand; ther champion. You ought to a bowt some for thissen.'

Others are boastful, like the young chap crossing a field with his lady love, who told her that he loved her so much he would climb the highest mountain, swim the deepest sea, go through fire and water and even face death itself for her sake. Just then a bellow noise was heard behind them and

lad and lass raced across the field and cleared the hedge just in the nick of time.

When she regained her breath, she said, 'I thought you said you would face death for me. And yet you ran away from that bull.'

'So I did,' said the young man. 'But you see, lass, that bull wasn't dead. It was very much alive.'

Odd ones are careful, like the lass from Pudsey who vowed that the chap who wed her would have to have at least one hundred pounds saved. When at long last she clicked, she told her sweetheart about her vow.

'Well,' said he. 'It's a seet o' brass, but Ah'll do me best.'

Six months later she asked him how he was getting on. 'Champion,' he replied. 'I've got thirty bob saved already.'

'That's near enough. T'rest isn't worth bothering about,' was an eager response.

R. W. Hornsey
(July 1950)

THE LAST RITES

FUNERALS FASCINATED the old Yorkshire humorists. The folk tales of the Ridings are full of them. The traditional funeral tea, where long buried family feuds are disinterred over the cold ham and fairy cakes, has provided a fertile pasture for humorous writers, past and present. We shouldn't be surprised at such a crop of jokes about a sombre subject. They say we laugh at what we fear most, so we laugh hardest and longest at death. For other than the family mourners, whose grief is close and real, a professionalism cloaks the

sadness of the occasion for outsiders. If you have ever chatted to the pallbearers from the undertakers as they idly wait by the empty hearse during the funeral service, stubbing out their cigarettes and grumbling good naturedly about the weight of the coffin, you will know what I mean.

Journalists have a similar detached attitude. Without it they would be overwhelmed by the sheer sadness of life. They are touched by the ridiculousness of the living, in the face of eternity, which is probably why there are more stories told in newspaper offices about funerals than any other type of assignment. Though some of the smaller weekly journals continue the practice, most newspapers have now abandoned the publication of long lists of mourners at the funerals of prominent pillars of the community. For the reporters involved, it was one of the most dreaded chores, though it had an excitement and unexpectedness all its own. One of its charms was the visiting card.

In a small town, funeral-going for some became almost a way of life. Any reasonably well-known businessman would be involved in several concentric circles of acquaintances. He would be a member of the Chamber of Commerce, if in a lesser way of business the Chamber of Trade, the Conservative Club, his firm's trade organisation, the Rotary Club, the Church and the Freemasons. His friends and acquaintances were likely to be members of the very same organisations. A Labour councillor, for his part, would be involved in his union, the Co-op, the Labour Club, the working men's club (where the beer was better), the Trades Council and possibly 'The Buffs', and his comrades and colleagues would be largely interchangeable.

So a veteran funeral-goer would present the eager reporter at the church door with a visiting card representing William Bloggs of the Fish Slice Manufacturers' Association, also representing Dr Alistair McNab of the local branch of the British Medical Association, who represented the Rotary

Funeral by horse-drawn sleigh on the moors between Otley and Horsforth in the winter of 1947. (*Ledbetter of Leeds*)

Club, including its President, Coun. George Crowther, who represented the Liberal Party and the Constitution Club and so on. Sometimes one felt that a single man bore almost the whole weight of the town on his shoulders. For reporters, visiting cards were the 'jam' of funerals. We tucked them in our notebooks, in our top pockets, in our wallets. When we returned to the office they cascaded out like confetti. The 'dry bread' were the names which had to be scribbled down hurriedly in a rain-spotted notebook, sometimes under the most arduous of conditions.

I still shudder when I recall the time I was sent to cover, alone, the funeral of some not-so-prominent local dignitary. The town was stiff with chapels. I got the wrong one. One look at the locked, spiked gates was message enough. I set out at a trot for the next likely candidate. It was half a mile up a hill, and by the time I reached it I was red in the face and the last of the mourners had disappeared within the chapel's huge oak doors. Disregarding all the unwritten rules about how a reporter

should disport himself, I set about discreetly collecting names along the back few pews. At my first glance inside the chapel, I was horrified. It was big, one of the largest. And it was full. We had miscalculated. The deceased, although little known locally, was associated with half a dozen regional and one national organisation.

I kept my ears cocked for the sound of the arriving hearse, and made a swift exit. I had barely two pages of my notebook full. There was nothing for it but to tackle the mourners as they emerged. Unfortunately there were two doors. Madly, I shuttled between them, borne back by a wave of black-tied humanity, intent on getting home early for dinner. I regretted I hadn't had the foresight or the cheek of one funeral reporter who, confronted with a similar situation, tied a gate shut with a piece of string and thereby forced the congregation to file past his out-thrust notebook.

John Hewitt
(May 1979)

5

FOLK OF THE BROAD ACRES

AT HOME WITH SIR TITUS

Few 19th-century textile barons have exerted such a hold on popular imagination as Morley-born Sir Titus Salt. His success in processing South American alpaca fibre, which led to the creation of an industrial complex and model village at Saltaire, is well-known. Less familiar are the celebrations that took place at Crow Nest, Lightcliffe, his home from 1844 to 1858 and again from 1867 until his death nine years later. They were described by J. A. Iredale and P. A. Townhill.

WHEN SIR Titus Salt moved to Crow Nest in 1844 his business affairs were prospering, and this large mansion offered many advantages to a successful entrepreneur. The house had been built in about 1780 on the site of an earlier dwelling, and the architect is reputed to have been John Carr, although Sir Nikolaus Pevsner queries this and suggests that Thomas Bradley was responsible. The name Crow Nest suggests an immediate link with the birds in the locality, yet we are told in Balgarnie's *Sir Titus Salt* that in fact no crows had nested in the neighbouring trees for many years, and that Salt was delighted when his use of decoy nests and food supplies enticed these birds to return near the house.

Crow Nest was stone-built, like other local mansions, having a centre block with a large wing on either side, and these were connected by smaller buildings. Over the years various improvements and alterations were made to the property, and a carriage drive was constructed across the park in 1861 to give a more secluded approach from the present Wakefield Road. A gateway with gateposts adorned by carved stone alpaca heads was later added, and a lake constructed in the grounds with an island for the shelter of birds. The conservatories became a prominent feature in the grounds of Crow Nest, the main conservatory having an elaborate rockery and cascade. Salt was a keen horticulturalist and took pride in his successful growing of unusual fruit, in particular bananas. Add to these exotic sights in Yorkshire the presence of llamas, alpacas and Angora goats kept in the grounds and the excitement can be imagined when Salt invited all his employees to visit him at Crow Nest on 20 September 1856.

The occasion was Salt's 53rd birthday, and the day must have been a memorable one for the 3,000 who attended. The proceedings began at 8.30 a.m. in the Saltaire millyard, where the workers formed a procession accompanied by the Saltaire Drum and Fife Band and the Saltaire Brass Band. Two trains then conveyed the party to Lightcliffe station, adjacent to Crow Nest. A gargantuan lunch was prepared, the details being recorded with great thoroughness by the contemporary press. An enormous marquee was erected for the

Sir Titus Salt's statue at Saltaire.

occasion reputedly containing 870 yards of tables and a mile of seating. The meal is stated to have required 1,380 lb of beef, 1,300 lb of ham and 520 lb of tongues and pies, together with numerous dishes of chicken, duck, partridge, grouse, lobster, turkey, veal, etc. After a tour of the grounds the visitors left at 4.30 p.m. to return to Bradford.

In the evening of the same day a *soirée musicale* was held in St George's Hall, Bradford, where the entertainment included vocal items by the celebrated Mrs Sunderland, and the climax of the event was the presentation to Titus of a bust of himself carved in Carrara marble by T. Milnes and standing on a pedestal of Sicilian marble. This bust occupied a prominent place in the entrance hall of Crow Nest for many years.

When Salt returned as owner of Crow Nest in 1867 he became more closely identified with local Congregational church affairs. He had always been an active Christian, and his attitudes are perhaps best exemplified by his concern for his employees, and his building of Saltaire. While at Lightcliffe he first attended Bramley Lane chapel, a small building; he then became active in the construction of the present, much larger Lightcliffe Congregational (now United Reform) church. The corner stones for this new church were laid on 22 August 1870, his daughters Helen and Ada performing the ceremonies. The whole Salt family were closely involved with this church project, reputedly contributing more than £2,000 towards the costs, and Sir Titus was chairman of the building committee. The new church was formally opened in October 1871, and it was here in 1873 that his eldest daughter was married. This church, one of the few remaining links between Sir Titus Salt and

Lightcliffe, is at present threatened with demolition but although architecturally interesting, being built in the Gothic style, it is very large and must be difficult to maintain in these days of high costs.

It was also in 1873 that Salt again indulged in his pleasure of offering large meals to his friends and employees. Massive celebrations were held at Crow Nest on 20 September when Salt held a party to celebrate his 70th birthday and also the 20th anniversary of the opening of his mills at Saltaire. On this occasion more than 4,000 work-people and visitors were transported to Lightcliffe by three special trains, but unfortunately the weather is recorded as having been dreary with threatening rain. During the day sports were held, balloons were sent up, and games, dancing and a Punch and Judy show all added to the festivities, together with an opportunity to view the alpaca which had been penned up for the event. The meal commenced at 2 p.m. and was on the same gigantic scale as before, the total seating on this occasion again reputed to have measured over one mile. Sir Titus and his family sat at the centre table, surrounded by 2,400 lb of beef, 500 lb of tongue, 140 pork pies, 125 stones of plain bread, etc., and 'cakes and fruit in rich profusion', in a marquee covering 4,200 square yards.

Although advancing in years he continued to lead an active life, but he died at Crow Nest three years later on 29 December. His obituary in the *Bradford Observer* covered seven and a half columns, and it was stated that between 100,000 and 120,000 paid their respects to his memory on the final journey from Crow Nest to the mausoleum at Saltaire. After the death of Sir Titus, Crow Nest again came on the market and was bought by Richard Kershaw, the Brighouse silk spinner, for £38,000.

Now, however, nearly 100 years have elapsed since Salt's death, and although his name is still familiar to Yorkshiremen by his endowments for educational, medical and religious purposes, the mansion of Crow Nest is demolished, the church is threatened and few visible relics remain in the area to indicate the former days of Salt's residence in Lightcliffe.

(April 1975)

DELIUS IN THE DALES

An utterly different kind of Yorkshireman to Titus Salt was the long-neglected Bradford-born composer Frederick Delius. His niece, Margaret de Vesci, revealed his love of the grandeur of the Dales and the characterful Dalesfolk.

MY UNCLE was the Bradford-born composer, Frederick Delius, with whom I lived in France. My mother, Clare, his favourite sister, was as gifted as he and had a glorious voice. Professor Procter-Gregg of Covent Garden wrote: 'She sang her brother's songs as he meant them to be sung.' My mother relates

in *Memoirs of my Brother, Frederick Delius* (with which biography I helped from beginning to end) how Delius brought his just-completed score of *Koanga*, for her opinion, to the Brontë country. It was while staying here that Delius and my mother rode over on horseback to look at Wuthering Heights. They were both magnificent equestrians. Delius discussed with my mother the possibility of making Charlotte Brontë's *Jane Eyre* into an opera.

When Delius was a small boy he visited the circus and, like many small boys, wanted to try standing upright on the back of a horse. He set off on Black Bess, an unbroken pony that my grandfather bought for my mother, and his son Frederick. The first day my mother rode Black Bess, she was five. Bending down, she cut the leading rein between her and the groom and immediately Black Bess bolted. Pursued by a frantic groom crying: 'Miss Clare, Miss Clare', Black Bess tore on and on and was brought to something of a halt by a funeral cortege. The horse's nose poked in the back of the hearse! This time, schoolboy Frederick Delius set off across Ilkley Moor. He stood up on the horse's back and put up an umbrella. With a scream of fury, Black Bess bolted and threw the young boy. His foot caught in the stirrup and he was dragged over those rocky paths and boulders. The injuries to his head and jaw were frightful, but he recovered without even a scar.

Delius was an advanced mystic. My mother related in the memoirs of Delius that Mr Tweedale, a Yorkshire incumbent, and writer of books on psychic matters that have been published and translated into various langauges all over the world, wrote to her. Mr Tweedale said that Chopin came to tell his wife, 'that Delius would die in six months and his dear sister Clare

would write his life'. Delius died in six months and she did write about him.

Here is a curious example of the tapestry of life. When Delius was a small boy, he came downstairs and heard his father playing Chopin. He was entranced, and clasping his hands, said: 'Oh, Papa, do let me play that.' Grandpapa replied: 'You cannot play it at once; it is difficult.' Frederick persisted, and grandpapa allowed him to sit down and try. He was astounded by the result. Delius played the piece beautifully. My mother said that after a concert he would come back and play the complete programme by ear.

Frederick, my mother and I had a deep devotion to the Yorkshire Dales. In her *Memoirs* my mother relates how she and Delius, while staying in the Brontë country, often rode on horseback to Skipton Castle, the home of the Cliffords and Vesci's, into whose family I was to marry. I often talked about the Shepherd Lord to Delius. It was in the Dales that there was an example of the loyalty and compassion of Delius. When he and his friend, the celebrated violinist, Halfdam Jebe, were staying with my parents in the old Brontë house they used to go for long walks on the moors and in the Dales. Jebe had his violin, my mother sang and Delius played his Amati violin; he would stand perfectly still listening to the moor birds and then play what he heard.

Years passed and one day, in France, Delius's manservant announced that Monsieur Jebe had arrived to see him. The manservant paused uncomfortably and added: 'He is very ragged and dirty, monsieur.' Delius at once replied: 'Show him in.' Jebe entered, and 'dirty' was a masterpiece of understatement. He stank, was incontinent and a hopeless drug addict. Delius acted exactly as my mother would have done. He discussed his friend with his wife and the staff and arranged for Jebe to be cared for.

There was in the character of Clare and Frederick Delius a love of the deep-rooted grandeur of the Dales. They frequently spoke of the loyalty, strength of character and lack of hypocrisy of the Dalesfolk. Delius and my mother loathed hypocrisy and lies. Delius talked to me about Arncliffe, Buckden, Skipton, Bolton, Barden, the Pennines generally and the staunch, upright vigorous Dalesfolk. He and my mother used to ride over to Barden Tower to discuss astrology and the search for The Philosopher's Stone, reputedly carried out by the Shepherd Lord. It was an outcome of this that Delius wrote, in 1889, a treatise on the effect of notes and pitches in music on the human body, of which I have a copy. At Barden and Bolton the Shepherd Lord had written a treatise on natural philosophy, a copy of which is also in my possession.

When people play the music of Delius, let them realise that in it lies great healing. In it lies the great strength of the moors, the fells and the peaty strength of the Wharfe. I recall one wild and stormy Bank Holiday when the Wharfe came tearing down in a torrent, black with moorland peat. I dived in and swam across to the amazement of the people lining the bank, who expected me to be swept away. I will always remember the vital sweetness and strength of that black rushing water of which I felt I was an absolute part. Delius swam in the Wharfe and fjords in Norway. He said: 'We are closely and deeply integrated and involved with Nature, and her laws, which we ignore at our peril.'

(April 1974)

MEETING WILFRED PICKLES

One of the most absorbing series of articles to appear in The Dalesman *was Frank Haley's 'Yorkshiremen in London'. One of his subjects, Wilfred Pickles, became regarded as the archetypal Yorkshireman through his programme* Have A Go *in the days when radio ruled supreme.*

WILFRED PICKLES is one man who is exactly like his picture, or pictures if you include films and television. His home nowadays is Brighton, with a 'working' flat by Madame Tussauds in London, 'but I can go back to when I was five, in Yorkshire. It was the first day I had to go to school. The school was at the end of the street where we lived, and naturally I didn't want to go! I say naturally because most children don't want to go. So my mother had the old-fashioned idea of whacking my behind with a strap all the way along to Parkinson Lane.' The headmistress looked at Mrs Pickles as she whacked Wilfred along and in. She was an imposing figure, dressed in black bombazine, black hat with a veil, and wore black

beads. Miss Helliwell told his mother: 'That's no way to bring a child to school!' Though she was rather terrifying, Mrs Pickles told her: 'You don't know him!'

When I asked him where he was born he said, '24 Conway Street, Halifax. A gag I've cracked before – there is a plate up outside the door, only it says "Gas main 15 feet". But the number 4 has played such an important part in my life. I was born at 24, we moved to 24, we moved to 54, that's been done before, and every telephone number we have had since we married has had a 4 in it.' ('We' includes the charming Mabel, should anyone need informing.) 'Then we moved to Brighton and were given a number that hadn't a 4 in it anywhere. I said, "Oh, my Gawd" – but I added the numbers up, and they came to 24. You probably noticed when you came

Wilfred Pickles.

here today that the number is 34, and our telephone number here adds up to 40.' His town flat is a brief turn off from the hair-raisingly busy, loud Marylebone Road, and more or less on top of the Tube station, but it was beautifully quiet.

I asked what happened after his sensational arrival at school: what had he excelled at? 'Well, I was never top of the class, and never bottom. I was always about medium. I excelled at what we used to call composition, I don't know what they call it now: writing – I could tell stories. But I still had a love for poetry. In those days I used to go to the school library for poetry books and hide them under my coat because I didn't want the other boys to see. Some of them thought you were a cissy if you were borrowing poetry books, rather than *Jock o' the Bush* or maybe *Two Years Before The Mast*. But I really did love poetry, and of course it came out later in my life, as you well know.'

True indeed. His virile but sensitive readings were strongly individual, a welcome counterpart to the precious, hyper-intellectual poesy flowering over on Radio 3. Our Wilfred was a force to be reckoned with. Thank God for plain men – with intelligence. Chatting with him, I suggested that he had done so many things – acting, writing, comedy, producing, poetry readings, the outstanding *Have A Go* shows, announcing, musicals? 'Yes, I have sung.'

There must be nothing he had not done, I said. 'Not a lot, no . . .' he grinned, adding: 'I never played the cinema organ. That's the only thing I ever missed!'

Trust that ready wit to give me an answer . . .

I wondered if Wilfred Pickles is his real name. 'Yes. Spell it –fred, mind! Pickles is my real name. Many an actor has said that it was a very good choice, but it was no choice at all; I was born with it. My father said if Pickles was good enough for him it was good enough for me! His name was Fred, and where Wilfred came from I'll never know. Except, the patron saint of Ripon is Wilfrid, spelt the Latin way. So it's a good Yorkshire name.'

What amount of his talent was inherited? 'My father always had the ambition to act. He used to recite at parties when he'd had one or two, which was very amusing. My mother was highly intelligent. She was brought up at Bluecoats School – she was an orphan – and learned there to appreciate music. A young fellow there, son of the headmaster, went to London, heard Gilbert and Sullivan – mind you, I'm going back a lot of years now, for my mother was eighty-five when she died – and played them on the piano.'

At a very early age Wilfred heard his mother singing the G. and S. operas, which deeply impressed him. He sang some snatches for me, *I have a song to sing, oh* and *Three Little Maids from School*, tunefully I must add. His mother was also fond of reading, and encouraged him to do likewise, always 'good stuff, which has stood me in good stead.' He was part of a big family circle – uncles and aunts and 'come to tea on Sunday sort of thing', which he is sure helped him a lot with *Have A Go*. His upbringing made him understand people. He went to the people, anywhere, never doing a show from Broadcasting House. People, he decided from the start, were to be the stars. He must be in the background, only ready to intervene if they dried up. He would not come out and be the 'big fella'. So many interviewers now dominate the talking. But, Wilfred maintained, the art of interviewing is knowing when to shut up!

All his family are builders, and his father expected him to follow on. But it did not appeal to Wilfred. 'The walls of Jericho were nothing to the walls I built.' His walls fell down? 'Aye – if they ever got up in the first place. My father one day in desperation said to a feller, "If you talk to our Wilfred about a drain pipe, he'll quote you a line of poetry."'

Prophetic father, since his son went on to quote lines of poetry in some style – but that at the time was not what he had in mind. Wilfred was not interested in building, though his two brothers now in Halifax are architects. 'I just wanted to act. Perhaps that is why I'm the best actor in my family!'

Something always happens, he recalled, which is bad luck but turns into good luck. 'My family moved to Southport, and I was taken ill. I was in digs in Halifax, still building, bad building, and not liking it very much. I was twenty-one, and acting with the amateurs, the Thespians. I went at Easter to stay with my parents, who sent for a doctor to treat me.'

His father was selling the house next door to a man who mentioned he had been a director of the Manchester Repertory Theatre. 'Go upstairs, will you, and talk to my son; he's mad about acting,' commented Fred Pickles, possibly a trifle wearily. The former director suggested to Wilfred he could watch him producing an amateur show at a church hall in the village of Ainsdale. Thinking it would take him out of himself, Wilfred agreed to go to the Sunday School theatre. The first thing he saw was a very pretty girl, or rather, the back of her. She had very pretty legs, he noted, and red hair. It turned out to be Mabel. That has lasted a long time, I mentioned. Wilfred smiled happily. 'We've been married forty-two years.

Known one another forty-seven years. You know, it was Mabel who persuaded me to go to the B.B.C. She said that my voice was so much better than a lot of the people you hear on the wireless; why didn't I try for an audition? I did . . .'

While discussing that distinctive voice of his with him – a voice you could pick out anywhere, not to be confused with others – he said: 'Well, I have a North country voice. And so have you – but I bet you come from further North than me . . . Newcastle?' The old expert at *Having A Go* had scored again, but he said he had travelled so much, and listened so hard to people, he could generally pick them out. 'It's not very obvious, not Geordie, but it's there. I knew it.'

I found him a friendly, homely man, yet with an uncanny precision of thought and word: no burbling or waffling. Wilfred Pickles is one of the shrewdest but kindest of men, and a greater artist than would appear.

(September 1973)

'BEN' OF HEBDEN GILL

For every famous Yorkshireman there are thousands of ordinary folk – and The Dalesman *has always emphasised everyday life rather than the doings of celebrities. In 1950 we held a competition inviting readers to write about 'the most interesting Dalesman I have met'. By one of those strange coincidences, one of the winning entries – by Herbert H. Fletcher – was a delightful pen-picture of Anthony Joy, great-uncle of the present editor. This book has been compiled at the 'small farm' in Hebden Gill.*

ANTHONY JOY lived alone at a small farm in Hebden Gill. When I first met him, he told me that he was the original 'Ben' in William Riley's novel *Jerry and Ben*, and he would proudly point to an old concertina hanging on the ceiling which he said was the actual concertina mentioned in the novel. Others discredited his claim, but after he told me I always called him Ben, a name which seemed to fit him far better than Anthony.

He was a true lover of the Dales, and particularly of his own neighbourhood. Occasionally he would take a trip to Liverpool or Chester, but he could not stay more than a day or two and was always glad to get back. He was very fond of reading and in the evenings would sit in his old grandfather's chair with a book in one hand and a candle in the other. He had a very strong objection to 'summer time', and never put his clock or watch forward. 'What reight have they to muck about with time,' he would say. I asked him what he would do if he had to catch a bus or train, and he grudgingly admitted that he had to start an hour too soon. Even when 'summer time' was advanced two hours he still refused to conform to it as far as he possibly could, and when it came to an end he would point proudly to his clock and say, 'Look at it, it's reight; and it's been reight all t'time.'

One could always be sure of a kindly welcome at his house. I remember once in pre-war days calling at his house to see if I could get some eggs for preserving. 'Aye,' he said, 'I wish you'd cumed sooner, though. I selled them this morning and I've nobbut ten left.' I said I should be glad to take those, and when I inquired the price, he said, 'They are 1s. 9d. a dozen, so that will be (scratching his head), that will be (still scratching), nay dang it all I'll goa out to t'hen hut and see if I can get two more.' Returning after a minute or two he smilingly said, 'I've getten 'em, so now we can do it.'

Not only had he an inherent love of the Dales; he was also passionately fond of his animals. It was not easy to keep his sheep out of the house. I remember once he was bottle-feeding two lambs. He became very much attached to them and called them Barnum and Bailey. They became such favourites that he could never part with them. Some years afterwards I asked him what had become of Barnum and Bailey. 'Oh,' he said, 'they're out on t'ill side. I'll call 'em,' and going out in the yard he shouted, 'Barnum, Barnum, Bailey.' In a few seconds they came running to him. His dog Roy was also a great favourite, and understood everything that Ben said to him. When I talked with Ben on one occasion, Roy persisted in barking, so Ben said to him, 'Roy, goa and fetch t'bulls.' These were some distance away from the house, but Roy went off at once and fetched them.

Once I took a party of a dozen or so to camp in one of his fields. One night we arranged to have a sing-song, and invited Ben to join us, but he was too shy to do this. Meeting him the next morning I told him he had missed a treat. I was much surprised when he replied, 'Noa I didn't. I sat at back of t'tent and heeard it all, it were grand.'

Since his death the Gill has never seemed the same. One misses his kindly welcome and the merry twinkle in his eyes; and somehow the very landscape, of which he formed a part, seems still to be mourning the loss of a dear friend.

Hebden Gill. (*W. E. Leadley*)   (*September 1950*)

KIT CALVERT – THE COMPLETE DALESMAN

A great friend of The Dalesman *for over forty years, Kit Calvert of Hawes was the creator of the modern Wensleydale cheese industry, founder of a unique bookshop, an authority on Yorkshire dialect and a great local benefactor. Norman Duerden recalled his treasured encounters with this complete Dalesman.*

THERE IS a spot on the Burtersett road which must be one of the most flowery corners in the Dales. With its uncut banks and damp flushes, the rough field has since become a place of pilgrimage at the end of summer, with its harebells, knapweeds, scabious, betony, and grass of parnassus. A tall and derelict barn-like building and a high hedgerow hide it, and give protection from the worst of the weather. It was this abundance of flowers which more than twenty years ago sent me to a small bookshop in Hawes, where the proprietor, an elderly gentleman, who chanced to be there at the time, satisfied from his overloaded shelves my enquiry for a flower-book. Above the door, a sign announced the name 'Kit Calvert' – a name respected, almost revered, throughout Wensleydale, though at the time unknown to me.

Much has been said and written since about this, the archetypal Dalesman, who, complete with his clay pipe, or with his pony and trap, was for long a familiar figure to Hawes folk. Historian, book collector, and sometime cheese-factory owner, the man, his work and devotion to the dale, were honoured by the Queen. At a subsequent meeting at his bungalow, he proudly showed me a coloured photograph taken in 1977 at Buckingham Palace on a very special occasion. I must confess that I felt more at home with his alter ego, comfortable in union shirt and shapeless trousers,

Kit Calvert, photographed at Bolton Castle.

who a few minutes later brought out a velvet-lined case containing his medal, awarded for services to the dale. With growing public acknowledgement and his microscopic knowledge of the dale, the popular Kit (Christopher on Sundays?) became a much sought-after personality, and the short drive to his house a muddy quagmire churned continually, one suspects, by the wheels of radio and television vans.

One day I returned with him to his home village of Burtersett, where I pointed out my field of flowers, commenting on the unusual proportions of the nearby building. He informed me that it had originally been a silk mill. Most folks remembered it as a candle mill, where its owner, 'Candle Willie', met the demand for tallow candles for domestic use, and for lighting in the subterranean quarry drifts. With string and water, and primitive equipment, some skill was required to produce candles of uniform thickness, but Billy Tommy Willie Metcalfe was a craftsman. 'Candle Willie's were good,' remarked Kit, 'but chap as follered 'im med pear-shaped candles!'

Kit's preoccupation with books, Burtersett, and by-gone days soon became evident; the village was his special delight. As we slowly wandered around he pointed out the two quarries, where ponies once brought out sandstone from the various levels – 'Red Gate', 'Fancy End', 'Peacock' – and the hill where the heavy slabs literally pushed the shire horses down towards Hawes station four times a day, on wagons with 'slippers' on chains ready to scotch the wheels. The quarries employed over a hundred men, many of whom would stop at Billy Willie's village shop, opened specially each morning at 7 a.m. for 'blow-up time' to see twists of tobacco at a halfpenny or a penny a 'screw'. There was also a butcher's shop with a 'hung' (slaughter) house, patronised by the Ivesons, Walkers, Dinsdales and Metcalfes of the village.

Kit spoke of great occasions in the 'good old days'; of the 'mell supper' after haymaking was completed; Guy Fawke's night and its bonfires of empty butter and tar barrels; and of the dispute between farmers and quarrymen which resulted in the laying of flagged paths through the fields between village and quarry. Kit had an endless fund of anecdotes. On the occasion of my first visit to his house, he began to talk, and then suddenly, spotting the unopened case of equipment which I was nursing, broke off in the middle of a sentence.

'Have you switched on?' he enquired. 'I'll start again . . .!' Well, I hadn't; and he did. That was the first of many rewarding sessions. Many of his stories were, to say the least, well rehearsed; only once did I see him lost for words, and that was during an account of his childhood and New Year's day when it was the custom for youngsters to make the rounds of the village collecting a gift – an apple, an orange, or even a silver threepenny piece. Fruit went into a pillowcase, money into a purse (and eventually to a Clothing Club run by a Hawes draper!). On one occasion they called at a house and were confronted by an old lady.

'Eh dear luv,' she said, 'Ah hevn't owt.'

The children turned away, patently disappointed.

'But wait a minit,' she called after them.

A moment later she produced a pot of jam, and gave each of the four youngsters a spoonful.

'Ah think of that wi' tears in mi' eyes sometimes,' faltered Kit, visibly moved. 'Poor old body had nothin' to give but a spoonful of jam apiece.' His subsequent reference to the 'modern generation' does not bear repetition.

(May 1988)

KIT'S LAST ARTICLE

Just before he died in January 1984, Kit Calvert contributed an article to The Dalesman *on 'gezlings' – goslings. In it he mentioned the time when his father, yardman at Hawes Auction Mart, went with two dealers – Ernest Myers and W. Smith – to Robin Jackson's farm at Duerley Bottom.*

FATHER PROMISED to take them to Duerley Bottom, which is the furthest farm up Duerley valley, some two and a half miles beyond Gayle. When they arrived next morning, the old farmer took them to a small paddock behind the home to look at the gezlings.

'Them's a fine lot; you'll nut find better in t'deeal.'

'Yes,' replied Ernest. 'What do you value them at?'

Robin asked what they thought was a ridiculous price – more than they would be worth at Christmas, and this was only August, They did not know what to do, as the old man had not shown them any sheep and they did not want to buy the goslings at shillings above market value and then be unable to buy the sheep.

'What have we to do, John?' Mr Smith asked. Father replied: 'Give him his price for t'gezlings and then tak it oot of t'lambs.' On this advice they bought the goslings and turned into a meadow to look at sheep and lambs.

'How much do ye want for the lambs, Mr Jackson?'

'Nay, ye'll kna best what lambs is worth. Your George gave me twenty-four bob last year. They may bi worth maar or maybe less. I doant kna.' A bargain was soon

(D. C. Smith)

struck for the sheep and lambs at very low value, but the goslings were far too dear.

As they drove back to Hawes, they asked father why the old man was so tough on the price for the goslings and yet so indifferent about the sheep. Father replied: 'Ah saw what he was after fra t'start. He wanted t'ga doon t'Gayle and tell all t'quarrymen what he hez meead ev his gezlings and t'booast that he bred t'best gezlings in t'deeal. He's satisfied and you're satisfied, seea it's been a good moorin's wark all roond.'

OPPOSITE
Geese and goslings at Gayle, near Hawes.
(*Robert Rixon*)

(*March 1984*)

HANNAH'S CHRISTMAS

The Dalesman paid a seasonal call on Hannah Hauxwell, who with the quiet resilience *of Dalesfolk survived the trauma of being 'discovered' by television.*

CHRISTMAS DAY is just another working day at Low Birk Hatt, in Baldersdale. This valley unfolds, endlessly it seems, to the west of Romaldkirk, beginning in the temperate zone of Teesdale and ending in the shadow of lean Pennine ridges which, at Christmas, usually have a crust of snow and ice. Hannah Hauxwell lives alone at a farmhouse standing a few hundred yards from where the river became a lake when water engineers plugged the dale. It is not the highest farm in these parts but is, none the less, at an elevation of over 900 feet, where easterly winds can have a cutting edge like a blade of Sheffield steel.

Hannah has been alone for nineteen years. She is solitary, but not lonely, for there are human friends in the local farming families and chance acquaintances among those who are trudging along the Pennine Way. Non-human acquaintances include a sprightly dog named Chip, two cats and the few cattle around which her daily round, seven days a week, is organised. A field track connects her with her nearest neighbours. A road just suitable for wheeled traffic leads out in another direction. Hannah rarely leaves the farm. Since last December there have been just four jaunts – two excursions to relatives living lower down the dale, one to Bolton in Lancashire, at the invitation of a schoolmistress friend, and the fourth to vote in the General Election. The Bolton trip was accomplished within a day. She milked her cattle when that day began and ended.

Hannah Hauxwell. (*W.R. Mitchell*)

Hannah achieved national fame through television. There was an astonishing response from viewers when Yorkshire Television presented a Dales documentary, *Too Long a Winter*. Later she was invited to attend a 'Woman of the Year' luncheon in

London – which she enjoyed – and television cameras followed her around for another documentary. Fame came to her nine years ago. It had been revealed that her income was then £150 a year, some of it derived from letting off most of her 80 acres and some from the occasional sale of cattle. Television focussed attention on her long, gruelling struggle against the land and the climate.

Hannah spends most of the short winter day tending her few cattle. She hand-milks them each morning and evening – there are no specific times, as she is not ruled by the clock – and the milk is available for the young stock, for her pets and, in modest quantities, for herself. Hannah is not very fond of drinking milk. During the week before Christmas last year, she tied up the cattle in the byres and resigned herself to the extra work this would involve. Hannah both loves and hates her cattle. She certainly likes them, but is sometimes weary of the demands they make on her time and energy.

She is now enduring her fiftieth winter at Low Birk Hatt, to which she was borne, from a nearby farm, as a small child. She has never liked winter, and often she dreams about what she imagines the Mediterranean to be like – blue sky, blue sea – as the gales pound her house, loosening yet more slates, and snowdrifts arch themselves against the buildings. Sometimes the wind whirls the snow in an action the Dalesfolk call 'stouring'. Last winter, the worst winter she can remember, left a legacy of work. Some of the walls that were gapped remain gapped. Some of the slates on the outbuildings are still deranged. You may recall that winter overlapped spring. The summer seemed pitifully brief, with the days apparently rushing by towards yet another winter. 'Only the weeds seemed to thrive,' she says. 'It's amazing how *they* recovered after the bad winter.'

Hannah is not an early riser. She copes with her little herd of cattle as best she can. She goes early to bed. The routine is familar to her, for she has known no other. Visitors – mainly summertime visitors – find the area appealing. The tewits (lapwings) call and tumble in the sky. The old thorn trees spread themselves with white blossom. Curlews drawl through the long summer days. Hannah, with a lifelong experience of life in the upper dale, takes such sensations for granted; they are a part of her life. She craves for unlimited sunshine.

No one called last Christmas Day, but there was a visitor on Boxing Day. Meanwhile, little groups of walkers trod the Pennine Way and bade her good-day. Hannah has a supply of electricity, but last winter the power failed for several days. The cold seeped through every stone of her house.

In normal times, she has a television set which offers a picture but no sound. Her radio is a close friend now that her eyesight is not strong enough for sustained reading. The main rooms are heated by electricity, and there is an electric stove. When the power failed, her trusty Army greatcoat – of 1939 vintage – insulated her from the sub-zero temperatures outside, and within the house she swaddled herself in clothes, as well as blankets, when she went to bed. She recalls that one of the items of clothing she spread over herself was a tweed coat that had belonged to her uncle. On each of the days she was without power she had but one meal – a cold drink and some corned beef, with a cold drink before bed at night. It was not that she was without food, but the effort of coping with the cattle in grim weather left her little energy to care for

herself. She could not light coal fires because the chimneys were in need of attention. Her only form of lighting during the power cut was a stable lamp.

Low Birk Hatt has no running water. Hannah collects water from a nearby stream – if it is clear of ice. There is not enough room in the outbuildings to hold all the hay for the cattle, and so some must be stored in another building. She concentrates on feeding the bales stored here before touching the supply at home. When the blizzards raged last winter, she hauled the bales across the glassy surface of the fields on a home-made sled. Incidentally, a kind neighbour mows her meadow and bales the hay.

Groceries are delivered from Cotherstone, being set down at a point within easy walking distance of the farm. The delivery is once a month. She is full of praise for the devotion shown by the delivery man during the last, long winter. Hannah could survive, in a fashion, on a stock of potatoes and 'tins and things', but she has a fondness for butter and cheese. Her routine does not permit her much time for cooking, but in the autumn of 1978 she baked 'tharf' cake and two apple pies.

When the Pennine winter regretfully loses its grip on the high fell country, and the tewits tumble and call, Hannah's spirits revive. Last winter it was 'a bit alarming' to spend several days without electricity. One of the memorable sights was when she became aware that the power had been restored by the valiant men of the electricity authority. Hannah had been cleaning out the byres. She was moving manure to a heap in the gloom when she saw a blaze of light from the farm up the hillside. She went into her house, and switched on the supply. A layer of ice in the electric kettle delayed her preparing hot tea; she had first to warm water in a pan to thaw out the ice. Slowly, heat returned to the rooms and made life within them bearable.

'I'm not really a Christmassy person now,' says Hannah, whose clear, rosy complexion speaks of days spent in the open air. Even on Christmas day, she is absorbed by 'beast-work'. As she reflects on the colder end of the year, she observes wistfully: 'I wish it was always summer.'

W. R. Mitchell (December 1979)

6

YORKSHIRE WRITERS
and a Very Special Artist

A GALAXY OF YORKSHIRE WRITERS

Dr H.C. Strick, the then Warden of Grantley Hall – an adult education college near Ripon, took a detached look at Yorkshire writers, including several featuring in the pages of this anthology.

MANY PROFESSIONAL writers have chosen Yorkshire as the setting for a story at one time or another. Not all of them have been born in Yorkshire. It is perhaps not very important to differentiate between those who were and those who were not, as if we were selecting candidates for the county cricket team. To differentiate in this matter anyway, involves a good deal of research. If you were to persevere in checking the antecedents of British novelists, dramatists and poets, you would find – as you might suppose – a formidable list of Yorkshire-born writers, the best part of a hundred of whom are well-known enough to have retained a readership of sorts. Two Poet Laureates were born in Yorkshire – Laurence Eusden (Spofforth, 1688) and Alfred Austin (Headingley, 1835) – though it is unlikely that many people will know

JOHN SELBY

much of their work. Can one legitimately start the list of poets with Caedmon of Whitby? He did not *write* anything, but his famous hymn is just about the earliest recorded literary work in the native language anywhere in this island, let alone in Yorkshire. Perhaps the finest of the native poets was Andrew Marvell, the 'Cavalier' poet, born in Hull. Yorkshire can also lay claim to the best of the Restoration comedies, *The Way of the World*, by Congreve, born near Leeds – though when it was first staged at Drury Lane in 1670 it was a flop.

To suggest who is the greatest Yorkshire-born writer would be to invite argument, but there can be little doubt that the most prolific was Joseph Smith Fletcher (Halifax, 1863). In the seventy-two years of his life he published over 230 books, according to the British Museum catalogue, most of them good-sized novels and most of

them about his native Yorkshire. That represents more than three books for every year of his life. Ironically enough, although he has a good clear and honest style and is easy to read, for all this impressive output his fame is slight indeed beside that of the Brontës, who produced only seven books among the four of them (if you include Branwell) but have a reputation which is international. The three Brontë daughters are almost the only women writers in our list before 1900. After that year there were many women novelists, with Yorkshire well represented by such names as Naomi Jacob, Winifred Williams, Phyllis Bentley, Lettice Cooper, Storm Jameson and Winifred Holtby. This phenomenon is no doubt due to the appearance in the first quarter of the present century of an emancipated and literate female readership, interested in novels written by women for women. Since the last war the proportion of women novelists has spectacularly decreased, presumably because the women's magazines now meet the demands of that same female readership.

Since the war the most noticeable feature in the work of Yorkshire-born writers has been the number of novels set in the industrial areas of the West Riding and written by men born there. *This Sporting Life* (David Storey), *Room at the Top* and *Life at the Top* (John Braine), *Billy Liar* (Keith Waterhouse) and *A Kind of Loving* (Stan Barstow) are among the examples. Sometimes condemned for their apparent preoccupation with sex, they have a fundamental morality which is frequently overlooked. They all concern young men who ruthlessly and deliberately ignore the feelings of others in order to get what they think they want from life, which is material gain, power and self-gratification; only to find, when they have succeeded,

that in fact they have failed. Their self-seeking has resulted only in the amassing of responsibilities which have to be met. The members of this contemporary group of Yorkshire-born writers are all concerned to pose this moral, that there is no real alternative in life but to face up to one's responsibilities – not because it is 'the thing to do' but for the very much more valid reason that there can be no real fulfilment otherwise.

The industrial West Riding has been well-served by native writers. In addition to the group mentioned above, Thomas Armstrong and J. B. Priestley have written about the region with the authenticity which comes from having been born in it. From the beginning of industrialisation, through the depression and two world wars to the Welfare State, family life in the West Riding woollen industry has been amply and compellingly depicted. Similarly, the Yorkshire coastal region has been adequately treated. The essence of the fishing villages and ports and the seaside resorts has been effectively distilled by writers such as Leo Walmsley from Robin Hood's Bay, O. H. Harland of Middlesbrough and Edward Booth of Doncaster, and in an earlier generation by Mary Linskill, born in Whitby in 1840. She sometimes used the alias 'Stephen Yorke'.

Have the Yorkshire Dales found their expression in the same way? They have had their writers – James Keighley Snowden, Mary Beaumont, William Riley, H. F. M. Prescott and 'Gil North', who uses them as a setting for the exploits of Sergeant Cluff. It is arguable, however, that few of them have been able to capture, or at any rate to maintain, the true and inimitable atmosphere of the Dales and Dalesfolk. Perhaps the remoteness and the romanticism of the setting have always over-excited the imagination of the writers. When the Saxons and Danes arrived as foreigners in the Dark Ages, their imaginations were carried away by what they found, whether the Wensleydale waterfalls which reminded them of Aasgard, the playground of the gods (we call it Aysgarth today) or the rocky valley by Greenhow which we still know as Troller's Ghyll, perhaps because the trolls haunted it – as also did the Barguest, the great ghostly hound which roamed the moors on wild nights. The Brontës had much this same feeling about the moors; *Wuthering Heights* gives them the same spine-chilling quality, both literally and figuratively.

Perhaps the writer who is remembered with most affection as a portrayer of Dales and Dalesfolk is Halliwell Sutcliffe, born in Bingley in 1870. It is hardly likely that anyone below middle age reads him nowadays, unless by accident or curiosity, for his manner and his style could hardly be less in keeping with the tastes of today – though this does not in itself necessarily prove anything to be wrong with his manner and style. He certainly has a profound affection for 'Wharfe River', as he persists in calling it, and for the moors enclosing it which he peoples with picturesque and frequently violent characters. Often the atmosphere is genuine, as for an occasion in *Storm* and *Peddlar's Quest*.

One warning – although he writes so much historical fiction, it is as well to treat his history as fiction rather than fact. He himself admits that legend, tradition and imagination are at least as valid for him as proven record. The strong element of romance in Halliwell Sutcliffe means that he gives a highly-coloured and larger-than-life picture of the Dales and their inhabitants even when he is writing what are ostensibly non-fictional accounts, such as *The Striding Dales* and *By Moor and Fell*. There are, of course, scholars and social historians who have together compiled an account of the Yorkshire Dales as comprehensive, detailed, accurate and compelling as has been produced for any other part of England. Arthur Raistrick, Bernard Jennings, Marie Hartley and Joan Ingilby are among those who immediately come to mind.

The Yorkshire Dales still await the writer who will do for them what Hardy did for Wessex or Mary Webb for Shropshire. It will have to be someone who, even if not a Dalesman born, has lived there a long time. The Dales and their inhabitants are too complex and too self-contained to be readily interpreted by the superficial observer.

(August 1969)

INTRODUCING THE BRONTËS

More has been written about the three famous Brontë sisters – and their infamous brother – than any other English authors since Shakespeare. Emily Brontë's Wuthering Heights *is the Yorkshire novel* par excellence *and illumines the strange wild country round Haworth like a beacon light. Phyllis Bentley, herself the author of a fine series of novels on West Riding life – including her most famous book* Inheritance, *explained why the Brontës have endured.*

THE BRONTË sisters wrote, in all, seven novels. Charlotte's four novels are *The Professor, Jane Eyre, Shirley, Villette*; Anne's two novels are *Agnes Grey* and *The Tenant of Wildfell Hall*; Emily's solitary but superb novel is *Wuthering Heights. Jane Eyre* appeared in October, 1847, *Agnes Grey* and *Wuthering Heights* were published – together, as they were not long enough singly to fill the three volumes then considered proper for a work of fiction – in December, 1847. *The Tenant* appeared in 1848; *Shirley* in 1849, *Villette* in 1853; *The Professor*, though the first of Charlotte's novels to be written, was not published until 1857, two years after her death.

Ten years, from 1847 to 1857; seven novels; it is a brief and in some respects a scanty flowering. Moreover, the hundred years between 1847 and today form a period particularly rich in English fiction. Most of the books of Dickens, the best of Thackeray, the novels of Trollope, George Eliot, Meredith and Hardy, as well as of the writers of the 20th century, Bennett, Wells, Galsworthy and so on, have appeared for the delight of readers since the Brontës' day. Yet the books of these three sisters from the bleak little moorland parish of Haworth still retain a very great popularity . . .

The Brontës' lives have a strange and poignant fascination because of the con-

Phyllis Bentley.

trast between their great inward genius and their narrow and frustrated outward circumstances. Charlotte, Branwell, Emily and Anne, with two elder sisters, were the children of a Cornish gentlewoman and an Irish peasant who had educated himself to be a curate. Mr Brontë became incumbent of Haworth when his eldest child was seven years old. His wife died there the year after, and her sister, Miss Branwell, came to live at Haworth Parsonage to look after the children. Miss Branwell brought the girls up well, but was perhaps rather chilly and pernickety and always grumbling about the Haworth weather; at any rate the girls never alluded to her with much affection.

As curate Mr Brontë had been a lively, prattling fellow, even a little flirtatious at times; but the loss of his wife and the remote situation of Haworth made him into a fiery-tempered recluse – he even ate his meals alone. He taught his children to read good books and newspapers, however, and to take a keen and informed interest in politics. The four elder girls were sent to a school for clergymen's daughters, and the two eldest died from consumption after a year there. Later, the three remaining girls took posts as governesses in private houses, and their brother similarly became a private tutor. The girls were unhappy in their posts and decided to found a school of their own; to acquire suitable accomplishments for this purpose Charlotte and Emily went to a school in Brussels.

How mild and ordinary it all sounds! But beneath this conventional parson's-daughter surface lay burning, passionate, turbulent genius, struggling fiercely to gain

Haworth main street. (*Terence Murphy*)

expression. The terrible conflict between this urgent genius and the restricting bonds of their narrow lives drove the weak Branwell to drink and despair, drove his sisters to the creation of their tempestuous novels, drove them all into an early grave – they all died in their early thirties. Mrs Gaskell's *Life of Charlotte Brontë*, which tells this story, is one of the most painfully exciting books in the English language. The story of the Brontës' lives had indeed so many facets, so much struggle, so much pent-up emotion, so much tragedy, so much fiery ardour, that large numbers of biographies, novels, plays, have been founded upon it, and film directors are beginning to discover its fascination too.

Now for a question: why are the Brontë novels still worth reading? The answer is quite simple. There are four main elements in a novel: the characters, the story, the setting and the words in which the story is told. In respect of all these four elements, the Brontës still have something fine and rich and rare to offer to the reader. The words in which they write are most powerful and fine. They do not write in a flowery manner, but in a firm plain style which is just as easy to read today as it was a hundred years ago; yet the way the words are arranged makes them deeply and splendidly impressive. If you read, for example, Mr Lockwood's dream of the dead Cathy tapping on the window, in *Wuthering Heights*, the words are so powerful that cold shudders run down the spine. I remember having to read this scene some years ago over the microphone in the Leeds studio; in spite of the prosaic surroundings, electric light and sound-proof curtains and well-padded chairs and settees, in spite too of the presence of the announcer, I felt the same strange fear and excitement as Mr Lockwood did when Cathy's ghost wailed:

'Let me in!' Scenes of similar power, which make unforgettable impressions on the reader, are the garden love-scene between Jane and Mr Rochester in *Jane Eyre*, and Lucy Snowe's night journey in *Villette*.

It is, of course, the Brontës' presentation of their Yorkshire setting, the West Riding moorlands, which especially endears their books to Yorkshire readers. The most 'Yorkshire' of the Brontë novels are Charlotte's *Shirley* and Emily's *Wuthering Heights*, but there are Yorkshire landscapes in all the novels – for instance, Anne gives a charming picture of Scarborough in *Agnes Grey*. Wuthering Heights, as everyone knows, is the name of a storm-beaten old mansion on a brow of the West Riding moors, 'wuthering', as Emily explains, being a significant Yorkshire adjective indicating the amount of weather they have up there. Emily describes the wild moors in all their moods; in all their seasons, in all their weathers. A great many of the incidents of the book take place out of doors, and even when the story moves inside the house, the power of the north wind is never far away – always 'the blast wails by' the windows. Indeed Emily's pictures of our moorland are unsurpassed in English fiction; wild, grim, sombre, perhaps, but majestic in power and sweep . . .

The special quality, the special flavour of the Brontës' writing is due to the mingling of Irish and Yorkshire in their mental make-up. No other novelists have written of Yorkshire with such Celtic power and fire. So the Brontë novels offer readers not only a highly pleasurable, exciting and instructive, but also a unique experience, which we can obtain from no other fiction. It is an experience no Yorkshire reader should miss.

(June 1947)

PRIESTLEY IN THE DALES

J.B. Priestley, who introduced the first number of The Dalesman *in April 1939 (see page 1), seldom visited Yorkshire in his latter years. An exception came in 1965, when he was commissioned by the prestigious American magazine* Life International *to write an article on the Dales. He called at* The Dalesman *offices and later made the following comments – in Swaledale one day in late May.*

J. B. Priestley on . . .

Dalesfolk

Talking among themselves they sound Scandinavian, rather like minor Ibsen characters. But they are good people, not yet corrupted by tourism.

His first visits

I knew the lower part of the Dales when I was a child, well before the First World War. Just after the first war, I got to know the upper valleys well. One of the first jobs I did when I came out of the Army was to have a walking tour for the *Yorkshire Observer*. Four or five articles. Guinea a time. I stayed a night in Coverdale. It was then very remote indeed. I remember that first walking tour well, for the weather was brilliantly fine and hot.

J.B. Priestley, photographed in Swaledale in 1965. (*W.R. Mitchell*)

Dales weather

The Dales are probably the most satisfying countryside in the world. But you need sun. When the sun comes out, it's magic. If there's no sun at all it's apt to be too grey. A mixture of sunshine and cloud is wonderful.

His favourite Dale

Wensleydale is my favourite Dale. It has perhaps more variety than any other dale. It's not as grand as Swaledale, or in some respects Upper Wharfedale. It has great charm, and the play of light on it is probably better than in any other dale. I regard Wensleydale as a sort of anchor-man to the whole thing.

Dales villages

On the whole, they are very tidy and well-kept. You don't get heaps of rubbish all over the place. I think they have changed less than any other part of England I know, with the possible exception of a small section of the Cotswolds which has been carefully planned and controlled. Bainbridge, where I have been staying, looks very little different from what it did forty years ago.

Food

I think the food was better years ago. There were not the caterers' tricks. The food was simpler, with less attempt to make an hotel meal out of it.

Pies

It is the essence of a pie, whether a meat pie or a fruit pie, that the crust is baked with the pie, and is part of it. It's now a great caterers' trick to stew some fruit or meat and add a square of crust done separately. This is not a pie, and it irritates me when I encounter it.

Painting

I love the broad open landscape of the Dales. The last time I was here I had some of the most successful paintings I have ever done. But you do need a bit of sunlight to bring out the colours. I've been painting for about ten years, and I've always done gouache. I only paint on holiday, and I get very cross when I can't do it. I've only done one sketch since I came, which makes me angry.

(August 1965)

A MAN OF THE MOORS

'Bolton Bridge sweeps in a comely arch across Wharfe River, brown with moorland peat; and the road goes forward, after its long stride, between quiet pastures where the cattle graze.' So begins Halliwell Sutcliffe's The Striding Dales, *a work heavy in legend and nostalgia. Norman Thornber recalled the high priest of moorland romances.*

TO INNUMERABLE lovers of Yorkshire's Dales the name of Halliwell Sutcliffe stands for moorland romances. His novels have made Yorkshire's moors known, not only as mere tracts of waste land or purple heather, but vibrant and living, in turn somnolent, repellent, fascinating and bound up with loves and hatreds. What manner of man was the author of these romances? To most people he is merely a name, an almost legendary word painter. Halliwell Sutcliffe to the general public was something of a recluse, but he was not a recluse in the tiny village of Linton, near Skipton. There he was a villager, one of the people and one who was in every sense a Dalesman. Had he preferred to leave the Dales for London he would have been lionised and could have made much money in the process. Halliwell Sutcliffe preferred to remain at Linton and continue writing those delightful novels. Once when asked to attend a series of functions in London he replied, 'You can have me, but you will not be able to have my books as well.' Ulti-

White Abbey, Linton, home of Halliwell Sutcliffe. (*Derek G. Widdicombe*)

mately he stayed at home and gave the world another novel.

Although he was actually born just outside Bradford, this man of the moors claimed Lee, near Haworth, as his true birthplace. It was there his family was residing, and there he attended the village school kept by his father. Later when his father was appointed to a headmastership at Bingley, father and son would walk at least once every week over the five miles of moors between Bingley and Haworth. From an early age he was so steeped in the traditions, history and environment of the Haworth country that it could be claimed that he was more 'Haworth' than the Brontës. Members of the Brontë Society may take umbrage at this but as Sutcliffe pointed out, the Brontës could not help but write. A mixture of Irish and Cornish, they would still have written books about

their environment even if they had lived in the East End of London.

The early days of Halliwell Sutcliffe were hard days. Having adopted writing as a profession, he had to struggle to make his way. Once a few of his books had been accepted, then the going was much easier. His first book was published in 1893 and thereafter he was a prolific writer. At first he tried living in London, but the urge to live on the moors, amidst the setting of his novels, could not be subdued. And so this Yorkshire writer came back again to the Dales, first to Embsay and then finally in 1907 to White Abbey, Linton.

At his house in Linton he was in his true environment. There he made a great rock garden. From his garden he looked across the pastures to the moors in the blue haze. The stream at the garden foot meandered underneath the trees and bridges past the village green where the youth of the village played cricket and football. Halliwell Sutcliffe spent days in that rock garden, tending it and making it a masterpiece of beauty. The scent of a flower, he said, was an inspiration to a writer. When someone pointed out some weeds Sutcliffe retorted, 'Why look at the weeds when there are other beautiful things to see.' I cannot think of anything more typical of the man than this reply. It was typical of his books, too, for his stories deal, not with the weeds in life, but the flowers, rocks, soil and pools.

Much of the drama in his work came from the Yorkshire Dales feuds, which Halliwell Sutcliffe sketches so faithfully and so vigorously. One can picture the enjoyment of the Eton boys when they dramatised *Shameless Wayne*. The story of the fights between Ratcliffe and Wayne appealed to these boys more than anything else. It is not generally known that the fight in the churchyard was written while Mr and Mrs Sutcliffe were staying at Haworth Rectory. Their room overlooked the churchyard of Haworth, a familiar scene to the author, peopled as it was with ghosts of the past – his past.

Besides writing thirty novels, Halliwell Sutcliffe was a writer of delightful verse. He also wrote several pageants, notably those for Lancaster and Bradford. His novels, too, were correct geographically. The best proof of this is in *Pam, the Fiddler*. A reader of this book, although a complete stranger to the district, found his way to Thorpe, near Linton, where the scene is set, by following the book. *Ricroft of Withens* was broadcast some years ago from Leeds. It was a pity that broadcasting in those days had not reached the audience it has today. Many hundreds would have liked to hear the author tell this Yorkshire story in his own words. To the few who did hear the six broadcasts, it revealed the author in a new light. It revealed a voice full of personality, a voice which was essentially that of the Dales.

Although Halliwell Sutcliffe preferred the Dales, the Authors' Club in London paid him a great honour when he succeeded Sir Rider Haggard on the Council of the club. He was also associated with West Riding ramblers' clubs and delighted to show visitors and visiting clubs his moors and dales. It was surprising that he was not more actively associated with cycling clubs. An ardent cyclist, he had no use for motor cars as a means of seeing the countryside. A bicycle, he maintained, was quite quick enough. On it one could meander at will, stopping to admire a view or capture some beauty and inspiration from the clouds over distant moors. When wanting exercise, or the details of a new setting, he would sally forth on his bicycle exchanging pleasantries with those moor-land farmers who he knew so well.

He worked chiefly at night. After dinner he would start his writing. Generally about 8.30 p.m. he would retire to his study and work until the early hours, putting on to paper all that he had felt and experienced during the day, either on his cycle ride or while working on his garden. When in January 1932, Halliwell Sutcliffe died,

hundreds attended the funeral service at Burnsall Church, for which he had such an affection. Halliwell Sutcliffe went back to the moors, for his ashes were scattered in the winds on those moors of which he had written so lovingly. The man of the moors had returned home.

(July 1939)

SEARCHING FOR YORLADALE

Dorothy Una Ratcliffe – or D. U. R. as she preferred to be called – was closely associated with the early years of The Dalesman. *When the magazine came into being, she was prompt to offer help and encouragement. She contributed stories and some evocative dialect verse, suggested useful contacts and put us in touch with all manner of people from gypsies to the National Trust! She was fascinated by the Romany world and had always something of the gay abandon of the gypsy in her own personality.*

Her writings have tended to be neglected since her death in 1967 but are now beginning to enjoy something of a revival. Jacey Bedford of the singing group Artisan came across a copy of D. U.R.'s Yorkshire Lyrics – and the result was an L.P. record Searching for Yorladale *which re-discovered musically the well-loved Yorkshire poems of a remarkable woman. John Adams, who made the record, wrote this background article.*

A MAP of the Yorkshire Dales, how-ever carefully examined, will not yield any clues as to the where-abouts of Yorladale. This magical spot, like Hardy's 'Wessex', existed only in the mind of this very imaginative and talented lady. Those who have been reading *The Dales-man* for many years will certainly have read some of her writings, for she was a regular contributor, but those who have joined the readership within twenty years may not recognise the name.

Dorothy Una Ratcliffe was Yorkshire by adoption. Although she was born in Sussex her father, George Benson Clough, was a Yorkshireman and she always considered this county her own. A prolific writer from an early age, she had forty-nine books published during her lifetime, including lyrics, dialect poetry, travel and autobio-graphical works. Her numerous articles in *The Dalesman* and *The Yorkshire Post* endeared her to many who shared her passion for the Dales and it was that readership that granted her the rare honour of being referred to by her initials – D.U.R.

Her writing was based closely on her observation of the characters and scenery of the Yorkshire Dales, particularly Wensleydale, which was her favourite area. Many of her poems mention specific areas such as Hawes, Yockenthwaite, Penhill and Leyburn, and her work is like a living gazetteer, filled with the love of the land and the life on it, and showing a genuine admiration for its people. Though her writings include accounts of her travels to Greece and Africa, D.U.R. always returned to her beloved Dales and few poets encapsulate the atmosphere of the region as she did . . .

As a child Dorothy had her first contact with Yorkshire when she used to travel North to visit her Grandfather Clough in Wasdale. On these trips she would often stay with her nurse Hannah Moorhouse and it was from Hannah that she first learned Yorkshire dialect. At home Dorothy was the motivator in the family group and at the age of ten or eleven led her three sisters in the production of the handwritten family magazine containing poems, essays, news and illustrations. This interest in publishing carried on into her married life for after her marriage, in 1909, to Charles Frederick Ratcliffe, nephew of Lord Brotherton of Wakefield, she was editing a magazine called *The Microcosm* which her sister Pauline had started some time previously, and which was produced to raise money for charity. Dorothy had moved to Yorkshire and it was there that a particular event sparked off a passion for rare books. *The Towneley Mysteries*, the Wakefield cycle of mystery plays, was offered for sale at Sotheby's in February 1922, and many North Country people were anxious to have it purchased for the City of Wakefield. Dorothy persuaded her uncle-in-law Lord Brotherton, then MP for Wakefield,

to bid for it. The bid was unsuccessful and the book went to a Californian millionaire. As compensation, Lord Brotherton bought a first edition copy of Andrew Marvell's *Garden Poems*. These poems by one of Yorkshire's finest poets was the first volume in the Brotherton Collection, now housed in Leeds University Library.

Dorothy's marriage to Charles didn't last and in 1932, after a divorce, she married Captain Noel McGrigor Phillips of Cobham, Surrey. For the first few years of their marriage they travelled extensively both abroad and at home. Dorothy loved the freedom which a caravan afforded and the couple spent as much time as possible touring the Yorkshire Dales from their home, Temple Sowerby Manor near Penrith. Sadly Dorothy's second marriage lasted only for eleven years. Noel, as the result of long-term kidney damage sustained in Gallipoli during the First World War, was taken suddenly ill and died leaving Dorothy heartbroken. Some of her loveliest poems were written in memory of Noel, *Croodle Beck* being perhaps the most outstanding for its simplicity. Croodle Beck is the local name for Crowdundle Beck, which flows through the gardens of Temple Sowerby Manor. In 1950, Dorothy gave her home to the National Trust and the gardens, known as Acorn Bank, are open to the public. With her third husband, Alfred Charles Phillips, she continued her close association with the Dales. They had a caravan sited on a farm in Wensleydale and spent much time there together. Wensleydale was probably D.U.R.'s favourite area and it was for this reason that Artisan adopted Dorothy's special name for it as the title of their musical tribute to her. Through Wensleydale flows the River Ure, hence Uredale/Yoredale/Yorladale . . .

Sadly we all missed meeting Dorothy herself by twenty years, as she died in 1967, but she still lives on in the memories of those people who knew her, and those who read her books. I hope that *Searching* for *Yorladale* will be another suitable memorial to a very remarkable lady.

(October 1988)

Will's Stead

'My stead's far end o' neeawheer,
Neea lass wud care to settle theer:
Afore she died, my Muther said,
"It's time, dear lad, 'at thoo wur wed.
I weeänt bide wi' thee fur aye,
Soa Willie, think on what I say.
What aboot Meg? Write her a letter,
(At butter-making theer's noän
        better) . . .
Theer's Joan, she'll hae a seet o' brass
Yan day, an' she's a gradely lass!"

'Aboot 'em baith, my mind's a-muddle
For neether lass, I aim to cuddle.
I wud far liefer gae a-coortin'
O' t'gamesome red-head, Jennie Norton,
But Muther says she's not mich use –
Yet happen she's yan I wud choose,
But then she'd nivver look at me;
I'se noy young Jennie's cup o' tea!

'On starless neets when nor' wind howls
An' young bull beals an' sheep-cur yowls,
An' I'se reet lanesome, then I goes
To t'byre an' sings to milkin' coos.
In t'ingle-neuk I mend my socks,
An' think on Spring at Coortin' Rocks;
Hoo lark 'ull trill an' curlew whistle,
Mavis, blackie, wren an' missel;
Hoo ivery bird agen an' agen
'Ull sing a luve-sang to his hen.
Meg is in Leeds, Joan's walkin' oot,
I'll nivver wed, I have neea doubt;
For wheer is t'lass 'at wud bide here,
In t'stead far end o' neeawheer!'

DOROTHY UNA RATCLIFFE
(December 1958)

FRED LAWSON: WENSLEYDALE ARTIST

Many of Dorothy Una Ratcliffe's poems in The Dalesman *– as well as several of her books – were illustrated by Fred Lawson, who went to Castle Bolton for a holiday in 1910 and stayed there until his death in 1967. It became a familiar sight in Wensleydale to see Fred painting in a battered old hat and jacket, and in winter muffled up in half-a-dozen sacks. For ten years each issue of* The Dalesman *carried Fred Lawson's* Letter from the Dales *– conversational in style, simple yet profound. It was accompanied by a mini-masterpiece of a drawing, invariably completed out of doors, and a piece of poetry selected with great care by his wife Muriel. Ralph Whitling penned this tribute to a happy philosopher and very special artist.*

I T WOULD BE impossible to recall how many times I have knocked on the door of the Lawsons' little house in Castle Bolton, but always it was with a pleasurable thrill of anticipation. There were two possibilities. Either the door would be opened, and there would be a warm greeting: 'Come in, come in, Ralph!' This from Fred, adding his characteristic wry chuckle. Or there would be a note pinned on the door with words such as: 'Gone to Bolton Ghyll' or 'Up at Fox Cover' or 'On at the Castle'. The door was always left unlocked. It was an open house, and there was a welcome for everyone who called. My heart warms at the recollection of my many visits to that delightful home.

The living room had a magical atmosphere of its own. There was always a selection of Fred's pictures hanging on the walls. Poetry books and geographical magazines were spread around the shelves, and on the table, and the drawers were full of Fred's water-colours and pen sketches, which I never tired of scanning. On the sideboard were various porcelain statuettes – a large Ho-ti, the Chinese embodiment of happiness and contentment, the Indian god Krishna playing his flute, and English

Fred Lawson. (*W.H. Womersley*)

traditional figures, all of which Fred had included in his still life paintings at some time or other. Looking through the window, one saw the magnificent view across Wensleydale to Pen Hill, which Fred loved and painted in so many moods at all seasons of the year.

I first met Fred almost forty years ago, at the studio in Leeds of a mutual friend, the portrait artist Jacob Kramer. Immediately I fell under the spell of this man and his individualistic art. I asked if at some time I could go with him on a painting expedition to have lessons in the water-colour technique. In those far-off days, when I made my first visit, I travelled up the dale by steam train, and from Redmire station I walked across the fields past the old vicarage to stay at the *King's Arms* with the hospitable Mr and Mrs Joe Alderson. It was good to watch the horses pulling loads of hay on sleds on the hill slopes; to see the donkeys laden with huge flat-sided cans coming from the pastures where the cows had been milked. Fred loved to paint these homely, rural scenes, and his work over the years must represent a record of local social history. One of his favourite subjects was an old steam threshing machine at Woodhead Farm.

One did not only learn the technique of water-colour painting from Fred – one discovered a way of life. All his beautiful pictures and drawings expressed a philosophy of life without the need of words. He said: 'If a picture is to be good it must have a fair amount of love in it, and also a little humanity.' Fred's paintings assuredly had both. Fred loved the people, the way of life, the countryside, the flowers, the trees and the varied moods of nature. Living a simple, almost frugal life, he worked with devotion to capture the beauty and to record the life of the dale. He identified himself with the country folk and they in turn respected him. Every cottage and farm house for miles around Leyburn, Redmire and Castle Bolton must have had two or three of Fred's pictures hanging on the walls.

In time, I was enriched by having the friendship of the other two members of the little family – Muriel, Fred's wife, a sensitive mystic and a talented artist in her own right, and their daughter Sonia, a serene child with raven black hair and a dusky beauty. She also is now a highly successful and widely recognised artist. Many times have we walked through the meadows and discussed art, aesthetics, poetry and the life of the dale. There were happy days picnicking by the river at Redmire Falls, sometimes paddling or swimming in the near-golden water. I am delighted to have one of Fred's watercolours of Redmire Falls in sunshine to remind me of those halcyon times.

Fred painted and drew every day, going out at all seasons and in all weathers, producing glowing snowscapes, storms, golden sunsets, lazy summer days, lichened tree trunks, the homes of the dale's people and the men at work – ploughing, felling trees, sheep shearing and many other rural occupations. He became a legend in his own day. People visited him and wrote to him from all parts of the world but, in spite of his fame, he remained humble, unaffected and unperturbed by the many visitors, who came to meet the man and to buy his pictures.

(March 1979)

FRED LAWSON'S LETTER FROM THE DALES

CASTLE BOLTON
March.

> While yet we wait for spring –
> Already in glimpses of the tarnish'd sky
> The sun is warm and beckons to the larch,
> And where the covert hazels interarch
> Their tassel'd twigs, fair beds of primrose lie.
>
> *Robert Bridges*

Dear Dalesman,

IT HAS been a cold, dull, wild day. A little sun now, at tea time. Yesterday was lovely like early summer. I sat painting some rocks and trees just above the village and had a chat with the farmer as I went up.

The trees are fine sycamores, with interesting roots twisting and gripping the rocks. After the farmer I saw no one all afternoon.

One of the village ducks walked past me. This one has started going by itself; it does not join in with the other three now. It was very dignified, that is the front half of it. It kept its near eye on me all the time, and when it got nicely past it flew off.

We have had some fine spring weather and I have had some good days painting up the ghyll. Primroses are plentiful. Snow-drops have made a fine show but are just about over, and now the daffodils are out. A neighbour higher up has a fine show all round his house. He has had big clumps of snowdrops in the grass all round. I think if he dropped bulbs out of his pocket they would dig themselves in and do well. I have set bulbs myself at times and I don't think that I have had one flower, just one or two green spikes for a year or two and then nothing.

I remember one wet spring stopping to watch a man who was baring a piece of his garden, making a new bed, each top grassy piece as it was cut was carried by his young son on to a pile. As I watched, the son came with one raggy piece that had lumps of wet earth dangling from it, and after a long look at it before putting it on the pile, said, 'By dad! That's t'muckiest sod I've ever seen.'

It's a pleasure to have longer daylight at nights.

One day I did this drawing of one of my favourite old buildings. It's the last build-ing on the north side of the village. After this there's rough land and moors till you come to the Swaledale villages about six miles away. There old buildings always stand well, and make nice silhouettes against the sky.

A man said to me one day, 'T'pluvvers have come back.' I repeated this to some-one and naturally said plovers, and got no response. So I mentioned who had told me. After some explaining they said, 'Nay, did he say plovers? Did he mean pluvvers?'

Have just been to the post, and heard they have had two inches of snow in parts of Scotland, and the sky in the west past the castle was one of the wildest that I have ever seen.

Muriel said to me one day, 'Have you noticed what lovely long lines of coloured washing are hanging out?' Big things like bedspreads and curtains.

The little girl next door passed with a small bunch of violets in her hand. Hens have been sitting in the middle of the road, sunning themselves. Lambing officially starts here this week-end.

It's difficult to write about anything but spring. Yesterday I loitered by a flowering currant bush. Hawkers have started again with mats and carpets. Birds still fly past the window or sit on the ledge waiting, and black crows still flap about in the apple tree. Our garden hedge is a feathery green.

Yours,
Fred Lawson.

(May 1961)

7

ON THE FARM

FARM LIFE IN BISHOPDALE

Within two decades the Dales' farming scene has changed almost beyond recognition. Elizabeth Large, farmer's wife, penned a wonderfully evocative picture of the haytime of old with horse-drawn machinery, haycocks and Irish labourers.

IT IS THE end of June. There is great activity in the tool room and implement shed, because the weather is settling sufficiently for haytime to start in a day or two. I am taking an hour of freedom before this becomes impossible, and decide to go for my favourite walk, up Foss Beck with its many waterfalls and thence to the top of the fells. As I climb, I often stand and look down into Bishopdale and far away at the blue hills in the distance. Shafts of sunlight pierce the drifting cloud shadows, illuminating patches of hillside with a radiance not of this world . . .

I first came here in May nearly twenty years ago, when I thought it was the most beautiful valley I had ever seen. Nor have I found reason to change my mind. Snow still lay in hollows on the tops of the fells, over which the curlews wheeled, uttering their wild, bubbling, spring-time call, and the beck foamed along the valley bottom. I often used to walk past our farmhouse in those days, but no inner voice whispered that one day I would live there myself. My husband also, often came walking down this dale as a young man, but he never knew that one day he would be a farmer and live in the house across the stepping-stones.

In actual fact the farm was started soon after the school, to supply the children

with tuberculin tested milk and teach them all about farming. The school broke up at the end of the war but we remained, and though the gooseberries no longer disappeared from the garden, we missed our merry helpers. It did not take very long to get in a field of hay in those days. The children used to rake up the field in a long line and when they arrived at the top they turned and raked down the field again. James, our musical prodigy, once got to the top and then proceeded up the hillside raking nothing at all for a good five minutes, while we leaned on our rakes to see how long it would take him to emerge from his entrancement of musical composition. Oh, happy brown-legged children, so far from the sight and sound of war! Now they are scattered, but they all remember Bishopdale with love and longing.

We have lived here long enough to witness the decay of the old era and the dawn of the new age. Electricity is coming up the dale at last, and the road is being widened to meet the needs of the heavy holiday traffic. I am saddened at the passing of the secret, hidden places that used to lie so far from life's fitful fever. I shall have to hie me to Himalaya or a remote Canadian forest if the Dales become too civilised. We never saw the scythe in sole use at hay-time. It is only used now for those odd little corners that machines cannot get at, but when we came to Bishopdale during the war tractors were unknown and all the old horse-drawn machines were in use. They were just like my grandfather's hay-making implements on the little farm in Nova Scotia where I was born.

In my childhood days the golden wagon loads were drawn by Prince to a great covered barn, where the hay would be well protected from the snows. You could take your time about hay-making in Canada, for the summers were hot. Up here in the high dales quick methods of hay-making have had to be evolved because of the heavy rainfall. Almost every field contains its own grey stone barn with a hay loft above and byres below. On very fine days when the hay makes quickly, it is rowed up by a

win-rower and then swept directly to the barn, where it is forked up without further ado. On more unsettled days the hay is often made into small cocks and from these forked up into big pikes which can stand up to a good deal of rain if they are well made. The pikes can be transferred to the barns at leisure when the weather improves.

After the school left, hay-time labour was very difficult to obtain, but we were able to hire Ukranians from a camp for displaced persons. They were a marvel with horses and it was wonderful to see them mount our cart-horses and go galloping over the fields bareback, for all the world as if they were once more on the great plains in Asia. The Ukranians mostly found their way to Canada in the end, so we eventually followed the example of our neighbours and took to hiring an Irishman for hay-time. For five happy summers John came to give us a hand. How the children looked

The traditional Dales haytime personified – an August scene in Dentdale. (*Geoffrey N. Wright*)

forward to his coming! He caught them baby rabbits and hedgehogs for pets and found them birds' nests.

On Sundays he taught them to tickle trout and they all spent one morning chasing eels up and down the beck, pronging them with my kitchen fork and putting them upstairs in the bath tub till they were ready for skinning. Our guest found them and nearly had hysterics. Late each evening after the day's work he set rabbit snares and provided us with many a tasty hay-time stew. This was before the days of the rabbit disease. What a splendid worker he was, too! The young Irishmen who go into the country for the summer demand a high wage, but the skilled ones are worth every pound of it. John was a farmer's son and had learned his craft from the age of six or

so. I must say, he knew his poaching too!

Now we do not have Irishmen any more because of the weather. Excepting for the remarkable summer of 1955, the last few hay-times have hardly seen a dry day up in these hills. We shiver in barns over the mugs of tea and cakes I bring out to refresh the tired men, and my husband drives the tractor well muffled in thick pullovers and scarves. If a fine day comes one might be lucky enough to get hold of that popular man, the baler. How exciting that is! The baling machine goes round and round the field, licking up hay at one end and spitting it out in neatly tied bales at the other. Everyone turns out to help or watch, and the cats all come to play leap-frog over the bales. For a few hours the hayfield looks more like its old cheerful self of the days when summers were summers.

We have made much of our hay on

Farmers at Penistone Mart. (*Simon Warner*)

tripods during the past few years, because by this method it can be put on half-green. Unless a howling gale sweeps down the dale blowing all the tripods over, very fine hay is made in this way. One certainly tries every possible way of fooling the weather, including silage-making, but nevertheless during some years lately we have not finished dealing with the hay-crop till the beginning of October. At least we can be thankful that it has all been gathered in – no rotting grass or pikes floating in the floods.

Because we tend to glamorise the past in retrospect, I know that in after years I shall gloss over the continuous rain and the acres of mud. I shall best remember our dale on a perfect summer evening, as a sort of earthly Paradise, a Shangri-La set in the English hills. My husband is standing beneath the damson tree playing his violin while his faithful hound lies at his feet. She sleeps warily with one ear cocked and one eye on her traditional enemies the cats, who are scatting madly round and round

the garden. Lambkin is standing on the wall pruning roses, tiger lilies, any herbage within reach, excepting mere common-place grass. The children run past the house twirling their bathing costumes, off for a last swim in the beck before bed-time. They will not need a bath tonight but they will be very hungry indeed for good milk and home-made wholemeal bread. No wonder they look so healthy.

The pleasure traffic has returned to the great industrial towns, leaving the dale to the dwellers therein, while over the hill the risen moon starts to brighten and the first owl calls softly. That is how I shall remember it all. But, as I sit outside the shooting-box, I wonder where it will all end, this new age we are coming to. Will the soil be heated by atomic power, thus releasing its marvellous fertility? Will there be summer chalets and helicopters all over the fells? Shall we all be shepherding the sheep by radar? Who knows – but I hope I shall not be here to see.

(June 1959)

TO BE A FARMER'S BOY

Irene Megginson, who now contributes a monthly 'Letter from the Wolds' to The Dalesman, *set down her memories of farm lads on the Wolds. Hours were long and work was hard, but there was a happy comradeship and a pride in doing the job.*

O N THE larger farms, often around 1,000 acres, the unmarried men 'lived in' at the foreman's house. This was good-sized and well-built, standing 100 yards or so from the big farmhouse.

Both were protected by the usual 'shelter belt' of hardwood trees, without which life would have been a bleak prospect on the high windswept hills. The foreman's house was known as the 'hind's house' and the

foreman's wife, the 'hind's wife'. It was her job to provide beds for the men, two to a double-bed, in a large dormitory-like bedroom, and to feed them at a long scrubbed table in the big kitchen. The beds were mostly joiner-made, with plain wood head boards and metal or wooden slats on which a hard mattress was often topped by a feather bed, with coarse sheets, and brown blankets. Furniture and bed linen were supplied by the farmer, but washing was done by the hind's wife and, of course, there was a constant succession of baking days.

The lads, perhaps eight or nine of them, had pies at every meal – yes, even breakfast, after a good helping of cold, boiled

bacon (mostly fat) with dry bread, and tea in an enamel mug. In earlier days they were only allowed skimmed milk, as that was always plentiful, and tea was considered a luxury. The milk was served in basins. Bread and jam was a treat for Sunday tea. Broth, a soup made chiefly from vegetables, was cooked in the old fire-coppers, and also appeared in basins. The main course at the mid-day dinner was always filling. Boiled beef appeared frequently, and large puddings – Yorkshire or suet – were served before the meat. Steamed or boiled suet puddings with treacle made a satisfying sweet and a change from pie – which also appeared at teatime, and was more often than not accompanied by cold fat bacon again! This five o'clock meal had to last the lads till breakfast time. It was considered that good (if tough) pastry lasted in the stomach far better than bread,

Farm lads at Eastburn, near Driffield, in 1914.
(*Florence Hopper*)

and made one strong, hence the derisive remarks about the weakness of 'narrow-chinned-bread-and-butter townies'!

Under a good foreman, the lads learned to 'look sharp' and not to waste time over meals. At one farm near Birdsall, where the foreman's house was some distance from the buildings, it was said that 'if you tumbled over a stone on the way to dinner, it wasn't worth going for you'd have missed it!' On farms not large enough to warrant a foreman's house, the unmarried labourers were fed in the farm kitchen, often the men's kitchen, while the farmer and family ate in the front kitchen.

The men's bedroom was always situated at the top of the back staircase often with the open rail at the top forming the entrance to the room. There were air vents in the ceiling, presumably to give air in days when windows would be rarely opened. Each lad had a wooden box by his side of the bed, and this contained his clothes and worldly goods, with a secret compartment for valuables. Money was scarce when wages were paid only at Martinmas, and if cash was needed for some particular purchase during the year one had to ask the farmer, or maister, for a sub!

Clothes were made to last. Shirts (collarless) of strong white cotton striped in blue, or black with long 'laps', as underpants were seldom worn, though warm vests with sleeves were used all the year round. Waistcoats, and 'fustin' jackets lasted a long time, and corduroy was so thick that breeches or trousers seldom wore out. They had cotton linings too – so perhaps it is as well that in those days of laborious washdays it was not considered necessary to wash these garments often.

The farmer's wife never washed the personal clothes. Some relation took on this chore, so one saw the lads setting off on a Saturday afternoon with their bundle of 'weshing'. Some were lucky enough to be able to bathe, in a tin bath before a kitchen fire. The only ablutions in the farmhouse were performed in an enamel bowl at the back kitchen sink, the cold water coming from the pump, and hot from a can filled from the boiler at the side of the big black range in which a fire burned, for cooking and baking, all seasons of the year. The outside privy, so cold in winter and odorous in summer, was not for the men either. They had to manage as best they could in a corner of the foldyard. This was also the tipping place for the 'closet' buckets, tipping being an unpopular task . . .

The leisure time of the farm lads was filled with simple pastimes – games of 'merrills' from a board cut out on the cornbin lid, playing darts, cards or dominoes or enjoying mouth organ melodies plus the constant interest in the beautiful shire horses, always their pride and joy. Sunday mornings were often spent in visiting other stables nearby and comparing teams. Sunday afternoons might mean a cycle ride home to parents, if they lived near enough, or to the town for the pictures. There might be a chance to go rabbiting. Courting took place in fields, lanes and around the buildings. When a lad married, he became eligible for a tied cottage and considered himself fortunate to get a primitive dwelling with a good vegetable garden and, often, a sty in which to keep a pig.

Large families were brought up on small weekly wages, with the perks of milk and eggs from the farm. Some children thrived in overcrowded rooms, and expected to leave home to be 'hired out' as soon as their short years at school were finished. One less in the home to feed eased the situation for younger members of the family. The

local market towns – Driffield, Malton and Pocklington – all held hiring fairs at Martinmas when farm lads and maids looked for work for the following year, if they hadn't agreed to 'stop on' where they were. Martinmas was also their annual holiday. When men and maids were away I have heard of the farming families moving their easy chairs into the kitchen to save cleaning the 'room'.

A young boy who wanted to work with horses might start as 'thoddie lad', working his way up to 'wag-lad' and eventually to the responsible and exalted position of waggoner. The shepherds, if their flocks were large enough, had a shepherd lad, and in the cowhouse there would be a cowman or 'bullocky'. Larger farms usually had a 'Tommy Owt', who was at the beck and call of everybody. The day's work began early. The womenfolk had to rise early, too, in order to get the fire range hot to boil the water for breakfast. With horses to feed, muck out, and harness up, before the long hours of field work, the young lads must have grown very weary before the time came to 'lowse out'.

Changing seasons brought changes of jobs – ploughing, drilling, harrowing and rolling. They meant a long mileage of walking behind horses. 'Plugging muck' was hard, too. I remember my late father-in-law saying: 'Well, they'll never get a machine to do this job!' What a relief it must have been when the great foldyards were cleared of the winter's accumulation of well-rotted straw and bullock manure. Hoeing the root crops was a change, also 'luking', a strange term for chopping out thistles from growing corn. Haytime and harvest, with still longer working hours, were relieved by the welcome sight of the "lowance' baskets, and brief rests beside haycocks or stooks in the golden fields.

Threshing days, perhaps the busiest of all, were dreaded by most farm households. The lads enjoyed the extra chat and gossip as men from neighbouring farms came in to help. The work was hard, especially for the 'corn-carriers' (eighteen stone sacks to be humped up steep granary steps) and for the poor 'caff lads' who spent their day in a cloud of dust as they struggled beneath a large 'sheet' of caff held by the four corners, and nearly burying the carrier. In the house all was a frantic rush, with extra baking beforehand, and a 'tea' to provide for the two men who arrived the previous night with the traction engine. They were at the farm early the next morning, 'getting steam up', and so they were in for their breakfast too. Then "lowance' to be ready by 9.30 a.m. for a dozen or more. Extra men attended the mid-day dinner (which often featured huge meat-and-tatie pies). "Lowance' came again at three o'clock and if the stack (or perhaps more than one) wasn't finished the same procedure continued during the next day . . .

Hours were long, and work was hard, in the old days of farming, but there was a happy comradeship, and a pride in one's work. Only recently, a middle-aged lorry driver called at our farm, and remarked that he'd been hired 'first year off' in the district. He recalled: 'Those were good days, and we enjoyed life; it's not the same nowadays.' What has happened in this affluent age? The demon of discontent so often raises his head, but still the modern farm worker is a good deal happier, I'm sure, than his town cousins. He has a variety of jobs, and can smell the good earth, even through diesel fumes, as his work follows the age-old pattern of seed-time and harvest.

(October 1977)

IT DID HAPPEN TO A VET

Well before an ever-expanding chunk of Yorkshire became known as Herriot Country,
The Dalesman *reported on the exploits of a Dales' vet, C. J. Martin.*

I SHALL ALWAYS recall the fact that, by a remarkable stroke of luck, my first ever professional visit took me right to the very top of the dale. It was not to attend some startling farm animal complaint, but simply to see a dog with a badly damaged paw. I have often believed that Mr Vernon, the vet for whom I was now working as assistant, sent me purposely so that I would get to know the whole length of the winding road in daylight and would get my bearings for future visits in darkness, snow or fog.

That first journey certainly gave me the lie of the land, but it was my 'bag punching' expeditions that really impressed the local geography firmly into my mind. 'Bag punching' was our term for what the Ministry of Agriculture termed 'clinical palpation of the udder' and it was, to me anyway, a pleasing task and one which had its rewards financial and otherwise. How soon one forgets that there were, just after the war, so many more dairy herds than there are now and that the herd that was tuberculin tested was the exception and not the rule. It was the task of the country vet in those days to examine the udder of all milk cows – looking not only for tuberculosis, but any other condition harmful to man. To this end we were furnished at regular intervals with lists of all herds for inspection and supplies of official postcards to notify the farmers of our visits.

Planning a 'bag punching' itinerary was, I thought at first, a simple matter. I was wrong – in the early days anyway. The lists were split into parishes. High Stonedale

Farm, I would have thought, would be somewhere near to Low Stonedale. I learnt the hard way. 'Nay lad, tha's miles away. Go back down ta t'village and take t'old quarry road back up yon side of t'dale . . . look – that's it yonder,' said the amused farmer, pointing to a spot about on the horizon three miles away. He was amused, I think, because we were then at the time when the small farmer was particularly fed up with the wartime 'snoopers' that had plagued him for so many years. My client here knew me as his own vet, yet I was nevertheless there on behalf of 'officialdom'. The thought of an official having to face these unforeseen difficulties appealed to his sense of humour . . .

I loved the journeys, particularly in the summer months when I would sometimes be up at five in the morning and away up the dale to the first call before six. The cows were, of course, Dairy Shorthorns,

(*E. Jeffrey*)

[117]

Ayrshires or a bit of both. We saw few Friesians. Cows had their horns left on and were fastened up in rows and well-bedded in clean straw. It was my task to handle each udder and feel for trouble. 'Watch that one,' the farmer would suddenly say, 'she'll kick like a mule; she's a devil to milk.' He wouldn't have said it had he known how often we used to hear the same tale. What he might just as well have said was: 'I hope you don't feel the lumps in that one; she's my best cow and I don't want to part with her.' Time and again those that I was warned to watch had to have samples taken for examination.

The detection of tuberculosis was one of our major tasks in those days – in fact the major task. Much as I long for those warm, comfortable cow sheds of twenty-five years ago, they were hot-beds of tubercular spread. One cow with that characteristic soft cough could well infect a whole herd. The Dales outlying barns look attractive and are useful for storing the hay from the neighbouring fields, but they were dangerous. It was common practice to tie up perhaps three or four dry in-calf cows in them and have a batch of young calves wintered there, right alongside, with the low roof just above their heads. By turning-out time one cow with her cough had so often infected the lot.

When I think back to the scores of open cases of tuberculosis that cropped up in the Dales there is little wonder that village churchyards carry evidence of so many childhood deaths in days gone by. Many were from tuberculosis contracted from milk. What an enormous victory has been the conquering of this foul disease – and how pleased I am that I played a small part in the battle. In this period of change, as the incidence of TB decreased, so the use of artificial insemination increased and

brought one of the most spectacular and wondrous changes in Dales farming methods.

Joe Smith was one of the first to make use of this bewildering innovation and became, of course, the centre of conversation whenever and wherever his neighbours met. The tale of Joe's cow was passed rapidly up and down the dale but I am sure, on looking back, that it was just one of the many fabrications woven around this particular topic at that time.

Joe, it seemed, had felt that, first insemination or not, he had to be at his uncle's funeral in the nearby town at approximately the same time as the inseminator was due to call.

'Artificial chap's coming this morning, Martha,' Joe informed his wife at breakfast. 'Look after 'im will thee – 'e'll want some warm water, a bit o' soap an' a towel maybe. I'll leave t'owd cow in the end standing.'

Martha, not wanting to be considered ignorant by her husband, sought to assure him as he left: 'Don't thee worry Joe – it'll be all right.' And away he went. Shortly afterwards the 'artificial' man arrived and Martha, trying to keep very calm, found and filled a bucket, took a new bar of soap from the cupboard and grabbing a clean towel set off across the yard.

'This way mister,' she said, 'cow's tied up ready at t'byre.' As she opened the cow shed door her embarrassment grew acute. She could no longer remain calm and collected. Quickly she placed bucket and soap on the floor and the towel on the window sill and retreated hastily with a quick 'yer'll be all right, mister, won't you?' and shut the door behind her. Halfway back across the yard she stopped in her tracks, paused to pluck up courage and retraced her steps. Opening the door gingerly, she poked her blushing face round and pointed to an old nail stuck in the lintel. 'Hang yer trousers on here, mister,' she said, 'an' keep 'em out of t'muck!'

Now whether this actually happened I do not know, but the service certainly provided many an amusing story. I recall the case of a particular cow that I had previously examined regarding a problem of infertility. She belonged to a client who was a personal friend. I had explained that the next time she was ready for insemination I wanted to give her a simple hormone injection first. 'Just phone me when you phone them,' I told him, 'and I'll be out first.'

When I arrived at the farm, John – my farmer friend – was out and had left his father, retired some five or six years, to attend to the cow. After assuring him that there was nothing I required, other than the cow, he went with me to the new byre behind the house and identified the cow as she stood there chewing her cud. He stood and watched in silent interest as I took the vial from my pocket and carefully filled the syringe. His only remark was one which I was quite accustomed to hearing: 'It's all t'needle these days.'

I agreed with him as I injected the cow, attaching no more than usual significance to his remark. It was only as I was taking off my Wellington boots and preparing to leave that it was suddenly brought home to me why there had been such depth of silence throughout the whole procedure.

'By gum, lad,' he managed to say. 'A've seen some amazin' things i' my life – but a never thowt I'd see owt like that.' I was puzzled but his thoughts soon became clearer as he continued – 'to think . . . one prick in t'neck and she's in calf . . . bloody amazin'.'

I couldn't help but laugh, poor old chap; he'd quite thought that I was the inseminator that he'd heard so much about and I hastened to correct him before yet another tale started up and down the dale.

(October 1973)

EWE'LL NEVER WALK ALONE

Sheep, cattle and pigs have all plodded their way through the pages of The Dalesman. *Kathleen Binns opens this series of extracts by observing a sheep gathering. 'They were a motley crowd' with 'just one thing in common – they all baa'd.'*

THEY WERE 'gathering the moors', when all the sheep were collected from the fells to be sorted and dipped. At first light the farmers went off with their dogs and their stout sticks; some had well over an hour's walk before they began their search and it was often around noon before they were back again. This was the second round-up of the year; the first was for lambing, the next would bring them down to the low pastures for the winter months.

Each man in his rough country clothing followed his quarry down the fells and along the lanes, his black and white dog padding at his heels or circling round

obedient to a whistle. Before him bounced a sea of humping grey backs rippling and rolling like corn under the wind. The hooves of the sheep beat a shallow tattoo on the hard roads like a drum-stick accompaniment to his heavy footsteps. Seen from the rear they were nothing but ragged bundles of lolloping wool; but stem that flood, face them about and then look at the assortment! For every sheep had been gathered in by the vigilant dogs regardless of owner or property. There were ewes marked with red and others with blue; some had a clear black letter stamped on

Tan Hill Sheep Show, held on the windswept 1,700 ft contour above Swaledale towards the end of May. (*Geoffrey N. Wright*)

their backs. Some carried bramble sprays spiked to their sides, some were hobbled, some were lame; others raced and climbed with sure-footed agility.

There were large, dreary sheep, small dapper sheep, sheep with horns and sheep without, and lambs with stubs just pushing through. There were black-faced coons and white-nosed blondes, lambs like overgrown toys on a nursery shelf, and older sheep with the dignity and bearing of a duchess. There were sheep that were frightened, angry, disdainful and curious, their fleeces hanging heavily upon them as they pattered along the lanes – fleeces grey and dun and patched with black in imitation of the limestone with which they lived. They were a motley crowd that were shepherded into all the pastures and pen-folds of the village. But they had just one thing in common – they baa'd. In every key and with every meaning they baa'd their way into each village and made the world take notice. They kept it up all day and part of the night. It was a chorus like the harmony of hounds giving tongue, or the welter of blows on an anvil.

As they poured into the villages by every route it was for all the world like the arrival of a day-trip at the sea – everyone anxious to get there first and make the most of a cheap excursion. They bumped and jostled one another, ran round, ahead and over each other; they dawdled to see all the sights and got hustled along by impatient neighbours. They moved in a mass, calling out anxiously to their families not to stray; they were on the constant search for something to eat. They bunched rather than queued to get in anywhere and all wanted to do the same thing at the same time. They were determined to see everything and miss nothing so they pushed into each gateway and round every wall. They had

no compunctions about leaving litter on the roadway. They were voluble and noisy.

Like any other holiday crowd they were easily led, so, following the invitation of the busking dogs, they sought pleasure in an open doorway and flocked impetuously through. Too late, they found they were booked for a dip. There was nothing for it now but to put on a bold face and go through with it. With startled eyes and dutch courage they fell into the pit and allowed the surge of yellow waters to cover them. Splashing and crying out with alarm, swimming a little, getting a mouthful now and then, and being blinded by the harsh sting of water on unwilling eyes, they braved it out. They kicked and floundered in the angry waves, and at last trotted out defiantly, shaking off the drips from their tossing heads. After a little lounging, and a snack or two on the sun-lit grass, they streamed out once more through the wicket gate tanned a glorious golden brown. It was well to do the thing properly on a day-trip; here at least was evidence of an outing spent beneficently in the open.

And so back to the fells. A little footsore and grim after the rigours of the day, they pattered their way homeward to the green

(E. Jeffrey)

slopes. It was good to be back again on the crisp hill grass by the lichened walls and the limestone boulders and with the scent of a fellside wind in one's nostrils. There had been a few minor accidents, of course, as in any holiday crowd; accommodation had been scarce and food difficult to find and children had been separated from their parents. Still, it had been a good 'off' and, Yorkshirelike, they felt they had had their moneysworth.

All the same, as they cropped the short turf and bleated incessantly across the wind, there was a certain restlessness among them. They all looked to be moving about in search of something. Somehow, the fells didn't appear to be quite the same, though it was difficult to say in what way – it was as though something very familiar was missing. The ewes were vaguely distressed and wandered up and down, hoarsely complaining.

No one had thought of telling them about the Lamb Sales.

(July 1950)

ACROBATIC ANNIE

I STARTED my working life as a butcher's lad in Halifax. My employer bought most of his beef off the hook, but would occasionally buy it on the hoof from local farms. One summer in the late 1920s he bought two 'farmer's heifers' from a Sowerby farmer. Two young cows each of which had had one calf. One was still in milk, but the other had ceased to yield. Early one Sunday morning he and I set off to walk three miles to Triangle village and another steep half-mile to Field House Farm. We arrived there at about eight o'clock, the arrangements being that we would take the one which had ceased to yield. 'That's her,' said the farmer, 'yon bonny marked 'un.' Bonny she was, a Dairy Shorthorn, beautifully marked in red and white, but her beauty gave no indication of her potential for mischief. She had no intention of leaving the farm on that or any other morning.

Reluctantly she went out into the lane which led to the main Halifax–Oldham road. Because there was an intersection with another lane near the farm, the farmer and his man came with us to see us past the intersection. We formed a semicircle behind Annie, as I came to call her, and I was on the left wing, the intersection side of the road. She must have sensed that I was a townie, because she neatly dodged through a stile into a hayfield, taking me completely by surprise. The hayfield was large, and unknown to me had a ditch across it. I was sent to head her back and as I belted across the field after her I fell in the ditch. As I regained my feet Annie eyed me cynically as though to say: 'You've got a hope.' She wouldn't go back by way of the stile, so a gate had to be opened. After much untwisting of wire and stinging by nettles, it was opened and Annie was driven into the wrong lane. Then she nearly succeeded in making a break for home when we reached the intersection. I stood by the stile until she was well clear of it.

Across the road was a wood, bounded by a dry stone wall. Without warning Annie swerved, put her front feet on the wall and heaved herself over into the wood. The farmer yelled angrily at me: 'You soft gawk, what the 'ell did you let her do that for?' I felt like saying that I didn't know cows could jump walls but restrained. It later transpired that he didn't know all there was to know about cows either. Annie made her way over to the far side of the wood and then cleared another wall with the ease of a professional. She was now in her home pastures and in no time at all was back with the herd. My boss had had enough as it was very hot and he was not in form for running about. He said it would save a lot of time and trouble if we were to take the milker.

'Nay, Archie,' said the farmer. 'Yon milker 'ull likely give many a gallon yet. We'll put a hayrope on this one and that'll stop her jumping. She'll go as quiet as a lamb, likely.'

Archie was persuaded and a ring with rope attached was put in Annie's nose. I was told to lead her out of the yard so I gave a pull on the rope. Annie didn't care a damn for the ring in her nose. She went smartly into reverse and for the second time that day I went flat on my face at her feet. With deceptive meekness she strolled out of the yard and down the lane. As she

trotted down the road the wooden knob at the end of the hay rope rattled on the stone setts. She was safely guided past the intersection, the stile and the wood, but not the chapel. Only a few yards from the main road, the doors of the little corrugated iron mission house stood open in the sunshine.

All things bright and beautiful rang out and Annie barged in. The consternation of the congregation was only equalled by the amazement of the organist, who didn't know why they'd stopped singing. The sound of the harmonium and the sudden flurry of the congregation were too much for Annie. She turned tail and bolted, leaving a memento on the floor of the porch as she came out. Reinforced by the local bobby, who had seen Annie go into the chapel, we had no option but to form a line and stop her from dashing madly into the main road traffic. She turned once more up the lane and despite the hayrope cleared the wall of the first field she came to. She cleared two more walls with the same consummate ease and then made her own way back to her pasture. The last time I saw her she was back with the herd, and there she stayed. Annie had won the day and the farmer had lost his milker. We had no trouble with her but arrived home very late for lunch.

Annie's acrobatics gained her an extra week of life, but on the following Sunday the farmer delivered her safely at the lairage. She had to be taken in company with half-a-dozen others, which had then to be driven back to the farm. During the eight years which I spent in the trade, we brought many more beasts in from local farms. There was never another like Annie.

Wilfred Haigh
(January 1970)

PIG KILLING

A gruesome spectacle was also a great social occasion.

OFTEN IN these days of our limited and unstable meat ration I recall pig killing day in the Yorkshire village where I spent my youth. That day was one of the few days when we did not have to provide our own entertainment, for that day always closed with a social evening and a supper. Early on the great day grandfather would be up lighting the copper fire so that the water would be boiling before Neb the pig-sticker arrived. The arrival of Neb was in itself a rare spectacle for he always arrived in a gaily-painted trap pulled by two milk-white horses. The trap's decorations included paintings of various breeds of pigs done by the skilled hand of a country craftsman famed for his skill in sign painting. After the customary greetings Neb would enter the house to partake of a glass of my mother's famed gooseberry wine, whilst he exchanged local news and pondered upon childhood reminiscences with my parents. Eventually we persuaded the elders to leave their talking and proceed with the business in hand.

Our cottage pig was no lean weakling but a pig in the region of forty stone. It had to supply a large proportion of our meals for the coming twelve months. Neb had soon arranged himself in his professional clothing and armed himself with several knives of various shapes and sizes. He had now to perform the difficult task of sticking the pig, for he had no 'humane killer' with which to first stun the animal. The pig was first persuaded to stand in the region of several large sacks of straw placed to break its fall, thus preventing any bruising. Then the knife fell hard and true, and the red deluge of blood passed into the waiting bucket, it being required for the making of black pudding – a succulent and enjoyable dish.

The pig was then rolled into a tub of boiling water and the scraping began. This consisted of removing the long coarse bristles by using the sharp bases of the kitchen candlesticks. Eventually the pig was hauled and hung on a beam, thus allowing the usual butchering arrangements to take place. After it had hung for several days, depending upon the weather, the secretive and complex matter of salting took place, and even to this day I do not know what ingredients were used, although I think that vinegar, pepper and black treacle, together with a dash of rum, were placed in the long wooden troughs where the hams and sides were placed during the salting process.

But the most enjoyable time always occurred that evening of the party. What food we devoured – pork pies, sausage rolls, faggot cakes, sparry pie, scraps, fried pork cakes and many others, served with potent home-made wines, such as gooseberry, sloe, parsnip and dandelion. After this meal the entertainment began: old ballads were sung, humorous stories were told, and two old shepherds would bring out their fiddles and we would dance well into the morning, when we would finally end by telling ghost stories. This was a very suitable type of closing for it always provided an excellent excuse for we lads to take our girl friends home.

Barrie J. Kaye (November 1953)

SHUT THIS GATE

Frank W. Dibb wrestled with the vast – and painful – subject of gate fastenings.

To emerge physically and mentally unscathed from attempts to open and shut many Dales gates brings a justifiable glow of pride akin to that Euclid must have known when he'd worked out one of his equations. For the fastenings on these gates are more complex in their infinite variety than all the products of Heinz.

Near the villages or towns in the valleys they are, in the main, inoffensive objects which bode the traveller no ill, but further afield they are out for your blood and very often get it. The better fastenings are often simple, large snecks of wood or iron which open and close with ease. Or they may be iron bars which slot smoothly into a hole in the stone gate post. Or those slightly irritating spring catches which appear on the gates of dwellings on 'Ye Olde' suburban housing estates. The spring catch in this form may bother or annoy you but it doesn't offer you physical violence or suggest that the man who put it there is some descendant of the Borgias who has inherited most of his ancestors' capacity for premeditated cruelty but little of their subtlety.

If you would seek adventure and danger in this matter of gates get into the hinterland of fellside fields and moorland roads. At the first stage you will find gadgets not unlike those I have described, but not as marked in their utility. The iron bar with a hole-in-gatepost won't go in because (a) the hole is clogged up, (b) the bar is bent upwards, downwards or sideways or (c) it is rusted at the propelling end and won't move. The iron lifting sneck may also have been bent. Who contrives to twist these strong metal fittings into unfitness for purpose is a mystery. I suspect the nocturnal machinations of some fiend who lives at the bottom of an (archaeological) Buttertub. Likewise, the wooden sneck has suffered from advanced senile decay and following the example of many medieval

English kings has died from a surfeit, this time of lichen, which has caused it to dissolve into thin air or to break off at a point where it is not even picturesque. The spring catch has, it is true, assumed sturdier proportions than the suburban variety, until it looks like the trigger of an ancient flintlock musket or an outsize in blunderbusses. Attempts to pull it back from its socket can result in distressingly unpleasant ju-jitsu effects upon the person of anyone who is foolhardy enough to touch these things. Even if you succeed in opening the monstrosity it snaps back with a loud report which instantly makes you duck for cover in apprehension lest you are riddled with small shot. Perhaps a bar-maid accustomed to working the handle of a beer-engine would be the person most capable of coping successfully with this blunderbuss.

Then there are the chain fastenings. These either drop over the stone or wooden gate post in a coil like a lasso or end in a hook which, theoretically, slips into a staple round the girth of the post. In practice this staple is at a height from the ground that renders effective handling possible only to a midget. In the latter case you'll find yourself projected through the bars of the gate like a penitent in the pillory with your hat dropping in the adjacent dung, and blood rushing to your head in an alarming fashion. The inventor of this particular device no doubt had a standing contract for the supply of instruments to the Spanish Inquisition. The coils drop with comparative ease over a wooden gate post, but if they are not sufficiently large in circumference a stone post causes them to stick at ridiculous angles so that you become as 'feltered' with them as, when drawing on a sleeved pullover, arms and neck appear through the same hole. Puck had not encountered these chair

loops when he rashly declared his ability to 'put a girdle round the earth in forty minutes'.

As you penetrate into remoter regions the situation deteriorates and, as Hamlet almost said, 'thus bad begins and worse remains ahead'. The chain loops are replaced by either rope ones like misshapen deck-quoits or those made of twisted fence-wire, a type which demands the fingers of an illusionist or the wire-cutters of an electrician to unfasten them. The rope varieties are usually soaked with moisture and caked with bird lime. When walking with the hearts-delight it is advisable, after handling one of these 'quoits', to wash the hands in the nearest beck, or she'll take a poor view of you.

Stylized and formalized fastenings are getting scarcer. You may come to gates held to their posts by bits of old harness, picture cord, even a child's rusty hoop, and such a collection of cast-off belts and braces as to make you wonder if all the trousers in the Dales are being supported by faith, particularly Joe Murgatroyd's since

all his top gates seem to be latched with pensioned-off suspensory articles.

Eventually all fastenings are discarded and some gates stay closed because their bottom bars are vegetating in a few inches of the earth beneath. Failing a steam crane

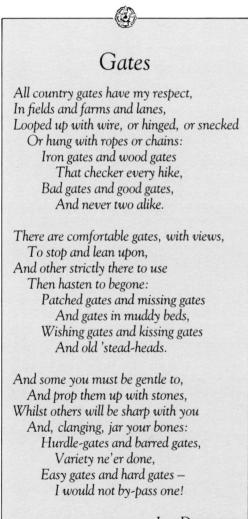

Gates

All country gates have my respect,
In fields and farms and lanes,
Looped up with wire, or hinged, or snecked
Or hung with ropes or chains:
    Iron gates and wood gates
      That checker every hike,
    Bad gates and good gates,
      And never two alike.

There are comfortable gates, with views,
    To stop and lean upon,
And other strictly there to use
    Then hasten to begone:
    Patched gates and missing gates
      And gates in muddy beds,
    Wishing gates and kissing gates
      And old 'stead-heads.

And some you must be gentle to,
    And prop them up with stones,
Whilst others will be sharp with you
And, clanging, jar your bones:
    Hurdle-gates and barred gates,
      Variety ne'er done,
    Easy gates and hard gates –
      I would not by-pass one!

IAN DEWHIRST
(March 1964)

or considerable ability as a music-hall weight lifter or brewers' drayman you let well alone and, provided the gate is attached to the post at the other end, climb over it. I write 'provided the gate is attached to the post at the other end' advisedly, because there is another species that isn't. The permanent and movable fastenings have both disappeared and the gate is kept in position simply by leaning it at an angle against the two posts. Do not, in this case, think that because of its tired attitude as it slopes towards you, you can gently hold it a foot away and slither through. If you try this it will fall away from you with an appalling crash which will make the walls of Jericho going down sound like someone dropping a slipper and its fall will seem to send all the sheep and grouse in Yorkshire bleating and squealing away from you in horror at your breach of the peace. Then you will feel that the persistent advice of the grouse to you to 'go back, go back,' which you have so far ignored, might well be worth heeding.

Finally, if you persist, you will discover a specimen of the most exasperating kind of all. Wind, weather and rough handling have done to it what Caesar did to Gaul and Shakespeare to *Henry the Fourth* – with the difference that Gaul and Henry were only divided into two parts. At the slightest touch the gate will disintegrate in a terrifying manner and make you feel as though you've upset a gigantic jigsaw puzzle on which someone had been working for centuries. This disintegration usually takes place when the farmer, perverse creature, chooses to be about and you stand there with oddments of gate at your feet, hooked over your arms and protruding from your hands, hoping, with all the housemaid's simple faith, that he'll believe you when you say 'it came to pieces in me hands.'

When you've finally assembled the component parts under his withering gaze (or, if he isn't there, piled them neatly alongside the track for kindling) you'll echo heartily the sentiment expressed on a Dales gate by some sorely-tried wayfarer who replied the farmer's curt injunction of 'SHUT THIS GATE' with a heart-felt footnote in chalk, 'MEND THE DAMNED THING'.

(March 1942)

8

SPORTING CHALLENGE

CRICKET IN THE CLOUDS

No book with a Yorkshire theme could be complete without reference to cricket. The Dalesman *has carried many erudite articles on the subject, but W. H. Marsden's account of a classic cricket match on the heights of Halifax was undoubtedly more entertaining.*

SITTING AROUND the dinner table and reminiscing with an old cricketing friend, I recalled a game of cricket which in retrospect was a classic of its kind.

My own club, Luddenden Foot, was away to a team (whose name escapes me), with a ground situated on one of the highest hills in Halifax. It was late April, a poor day for cricket, low cloud, light rain falling and a cold wind. The home team won the toss and elected to bat. We trooped out to join the one umpire present, wearing our thickest sweaters. Play began quietly enough. Runs came and wickets fell at regular intervals. The weather conditions, however, began to deteriorate. Clouds came lower and a mist began to form on the outfield. At the conclusion of the home team's innings, the mist was so thick the pavilion was barely visible from the wicket.

We took tea and considered if further play was possible. The home captain and the umpire thought it was. I did not, but was out-voted. When play recommenced, the mist became thicker. From where we were standing by the pavilion we were unable to see the pitch. We could hear the crack of bat hitting ball and the sound of the players running about. Obviously the match was developing into a farce. Shortly

afterwards, it was my turn to bat. I walked through the mist to the wicket, took a guard, played the first ball back to the bowler, and then asked the umpire to stop play as conditions were impossible, especially for batsmen wearing spectacles as I did. The umpire declined and told me to play on. Reluctantly, I did.

After a further five minutes, during which the mist again became thicker and the umpire was a vague shape at the other wicket, I appealed once more to him, saying I could not see the bowler, let alone the ball. The umpire pointed out to me that my fellow batsman, Dennis, was having no trouble in hitting the ball to all parts of the ground, and therefore I should make no more requests and play on, a remark which was endorsed by the home captain. He told me to pipe down – which I did.

Things had now come to such a pass that the fielders were just ghostly images flitting in and out. The pavilion and boundary edges were a memory. When a shot was, say, hooked to the leg, it would be returned by a fielder and he would tell the umpire if it was a boundary or not. The umpire would then yell to the scorer what had been scored and by whom. The scorer's answering cry echoed back through the gloom. My fellow batsman, Dennis, was

[129]

eventually out after an excellent innings. The next man in was a character called Ted, who had a metal artificial leg. With the conditions being damp and cold, the joints in this limb had begun to seize up. Every movement Ted made was accompanied by loud squeaks. Ted wore glasses. He asked the umpire if he could see through his, Ted's, glasses. The umpire took a look, admitted he could not and told Ted to wipe them. Ted did, and put them back on his face, took them off again and handed them to the umpire who solemnly put them in his pocket and motioned us to resume play.

Ted and I played quietly for a time, the only interruption being an old gentleman, complete with umbrella and gumboots, taking his dog for a walk. He loomed out of the mist, paused in the middle of the wicket, looked around him, shook his head in bewilderment and vanished into the mist as suddenly as he had arrived. My dismissal came in the following manner. An overpitched ball was driven hard in the direction of cover. As it went from sight in the mist, Ted and I began to run between the wickets. Ted's progress was a series of great lunges and hops accompanied by ear-splitting squeaks. For every yard I made, Ted made two. On the third run the ball was still not in sight; on the fourth run Ted was behind me and coming up fast; on the fifth run, puffing and panting, we were level. As we neared the wicket, a fielder, one hand on hip, holding the ball in the other, ran us out by yards.

It's not cricket! – well it is, at Alwoodley, Leeds, once the pitch has been cleared of snow in 1956 for the traditional Boxing Day match. (*Yorkshire Post Newspapers*)

Dismissing the fielder's claim for us both to be out, the umpire pointed to me. Returning to where I assumed the pavilion was, I missed it by twenty yards. The first thing I noticed, having removed my pads, was the scorer, who was wearing overcoat, hat and gloves. He filled in the score sheet by torchlight. The match was climaxed by the sound of galloping hooves. Into our vision came two ladies on horseback, riding furiously across the misty field towards the wicket. There were startled shouts and curses as the animals drove through. Eventually this extraordinary match was concluded and we were just ten runs short of victory.

(April 1974)

Dilemma of an Exiled Yorkshireman

Dear Mother and Dad,
Once again our family prepare for an offspring, and as we go through the routine patiently, the inevitable question comes uppermost in our minds. Will it be another daughter, as pretty as our firstborn, dimple, freckles and all? Or will it be another son to tease the life out of his brother with his leg-breaks and his googlies?

Last night, in my dreams, we had another boy and I dreamt of our two sons. The first was born on Don Bradman's birthday in the borough of Pudsey – gem of the West Riding, and renowned for producing illustrious cricketers. What better start could a man have! It was realised, however, despite his many other virtues, the sound of bat against ball was not pure music to this young man. By the time our second son was due, we had moved to Cheshire – more renowned for making cheese than cricketers, but as he grew up it was realised that this was a cricketing genius.

List all the finest thoughts and deeds of Fuller, Pilch and Grace, Hobbs and Bradman, and especially Sutcliffe and Hutton – this lad had the lot!

Then my dream turned into a nightmare when it was realised that this cricketing colossus could never don the White Rose cap. He suffered from 'birthwrong' – which is a new name I've just invented for when one is born in the wrong place. And all because an old man did not have the foresight to wheel the missus over the Pennines at the critical time of his birth!

Ah! Woe is me! Whoever heard of Cheshire winning the County Championship!

Your affectionate son,
Ron.

(November 1964)

LYKE WAKE CHALLENGE

For many years Bill Cowley contributed a 'Farmer's Diary' column to The Dalesman. *In 1955 he challenged any reader to cover the forty miles across the North York Moors from Scarth Wood Moor, above Mount Grace Priory, to Ravenscar in a day. Ten men and three women responded to the challenge – and the Lyke Wake Walk was born. By the end of the 1970s it was being traversed by some 10,000 people a year, creating severe erosion problems.*

The Challenge

YOU CAN get up to the 'tops' above Swainby, and walk due east on heather all the way except for crossing one main road at the head of Bilsdale, and one or two minor ones. You would cross Carlton Moor, Cringle Moor and Cold Moor; Botton Head and Bloworth; the long flat expanse of Stony Ridge – I spent a night up there once, above Westerdale – Flat Howe, Loose Howe and Shunner Howe.

That would bring you to Glaisdale Head in about twenty miles of tough walking. It is twenty-eight by road. But you could still keep on across open moor, keeping south of Wheeldale Gill, over Howl Moor and Simon Howe, by Tom Cross Rigg and Snod Hill to Lilla Cross, then over Fylingdales Moor (at your own risk) to the sea. And if you did that in September you would kick up a cloud of pollen from the purple heather at every step for forty miles.

There are plenty of springs by the way – including a chalybeate one at the head of Wheeldale Gill, Red Keld – and you might never meet a soul for the two or three days it would take you. I challenge anyone, Three Peaks champion or no, to do it in one! I think I might even present a cup – an inexpensive one – to anyone who can get from Scarth Wood Moor above Mount Grace Priory – the most westerly point of this range – to Wyke Point at Ravenscar, the most easterly, in twenty-four hours on his own feet! Notices of attempt to be given one month in advance to the Editor. Shelter may be had half way, at Glaisdale Head, in the event of exhaustion. The distance is actually about thirty-five miles as the curlew flies.

(August 1955)

The First Crossing

At noon on 1 October seven men and three women (members of the York Mountaineering Club), two Senior Scouts from Middlesbrough and one Forestry Engineer from Guisbrough set out with me to try to do this complete traverse of the moors in twenty-four hours. There was no question of racing. We meant to enjoy the walk. But we knew it would be a tough test – a minor Everest of our own making.

We had all lived with maps in hand or mind for days, weighing alternative routes. Now came the final choice – and the weather was perfect. One fine but difficult route over Whorlton and Snilesworth Moors to Chop Yat was ruled out by a shooting party, so we plunged down to Scarth Nick and into a sea of bracken. A convenient tree trunk over Scugdale Beck,

Route of the Lyke Wake Walk. (*Alec Wright*)

a stiff climb up Live Moor, and the long front line of the Cleveland Hills was before us. We took the alum miners' track round the face of Carlton Moor, Cringle Moor and Cold Moor, with the Cleveland Plain spread out below in a gigantic patchwork quilt of pasture and stubble fields stretching away to the Pennines by Cross Fell or across smoky Tees-side to the Durham hills. Four of us reached Clay Bank Top in two and a half hours, glad of the mobile bar that awaited us! Two more were not far behind, but the others, travelling more slowly, had taken a different route from Carlton Moor to Chop Yat.

We reached the high point of Botton Head (1,489 feet) right on schedule at 3.30 p.m. Now we were deep in the moors and deep in heather. All our concentration was required to find the easiest and the shortest way through, a Bronze Age mound or a leaning stone our guide, to the Smugglers' Trod, its stone flags now heaved crazily about by heather roots, Bloworth Crossing, and the old railway track that used to bring iron-ore out of Rosedale for the blast furnaces of Middlesbrough. We strode along this level going at a rare pace, and came up across South Flat Howe to Ralph Cross just on 5 p.m. Here Dennis and Mary from Glaisdale Head met us with hot sweet coffee and sandwiches, a wonderful interlude. Like new men we skirted the head of Rosedale past Fat Betty, and –

another bit of lucky timing – met Mr T. L. Goulton, delighted to see the middle of this walk as well as its end at Ravenscar next morning.

We were just beginning to think we might do it nicely, and it was in great spirits that we struck off across Loose Howe and along the line of white boundary stones that lead, past another ancient Causeway, to Shunner Howe. Darkness was just closing in on us as we reached the top and saw the lights and tents of our bivouac round the ruined inn of Hamer. The Cleveland Lyke Wake Dirge came to our minds –

> This ya neet, this ya neet,
> Ivvery neet an' all,
> Fire an' fleet an' cannle leet,
> An' Christ tak up thy saul.

We gave a great shout and rushed down through the heather. We had covered twenty-one miles in seven hours and had earned a rest. The others came in two hours later at 9 p.m. Few of us got much sleep. The worst part still lay ahead. Five, determined to get through even if they crawled, left at midnight; some others at 3 a.m. For three of us left in my party the real testing time of this walk started at 3.30 a.m.

Before us was the wild stretch of Wheeldale Moor, with never a track across it – just four miles of knee-deep heather till we reached the Roman highway at the other side. The moon was veiled by clouds. The

[133]

light and the contours were most deceitful. We felt rather than saw the sudden drop into Wheeldale Gill, our guide to the left. To the right was only the cold night wind on our cheeks. We kept checking our course by compass, slightly south of east – one solitary light far off in Goathland gave us another check – then suddenly an intake wall loomed ahead by the Snape road. Beyond was Wade's Causeway and the steep track down to a dark and silent Wheeldale Lodge. At 5.30 a.m. we were

Lyke Wake Lament

Two earthly ghosts, we trudged along,
Mumbling dirge and funeral song,
Feet entombed in evil mud,
Creeping on through icy flood.

Vicious rain with Devil's power
Like shivering fingers at the witching hour,
Frozen body of a rotting sheep,
Forever still in everlasting sleep.

Legs like stumps with muscles screaming,
Nightmare for sure, but we weren't
    dreaming,
Visions of Druids, floating by,
Attacked our dazed, unblinking eye.

Insanity has surely come,
Our senses warped, our bodies numb,
But the end in sight we felt at rest,
With sweet success our bodies blessed.

K. M. DEIGHTON
(April 1978)

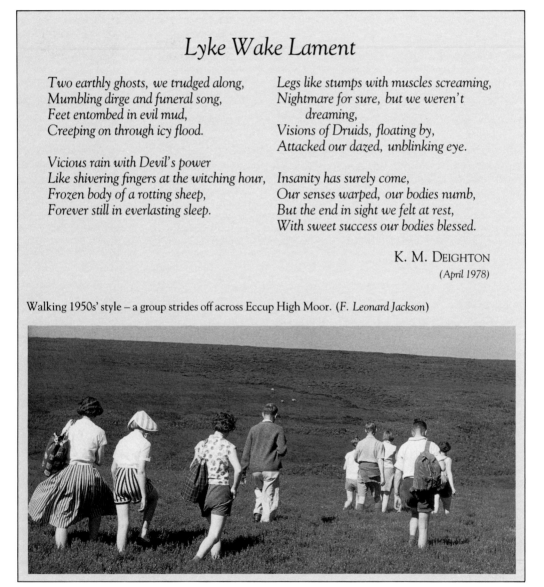

Walking 1950s' style – a group strides off across Eccup High Moor. (F. Leonard Jackson)

sitting on the stepping stones chewing chocolate, the wide stream a subdued silver between rustling trees.

There was another hard climb through rocks and bracken on to Howl Moor. Dawn broke slowly as we approached the railway cutting at Ellerbeck. We crossed by Fen House, over Tom Cross Rig to the Whitby road. A rest and a cold breakfast, and we set off along the Salt track for Lilla Howe. The Army had given us clearance over Fylingdales south of this, but there was no firing yet anyway. A mile off we saw figures by the Howe – our main party. We slanted across the heather to join them on Brown Hill Rigg south of Bloody Beck. One of the three girls had dropped out at Goathland with bad blisters. That she had started the second half at all was a token of great courage and Wheeldale Moor must have

been very painful to her. It was 10 a.m. as we crossed the Scarborough Road near Helwath Bridge and knew we were well in time. Even so, the last rough patches of heather over Rigg Howe were a sore trial, and it was with weary limbs, sore heels, but glad hearts that we tramped into Ravenscar at last down the road from the old windmill.

We celebrated our triumph with the Goulton Tankard and formed the Lyke Wake Club.

(December 1955)

THE WAY DOWN ALUM POT

Ian Plant joined The Dalesman *editorial team for a few brief years before moving on to the* Craven Herald *weekly newspaper where he became its youngest-ever editor. He was passionately fond of underground exploration – and died tragically in a cave-diving accident. His account of a descent of Alum Pot in Ribblesdale was one of several articles he wrote on potholing – a sport with an enormous following in the limestone wonderland that lies beneath large areas of the Dales.*

A HUNDRED yards north-west of Alum Pot a stream enters Diccan Pot and descends a series of deep shafts to the terminal chamber of its neighbour. Further along the wall running due west of Diccan, a party of potholers is preparing to descend Long Churn Cave. They gather their equipment, then scramble over the boulders opposite the entrance to Upper

Long Churn, a large and interesting cave passage which terminates at Dr Bannister's Handbasin, a waist-deep pool into which a water-chute thunders. It is possible to climb the waterfall and emerge on Borrins Moor.

Following the boulders beneath a large rock bridge, the potholers enter the cave mouth, where water from Upper Long

Churn on the right joins the cave passage. The explorers splash along the stream bed, revelling already in the delights of the underworld. Soon they are wading in the deeper water of Dam Pool where the passage forks to the left, the stream entering a low tunnel leading to daylight and the entrance to Diccan Pot. Scrambling out of the pool, the young men enter a roomy, dry passage, carved out of clean, waterworn limestone. Explorers wishing a dry descent of Diccan Pot divert the main stream along this passage. Here, the only sounds are the squelching and scraping of boots on rock as the party hurries onward. Every corner reveals an attraction of added interest, whether it be the ox-bow passages abandoned many years ago by running water, or the calcite decorations adorning the recesses of the main passage.

The passage ends above the Double Shuffle Pool, but a simple traverse round the side of the pool rejoins the main passage at the other side. After a few yards the passage halts again before a similar pool, spanned by a narrow plank which the explorers cross cautiously. Neither Plank Pool nor Double Shuffle Pool are very deep and a slip would result only in a mild wetting. Some potholers, however, pause to 'fish' around in the pools for tackle dropped by those uncertain of their depth. In Girder Pool, a deep trough above the first pitch in Diccan Pot, a potholing party once found 30 feet of good ladder. On the same day, a nylon sling and two new karabiners were 'fished' out of Plank Pool.

After a short length of passage the party enters a small well-decorated chamber. The potholers descend a narrow rift and scramble down a short drop into a larger chamber spanned by a wide but shallow pool. Two water-filled potholes, containing rounded pebbles which in times of flood

continue their drilling action at the far end of the chamber, are the Dolly Tubs. Here the potholers must assemble their tackle for the 45 feet descent which follows. Two lengths of ladder are belayed through an eyehole in the rock further round the brink of the shaft. Looking down the potholers can see the first glimpse of daylight filtering from the main shaft of Alum Pot. The ladder tinkles as it is lowered. The first man ties on a length of rope let out by a companion and gropes for the rungs beneath his feet. The climb is effortless but is hindered part-way down by an awkward rock flake which he must straddle in order to remount the ladder. In no time the man has untied the lifeline and is climbing the last few feet to the boulder-strewn floor overlooking Alum Pot.

Before his eyes is one of Craven's classic pothole views. The potholer can turn off his headlamp for the daylight streaming down the shaft is sufficient for the whole party to continue without. The spray of Alum Pot Beck rises in clouds of mist at the far end of the hole, plummeting a further 60 feet to the bottom. The ladder which the potholers must ascend on their return journey hangs limply in the spray, and fills one or two members of the party with some trepidation. In the centre of the shaft, the infamous Bridge nestles on two ledges, shortly to be crossed by the party. The sight on the moss-covered ledge, which falls steeply to the edge of the shaft on the left of the party, adds a touch of melancholy to its descent. The bodies of young sheep, victims of their own adventurous spirit and the carelessness of man, are seen in large numbers amid the scree on the ledge. Stones thrown off the walls by visitors create gaps which appeal to the inquisitive nature of young sheep. A fall from the brink of Alum Pot is always a fatal one. The practice of visitors who throw stones down the shaft is not only exasperating to the farmer who has to repair the walls but in 1936 it proved fatal to a woman potholer who was struck on the head by a stone hurled, it was stated at the inquest, 'by a silhouetted figure in shorts'.

The explorers turn to their descent. A 12 foot ladder belayed to a large boulder

The Bridge, Alum Pot. (*P. R. Sanderson*)

descends a wide ledge nearer the brink of the shaft. The potholers cross the slippery rock and scramble on to a narrow terrace running along the west side of the shaft. On their left is an 80 foot drop to the stream bed. The Bridge is reached and a handline is attached to a belay as a safety measure. Many explorers shun the use of a rope while crossing the Bridge but more than one accident has been caused by a slip on the rock. The Bridge is exceptionally

treacherous after rain or frost. The potholers descend a scree slope at the other side of the Bridge to the head of the next pitch, a descent of 60 feet. Their ladders are belayed to a metal spike driven into the rock. One at a time, the explorers descend the easy climb to the stream bed. Here, Alum Pot Beck comes to rest at the foot of the main shaft before swirling over several short cascades down which the party now proceeds. Unless the weather is bad, a lifeline is not required for these easy descents.

The potholers halt on the brink of a shaft requiring a long belay and 25 feet of ladder. Above their head a small cascade splashes down from Long Churn to augment the waterfall which accompanies their descent. The climb is easy and soon the explorers are rushing along the stream bed where the water channels along the floor of a high tunnel. The limestone here is black and enhances the gloom of the cavern. Daylight fades as the stream slides over a flat bed of rock, swirls in a deep pool, then leaps over a sheer waterfall, 10 feet above the terminal chamber of Alum Pot. The descent to the floor of the chamber requires no tackle but some of the party, not wishing to receive an undue soaking, descend a narrow tunnel beneath the left-hand wall. A deafening roar is the waterfall from Diccan Pot, falling 100 feet and pounded by protruding ledges throughout its descent. Running the gauntlet of spray flung out by the waterfall, the potholers dash to a gloomy corner of the cavern. The sump is an insignificant, scum-covered pool. Here the waters of Alum gather before beginning an underground journey of a mile and a half, passing *beneath* the River Ribble to Turn Dub, on the other side of the valley . . .

The party now turns to its ascent, when it must return by way of the short ladder pitch and the cascades to the foot of the main shaft. There is a whirring sound and a lifeline snakes down from above. Tentatively, one of the explorers fastens the lifeline and signals his companions above. The lifeline man at the head of the shaft is belayed to a tree and pulls in the rope as the climber begins to ascend. The lifeline man's muscles are tensed to take any strain on the lifeline. He must be prepared to hold the rope in the event of a fall for if a mishap occurs it may well be a fatal one. Only recently a potholer plunged to his death down the shaft. The man on the ladder passes the ledge he descended from previously, and begins to climb in the open shaft, well out of reach from the wall. Beneath his feet the ladder dances in the spray of the waterfall. His muscles strain to attain a climbing rhythm. Soon his fears succumb to a vast appreciation of his surroundings, which he can view without the need of a headlamp. The pitch is probably unique in this way. The big pitches of Juniper Gulf and Spectacle Pot (Kingsdale), impressive though they are in the opaque blackness of their environs, do not provide a panorama such as this.

The wall of the shaft leans once more towards the ladder and the toes of the climber's boots are soon scraping against the moss which clings to the rock near the head of the shaft. In no time he is helped off the ladder by his companions and is recovering from the ascent. Now there are his companions below to be lifelined, ladders to be rolled, and ropes to be coiled before he can return by the grassy track to Selside. He will return again and again to Alum. Such is the attraction of this 'siren' of Yorkshire potholes.

(January 1968)

WHITE CLIFFS OF YORKSHIRE

Diametrically opposite to potholing is the equally challenging, if less claustrophobic, sport of climbing. Anthony Greenbank looked at Yorkshire's answer to the Italian Dolomites.

ASK ANY expert climber today what he thinks of Kilnsey Crag, and you're sure to get a reply that makes you wonder if he has heard your question correctly. He will probably start talking enthusiastically about expansion bolts, rock boring drills, chisels, peg hammers and miniature rope ladders – the kind of equipment needed to do the hardest climbs in the Alps and other great mountain ranges.

In the last three or four years the great crag (for the climbing of which permission must be sought) has gained a wide reputation among cragsmen. They call it the answer to the Italian Dolomites. In fact, this tremendous cliff only differs in the colour of its milky limestone walls from the yellow-tinted towers of the Cima Grande di Lavadero, and other North Italian giants. The cliff overhangs so much that walking underneath you can spot old pieces of rope hanging from the walls, and swinging clear, plumbline fashion.

The climbing is so spectacular that motorists in the past have been asked to move on by the police as they were causing traffic jams. They could hardly be blamed. The sight of men like Joe Brown – a Manchester plumber, and reputed to be one of the six finest mountaineers in the world – sitting in nylon stirrups as he stitches himself to the huge overhang with steel, or alloy pegs and expansion bolts, would bring the most enthusiastic motorist to a stop. Joe Brown climbs best with a few hundred feet of thin air below his boot soles. He has fallen over half a dozen times

– once for 300 feet, but he has only badly injured himself once. A tea urn was brought into his hut when he was in the Army, and in the rush he broke his leg in three places. Certainly, in the last ten years he has advanced climbing to a degree unheard of before. Thanks to his skill and initiative no face can now be said to be unclimbable.

An instance of this is the ascent of Malham Cove. Not long ago any attempt on this 330 foot precipice would have been treated as stupid and foolhardy – despite the fact that Charles Kingsley, in his book *The Water Babies*, had written of Tom, the young chimney sweep, descending the bulging water-stained face. In reality it looked hopeless, yet Peter Biven and Trevor Peck climbed it in fifty-eight hours. Their equipment? – eighty-five ringscrews, twelve pegs and twenty-four battered chisels, as well as plenty of nylon rope. It takes lots of nerve to climb these limestone faces. And it's a comparatively new technique. The rope is threaded through rings on the pegs, as the leading climber inches his way upwards. He is held by the tension of the rope, while his companion keeps the rope tight. It's seldom a peg flies out under the strain, but when it does, the falling climber is still saved by the ones he has hammered in below.

During the first ascent of Malham Cove a large metal ice cream sign appeared on the face – in full view of the road. There was much comment in the Press criticising this kind of behaviour from climbers, but in this case the mountaineers concerned

OPPOSITE
Kilnsey Crag, the setting for many climbing exploits.
(*Geoffrey N. Wright*)

had tried to remove it. As one of them slid down a doubled rope to remove the sign, he found himself swinging in space, and unable to reach the face. The overhanging rock at the top was pushing him away. He suddenly stopped – and the metal clip which attached him to the rope had become so hot due to friction that it melted all but one strand of the nylon. There was still 100 feet below, and naturally all thoughts of retrieving the sign vanished. He just made it back to the ground.

These crags in the Dales are some of the toughest in the country, and they give the kind of thrills which previously could only be obtained by saving £50 for a holiday in the Dolomites. The situations are often identical – as is shown by the climber who had to spend a night clipped to a peg on Gordale Scar. He dozed off safely, then as dawn broke he carried on to finish the climb.

(June 1960)

'GATERS' AND 'RINGERS'

'Ringers' are in fact less effective opening shots than 'gaters' which sometimes turn out to be 'pots' or 'quews'. It all sounds utterly perplexing but not to those who indulge in the rural sport of quoits. Paul Pearson observed the idiosyncrasies of a game that has always been most popular in the north of England.

THE THUD of iron in clay breaks the silence of the evening air in summer as a quoits season develops in villages around the Esk Valley. From the beginning of May until the end of August a dozen local quoits clubs compete for the Winterschladen League Cup, just as they have done since the 1920s. In fact, the game of quoits was a popular pastime for people in North Yorkshire, and particularly in Eskdale, for many years before that. Quoits clubs, such as the one at Danby, have existed in an organized form since before the 1914-18 war, but we merely speculate about the origins of the game. Quoits was probably first played by using two horseshoes 'clagged' together by the local blacksmith. It is possible that the game may have been devised by Roman soldiers who occupied Britain as far back as the 2nd century A.D. However, this theory is flawed by the fact that horses used by the Romans were rarely shod and any iron available would be used for more practical purposes than manufacturing sports equipment.

Another interesting, but highly improbable theory, maintains that the game might possibly have originated from the practice of the ancient Sikhs of India using sharp throwing rings as hunting and fighting weapons. Quoits may have been invented by the Romans after watching demonstrations of the Sikhs' skills. However, this

is an extremely far-fetched, if romantic, theory with little real evidence available to back it up. Whatever its origins, quoits has always been most popular in the north of England and probably sprang up in the Border country between England and Scotland. During the Middle Ages, quoits developed into a popular tavern and village green activity enjoyed by large numbers of medieval English peasants.

The game was prohibited during the reign of Edward III. At this time, men were allowed only to take part in sports such as archery, which would have some use on the battlefield. It was decided that participation in any other games or pastimes would distract men from practising their battle skills, which were regarded as being of the utmost importance.

In 1545, Roger Ascham declared that

BELOW AND OPPOSITE
Quoits match in progress at Lealholm, North York Moors. (*Werner Kisling*)

'quoiting be too vile for scholars'. This certainly suggests that quoits was a game enjoyed mostly by the working classes and also, possibly, that Mr Ascham was not too clever when it came to demonstrating his quoiting skills. The popularity of the game reached a peak during Georgian times, but it has declined fairly steadily for most of the last century. The depression after the 1914-18 war possibly caused a revival in industrial towns. It was a relatively inexpensive pastime. Quoits, which is now largely a rural sport, survives today in an organised form only in a few small areas, mainly in the north of England. In recent years the sport seems to have enjoyed a new surge in popularity and, according to Bob Cornforth of Fryup End Farm, Fryup – who is a member of Danby Quoits Club – it is now 'spreading like wildfire'. New leagues are being formed away from the well-established Eskdale League.

Despite the recent growth in the popularity of quoits, it is becoming increasingly difficult to acquire new sets of quoits

because fewer firms are manufacturing them. The main suppliers of new quoits for clubs in the Esk Valley are Guisborough Foundry and a new set is likely to cost around £30.

Mr Cornforth first began playing quoits at about the age of five. During the many years he has been taking part in serious competition, he has accumulated much experience. Modern quoits are lighter and not as long-lasting as older quoits. Mr Cornforth recalls when special sets of quoits were made for youngsters until they became strong enough to graduate to the heavier variety.

Local people derive a great deal of pleasure from the game, both from its challenge as a test of skill and from the opportunity it provides to meet with friends. Geoff Dowson began playing quoits for Fryup in his late teens and has been captain and secretary since 1955. As far as he is concerned, one of the main attractions of playing quoits is the chance it gives him to join in the good-natured banter which invariably takes place between the players. Competitive matches are usually played in a friendly spirit, and the most popular custom takes place after the match has finished, when players from both teams head for the local pub. Quoits teams are always full of interesting, colourful characters and Mr Dowson says they also include many players who possess exceptional and unique skills, able to direct quoits 'reet where they want 'em'.

To a casual observer, quoits seems to be a fairly simple game. One hurls iron rings with strength and accuracy at an iron post driven into the ground. There is much more to it than that. The quoits themselves are cast-iron rings, usually no more than eight inches in diameter. They have a raised upper surface, known as the 'hill', while the lower concave surface is called the 'hole'. The weights of different quoits can vary considerably but those used in the Esk Valley usually weigh around 5¼ lb. Quoits pitches are 11 yards long between two iron posts which, known as 'hobs', are

set in 3 foot square beds of clay. This represents a considerable distance over which to throw heavy iron quoits and strength is as important a quality as skill. Teams usually consist of two or four players who take alternate throws. The ultimate aim is to cover the hob with the quoits of one's own team, excluding those of the opposition.

Two points are awarded for a quoit which encircles the hob, and is known as a 'ringer' and one point is earned by any quoit which is closer to the hob than that of an opponent. To decide who throws first, a player calls out 'ill' or 'ole' as a quoit is flipped into the air, in much the same way as a coin is tossed. The call is correct depending on which way up the quoit lands. Usually, the game ends when one team reaches twenty-one points, although, if time is running out, the game is sometimes shortened to the first team to reach fifteen points. often, games go on in semi-darkness, when the hob has to be chalked for it it be visible.

Many different terms, unique to the game of quoits, can be used to describe a quoit which has landed in a certain way. For the most part, the shots played are named according to whether the quoit falls to the right or left of the hob and whether it rests with the rim facing downwards or upwards. The main shots are the 'side quoit' and 'pot' to the left of the hob, and the 'quew' and 'Frenchman' to the right. A quoit landing on edge directly in front of the hob is known as a 'gater' and is the most effective opening shot, more useful even than a 'ringer'.

Tactics are as important in quoits as in any other sport; a game between good players is as much a battle of wits as it is a battle of skill. Throwing 'ringers' is not particularly difficult for the top players and superior tactics could be decisive in a match between players of equal skill. A considerable advantage can be gained from throwing first, but it is not usual to attempt a 'ringer' first throw as it may be cancelled by an opponent's quoit landing on top. There is rarely room for a third 'ringer'. The most effective first shot is a 'gater' which defends the hob and presents an obstacle from which opponents' quoits often glance into bad positions. A 'gater' can also be knocked down into a 'ringer' on the next throw. Mr Cornforth is a greater admirer of the 'gater' as a shot played by the 'master quoiter', but he also praises the 'wibbly-wabblers' thrown by some players as more unorthodox, but effective, shots. Such a shot is hurled in a manner which makes the quoit fly on a flat trajectory directly on to the hob.

There is no shortage of humour at quoits matches and most of it derives from the comments of players and spectators. Mr Cornforth can recall amusing incidents, such as when wayward quoits have caused 'one or two bruised ankles', which add to the enjoyment of participants and onlookers (apart from, presumably, those on the receiving end). Nevertheless, competitors always play to win and Mr Cornforth can remember watching as fights broke out between opponents who disagreed about something. However, such incidents are few and far between. Quoits is traditionally a sporting game, played in a friendly atmosphere.

It is certainly a game of strength and skill. Competition between the quoit clubs of the Esk Valley is as keen as ever during the quoiting months. Anyone who enjoys good company on a warm, summer evening is not likely to be disappointed.

(October 1984)

FRESHWATER LOBSTERS

T. K. Wilson, who as 'Broughton Point' was The Dalesman's *first angling correspondent, penned this relaxed account of an expedition in quest of crayfish – 'not one of the highest forms of sport but a pleasing way of spending an hour by the riverside'.*

CRAYFISH are to be found in most of our Dales rivers. The Yore, Wharfe, Aire and Ribble are fairly well stocked in their deeper, stony stretches, though nowadays probably few folk are acquainted with the presence of these freshwater lobsters save anglers who find them a source of annoyance when bait fishing in the evenings. Both herons and others include crayfish in their diet, and occasionally by the riverside you will come across evidence of their fishing. It would also seem that they are fairly numerous in such inland sheets of water as Malham Tarn and Lake Semerwater. On one occasion we had a good haul of perch from the Tarn, and almost without exception they had crayfish in their stomachs; one weighing 1½ lb had eaten no fewer than eight. The same year we camped on the shores of Lake Semerwater, and one morning found over a hundred dead bream and rudd near the side. Each corpse was being attacked by crayfish, and some had been half eaten from the tail upwards.

So far as I have been able to ascertain it is only in the Yore that crayfish are protected. Both the Wensleydale and the Hawes and High Abbotside Angling Associations have a by-law that stipulates that 'the crayfishing season shall begin on 10 August and end on 30 September. Any person not being the holder of an Association ticket shall be charged 1s. for a crayfishing ticket.'

Fifty or sixty years ago crayfish were sought after in Wensleydale, and very tasty

Catching crayfish. (*Werner Kisling*)

they are too, though, as one of the natives put it, "tis a fiddling job for so hard an eat'. Only the claws and flappers contain edible flesh, and the former have to be cracked with a hammer.

Crayfishing may not be one of the highest forms of sport, but a fellow angler and I found it good fun and a pleasing way of spending an hour by the riverside. We landed at Hawes about tea time, collected our friend 'Jim', who had a lump of liver

[145]

that was to serve as bait, and made for a stretch of the Yore on the low side of Sandy Wheel. The bottom there is well strewn with boulders and stones under which the crayfish find ample cover and protection from their natural enemies. The liver was cut into six pieces, tied to a yard of string and stick, and then moved to the bank, each bait resting on the river bottom about a yard from the side. By the time the last one was in position, a crayfish was sampling the first. At the outset only ones and twos were collected, but gradually the liver enticed the crayfish from their hiding places. Slowly but surely they ambled around or over the stones to the feast. There were fourteen at one bait, and all but two were safely netted.

When netting one lifts the liver and the feasting fish gently upwards until a landing net can be inserted underneath. Patience and a steady hand are essential. Try hurrying, and the crayfish become suspicious – a little shake and they shoot backwards well out of harm's way. Six dozen or more crayfish

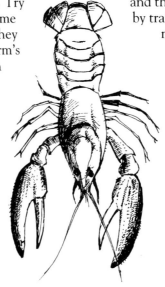

were collected before we ceased operations. They varied in size, and the biggest were as big as a man's hand. On arriving home they were plunged into a bucket of boiling water to which had been added a handful of salt. They went in green and came out red.

Though crayfish are plentiful in the Yore, they are not always to be tempted. On a bad day the angler may have to be satisfied with a score; on a good one he will quickly collect a couple of hundred. The record haul, made some sixty years ago, stands to the credit of Jim's grandfather, 'Sproates Blades', who was commissioned to provide a thousand live ones for the stocking of a Scottish reservoir. He and Jim's father had £10 for the job, and obtained the required number in one evening under two hours. Overnight the fish were kept alive in bags sunk in Gale Beck, and they made the journey next day by train in milk cans. What is more not a crayfish died on the way.

(July 1943)

9

A NATURALIST'S YORKSHIRE

THE ISLAND I LIKED TO VISIT

F. A Carter wistfully remembered a little patch of Littondale with its yellow mimulus and the staccato squawk of oystercatchers.

THE ISLAND I liked to visit is situated on a little-known stretch of that little-known river, the Skirfare, in that little-known part of Craven, Littondale, and though everybody calls it 'The Island', it isn't really one at all, but just a piece of rough land and shingle enclosed between a bend of the river and a high wall. In practice, however, it might almost as well be an island, as much the easiest way of reaching it is to wade across the river – in gumboots for preference, as the pebbles are not kind to bare feet.

'The Island's' vegetation has a way of running to extremes – coarse, tussocky grass, wild rhubarb, and knapweed at one end of the scale, and at the other, the yellow Welsh poppy and a remarkably showy red and yellow mimulus or monkey-musk, neither of which I had seen growing wild anywhere else, though I have since

Oystercatcher. (*Herman Hemingway*)

found that particular mimulus in great profusion by a little steam in Upper Wensleydale. But my chief interest in 'The Island' was its bird life, and especially in spring and summer. A pair of oystercatchers had nested there for several years running. As soon as anyone came near, one or both of the birds would begin to fly round in circles, giving shrill, staccato little squawks. At first I assumed that this performance was to divert attention from the nest, and, after hatching-out, from the young birds, but I found later that they went on doing it just the same when the youngsters could fly almost as well as their parents. However it began, it was a very pleasant habit from my point of view, as they often flew close enough to give me quite a good view, even without glasses. What attractive birds they are, with their boldly marked black and white plumage and orange-red legs and beaks! Most obliging birds I always found them, too, for not once did I take anyone to see them when they didn't show up.

I understand that informed opinion doesn't take their name very seriously, and that the nearest they ever get to oystercatching, when they go back to the seashore for the autumn and winter, is opening and eating mussels. Alas, they seem to have rather overdone this, for not very long ago the mussel-fishers, finding their livelihood threatened, persuaded the Home Secretary to withdraw the bird's legal protection. What effect this has had on its numbers I have no means of knowing, but I hear that a couple still turn up on 'The Island' in due season, and I have seen a few in Upper Wharfedale since sentence of outlawry was passed.

Then there were sand-martins from the holes in the bank, racing and darting over the river, one or two sandpipers poking about in the shallows, yellow wagtails looking like long, elegant canaries, and, usually, curlews and peewits wheeling and calling overhead. In fact, they did so much of this that I sometimes wondered how they found time to pick up a living. I occasionally saw a heron, but never for long. It's a wary and mistrustful bird, and always seemed to see me first, and to be just 'taking off' as I arrived.

At one time there seemed to be a threat to the peculiar status of 'The Island'. Three or four 'locals' turned up with picks and shovels, and began to dig a channel to cut across the bend in the river, and so prevent the current from making it still wider by eating away more and more of the field on the outer curve of it. Perfectly sound economics, if it didn't turn out too expensive a job, but I couldn't help wondering how the oystercatchers and sandpipers would take to the new conditions.

However, I needn't have bothered myself, for although that was a few years ago, and I haven't lived near enough since then to keep an eye on things, I hear from my spies that there are no new conditions. After a week of toilsome but unrewarding work in the difficult and stony ground, it had to be put to one side for sheep shearing and, following that, haymaking, and I wasn't at all surprised to hear that it was never restarted; for apart from all the interruptions bound to be provided by seasonal work and 'seasonable weather', it must have been rather like the kind of book mentioned in one of A.A. Milne's plays – 'Once you put it down, you can't pick it up again.'

OPPOSITE
Tawny Owl. (R. Duffield)

(July 1958)

A CURLEW CHICK GROWS UP

Selecting just one of the dozens of articles by W. R. Mitchell on the bird and animal life of Yorkshire was an onerous task. The final choice fell on this glimpse at the world of the curlew – one of the most conspicuous of nesting birds in the Dale country.

OF ALL the birds that nest in the Dale country of the North, the curlew is the most conspicuous. This is Europe's largest wader, clad in a streaky-brown plumage, with long neck, relatively small head and a beak curved like a scimitar. The length of the beak varies with individual birds (some curlews have very long beaks), but five inches is a good average size. The curlew parties return to the Dales in late February or March, often when there is mist, which signifies a thaw. A Dales farmer told me: 'Thou allus knaws t'back o' winter's brokken when thou hears t'curlew shout.'

Another farmer reported this spring that 't'queerest-lookin' curley I'se ivver seen' had touched down on his land. It was an albino, light fawn rather than white, with brown entirely absent from the plumage. This bird went into an injury-feigning routine I had not seen before, apparently attempting to fly but with laboured wing beats, then toppling to the ground. I thought it had some nervous or muscular complaint until I walked towards it and saw it zoom skywards.

The cock birds establish territories, court with the incoming hens and help to incubate eggs which lie in 'scrapes' on the ground. A curlew is least conspicuous when it is on the ground with the dun colours of a moorland or fell around it. The bird cannot be overlooked during the territorial flighting in spring. Sometimes it hangs on the wing with rigid wings, like a feathered kite. A bubbling song is uttered as it glides towards the ground. The notes change to angry barks when a man strays close to where its youngsters are crouching.

Forty years ago most of our curlews nestled high above sea-level. To see them you had to move to the hills. Now they often pick nesting sites in the Dales – in meadows or pastures, sometimes on grass edging up to roads and, ever more frequently I have noticed, in young wood-

Curlews in Wensleydale. (*Peter Allis*)

land. Two nests I found this year were set in rank grasses where spruce or larch were thinly spread. A curlew which nested in a young plantation caught a foot in bramble as it rose and was brought down heavily on its eggs, two of which shattered. The bird nested again – outside the wood.

A curlew sits very tightly on its nest when hatching time is near. A climax of its year is reached when it hears the pre-natal calling from within the shells; when it feels the rapping of egg teeth wielded in lusty spasms by the unborn chicks. As a chick struggles clear, the down is moist and draggled; it is possible to see the soft pink of flesh underneath. The chick soon dries off and begins to move around. Less than

Young curlew. (*W.R. Mitchell*)

an hour after hatching it has the strength to go into cover near the nest. On a fellside nesting site the chicks scrambled under the fronds of bracken when the parents sounded an alarm. The parents provide grubs, larvae and small worms, which the chick receives with excited fluttering of its stumpy wings and shrill 'peeps' for more. The chick is itself capable of snatching morsels of food with its short beak.

Now that the precise nesting site has no significance, the chick is led about the home ground. Food is varied and rich in the ever-moist meadows. Down is slowly replaced by feathers, and wing-flapping brings strength to the muscles and dislodges the hard, blue quills in which the flight feathers have been encased. The stumpy bill continues to develop but is yet inches short of the full curve of an adult. About six weeks elapse between the hatching of a curlew chick and its first flights. In that time the young bird is vulnerable because it is totally an earth-bound creature.

Curlews which nest in meadows suffer from harvesting operations, and particularly the late Maytime mowing of grass for silage. When the more traditional haytime takes place (and 85% of farmers are still haymakers) a chick can escape death by seeking out the field edges where the grass remains long. When I first helped with haymaking on a Dales farm it was a matter of pride for the 'dykes' and wallsides to be cleaned out; today the grass is invariably left standing and is eaten off by the stock turned into the field after the clearance of hay. This favours the curlews. A chick crouches, still and silent, when the parent birds bark a warning that a fox is on the prowl, but many birds perish as a fox's jaws close around them.

Soon the long wings of the young curlew

Brooding curlew in a Pennine meadow inclines its head at the approach of an aircraft. (*W.R. Mitchell*)

are lifting it over the walls; it must still return to earth to feed, to preen and to sleep, but no longer is it restricted to a small area. Family parties join up, form ever-larger groups, linger for a while where there is soft ground and feathers can be moulted in peace, and then move south-westwards for winter. The curlew chick hatched out in a Dales meadow may survive to spend the colder months on estuary or marsh in Eire.

(*August 1969*)

CLIFF 'CLIMMERS'

One of the great spectacles for Yorkshire bird-watchers is provided by the lofty white cliffs between Scarborough and Bridlington which in spring and summer are a jostling mass of 'sea fowl'. Bird populations have been threatened in the past, especially by the practice of 'climmin' – lowering men down the cliffs to collect eggs. It was still legal at the end of The Dalesman's first decade, as A. Norman Handley recounted.

THERE ARE several gangs of climbers on Bempton, Buckton, and Speeton cliffs, each gang has its own working ground beyond which they must not tres-pass. A gang is composed of four men, the climber and three top men. Strong hemp ropes, about 300 feet in length, are usually used; in wet weather these become slippery and so difficult to handle that little climbing can be done. The outfit consists of a steel or policeman's helmet to protect the climber's head from falling stones, plated or studded boots to enable him to walk on slippery ledges, and harness. The harness consists of broad loops of flat rope with a belt attached which buckles round his waist, to the front of the belt is fastened the body rope. An iron stake is firmly driven into the ground and a guide rope fastened to it, the slack being thrown over

'Climmers' in action on the cliffs of the Yorkshire coast.

the cliff. The rope passes over a leather belt round the climber's waist, behind him sit the other members of the gang. The climber grasping the guide rope in one hand walks backwards, driving into the cliff edge an iron stake with a running pulley at the top. By placing the waist or lowering rope over the wheel the danger of chafing and cutting by rock edges is eliminated.

The man going over the top quickly disappears as the 'lowerer' slacks away and his appearance causes a terrific commotion amongst the sea fowl which fly from the cliff face. The noise of their varied calls is

deafening. Eggs are transferred from rock edges into canvas bags. Iron pegs have been driven into the cliff face in difficult places so that the climber can wind his hand-rope round them to assist in reaching otherwise inaccessible eggs. When he has collected all available eggs he gives a single tug on the waist-rope. The top man grunts 'Up' and the three top men, seated one behind the other, haul away, their body action resembling that of three men rowing a boat. Sometimes a winch is used. The climber keeps kicking himself clear of the rock until he can assist those above by walking up the cliff face. Reaching the top he picks up the iron stake and joins his comrades, putting the eggs in large market baskets while the others coil up the ropes ready to move further along. At the end of the day the eggs are shared out, the danger man having first choice. When part of the cliff gives a poor yield it is usual to leave it alone for a couple of years to allow it to recover.

These days the best known egg-climber is Bob Hartley, he has been climbing for the last sixteen years and his territory covers the main Bempton Cliffs, a frontage of two large fields and four small; for the large fields he pays a rental of 200 eggs each and for the small fields a rental of fifty eggs each, for the privilege of working the adjacent cliffs. Harold Robson and his gang work the cliffs nearer Flamborough, while the Buckton Hall farm cliffs are now worked by a gang of Filey men.

(June 1949)

A naturalist in Yorkshire seeks many things that creepeth unseen, ranging from slugs to badgers . . .

SLUG-HUNTING

THREE DIFFERENT families of British slugs have evolved from snaily ancestors, one of which is composed of carnivorous nocturnal prowlers living underground by day and feeding chiefly on earthworms. The tail end of each is protected by a small external shell. Then there are the roundback slugs, the most familiar being the large black slug and its numerous colour-forms including cream, red and brown varieties, found everywhere in Yorkshire from upland pastures to the lowlands, often in great numbers among grasses, seedlings and cultivated plants. A species of good size known as the Lusita-nian slug had been noted in two English localities – Durham and Nuneaton – but recently turned up in other places, the first Yorkshire site being the centre of Leeds!

Personally, I find the keelback slugs of special interest because they possess small flat and oval shells internally. The netted field-slug is the leading pestiferous member of the family, often swarming at dusk on lawns and in gardens. Insignificant and unobtrusive, a small dark kind lives in marshy places, while a large watery-looking slug crawls on trees and walls feeding on fungi and lichens. Another, a larger edition of the marsh slug, is known as the

Maltese or Caruana's slug. This was a wartime contact of mine in Cornwall and I provided the first Yorkshire record at Boston Spa. Since then, it has invaded many parts of the county. A long and slender creature quite unknown in my younger days has spread and become a serious rootcrop pest. It is the Budapest slug, and on one occasion a friend collecting on an allotment found eleven living happily inside a big potato, which had been almost completely hollowed out by the obnoxious animals.

Found in a variety of habitats, the great grey slug lives in plantations, parks and gardens, feeding on fungi and decaying matter. Its country cousin, the ash-black slug, occurs in wild places, both among old woodlands and up in the windswept Dales. it is a rarity, but on a memorable occasion a small party of conchologists found several above Grassington. The yellow slub is a garbage lover of a greenish-yellow tint, often hard to come by. For some years we knew of a strong colony under wasteland litter behind hoardings in Wellington Street, Leeds. Unfortunately, the place

was converted to a building site and now we are obliged to visit Leeds Market at night when we require a few specimens.

For many years, *Limax tenellus* – otherwise the Slender or Tender Slug – eluded me. I then located it in plenty in a sombre wooded ravine near Pateley Bridge. No convincing record had been made in Yorkshire since 1904. The site, known locally as T'Muck Hole, is well named during a typical wet spell in autumn. The slug is a yellow and rather elegant creature associated with toadstools growing in ancient woodland, both deciduous and coniferous. It is always scarce and difficult to find during the greater part of the year. It reaches maturity normally late in autumn, and those first found were crawling over the red-capped beechwood form of russule known to mycologists as *Russula mairei*. During a dry autumn, the tender slug is down in numbers, and a frosty period will restrict fungus development; but the colony described is never in danger of extinction.

John Armitage
(August 1975)

BUMPING INTO BADGERS

I KNEW there were badgers in our district. I had heard a farmer grumble about the damage they had done to his wheat. He said they rolled on the stalks to bring down the ears to mouth-level. Tom McCabe, the porter-signalman had shown me a skin of a badger he had shot, and every time we passed a clump of gorse bushes near the cliff edge my dog whined and sniffed, running around with his tail and hackles raised.

The peculiar scent was strong sometimes. But I'd never seen a badger alive until, on a black wet autumn night with a gale from the south-west, I saw not one, but two.

It was nearly 2 a.m. I was on my way to the coastguard watch hut on the high cliffs at Ravenscar, to relieve Ron Rennison, the Station Master, who had done the middle spell of bad weather watch. I could almost lean on the wind. Outside the bright beam of my torch the blackness was solid. My thoughts were still back in my bed, when I stopped, my hair on end. Only three yards away in front, were two big badgers. One was close against the other's rump and both had their white streaked noses raised in my direction. I wanted to turn and run. I'd heard and read a lot about badgers, how they can crunch a dog's leg or a man's finger. Were my rubber knee boots any protection? But they wouldn't attack without provocation, surely. My curiosity kept me still.

For fully half a minute we studied one another, then the rear badger grunted, gave his mate a nudge with his nose, and they trundled off into the gorse bushes, my torch beam following. I hurried on to the watch hut, for I was nearly late. The Station Master, who was used to punctuality, and who carried a large old-fashioned pocket watch as well as a modern wrist watch, would be getting impatient.

When I returned on the cliff path it was dawn. The sea, 600 feet below, was grey and white-flecked and merged with the sky. Two trawlers, close in to miss the off-shore gale were plunging northwards, their black smoke seized by the wind and hurled seawards as soon as it emerged from their smokestacks. I stopped at the gorse bushes. There were signs of badgers, although the hole I found was probably not the main entrance to the sett. Some old bracken had been deposited in a hollow and there were plenty of five-toed foot-marks in a patch of wet soil behind one of the bushes. But breakfast called, and I hurried to answer it.

I made many visits to the badger holes after that, at all hours. I saw foxes twice and one early morning in spring I watched a vixen playing with two frolicsome cubs. But there were no badgers to be seen. I had to wait until the deep snow for them. There is an old legend that on Candlemas Day (2 February), the badger awakes from his long winter sleep and comes out of his hole. If the day is cold he stays awake, but if the sun is shining he knows the worst is yet to come and goes back to sleep for a few more weeks. One particular badger did not come out until late February and though the sun was shining, the weather was intensely cold, with very deep snow. This combination probably puzzled him for he went for a walk and appeared in my garden.

The snow was so deep at the back of the house that we could not open the door. By a freak effect of the wind, the front, facing the sea, was practically clear and early one morning I opened the front door to see if there was still a way out. I took one glance, then closed the door quietly and rushed upstairs to rouse my family.

'Get up,' I called, 'there's a badger at our front gate.'

Carefully we opened the door and watched. He was inside the small front garden, chewing at the bottom of the heavy wooden gate, apparently with a view to creeping under it, although the gap was no more than two inches. He was big, possibly 2ft 6in from nose to tail, and he looked all of 30 lb odd. I walked out close to him and he turned and gave me a sidelong glance, then grunted and returned to gate demolition. His legs and feet were black and his claws very long. His white streaked nose was pig-like and his ears small and white-tipped. His heavy round body had a sort of grey coat, although I believe the actual hairs are part black and white. There was a strong musky smell which is said to be emitted from a gland when the animal is frightened or excited.

I did not like to see my gate being damaged, much as I disliked disturbing Brock, so I moved towards him and made noises. Very deliberately he turned and trundled past me round the corner of the house, on his way to the big snow-choked back garden. I raced through the house to the kitchen window to see where he went, but no Brock appeared. Back I went and out into the garden. He was under the side fence where the snow was only a few inches deep and appeared to be asleep. I watched him a while but he made no movement. I was nearly frozen, so I left him.

Half an hour later, while in the kitchen, I heard shrieks and from the window I saw the brave lady who battled with the snow to deliver our mail, scampering away over the drifts with old Brock lumbering a few yards behind her. But she was not being chased. Suddenly he swung aside and went over the fence, the snow being level with the top, and disappeared across the field in the direction of the cliffs. Apparently he had remembered where he came in. Why he had spent so long trying to eat a way under the front gate only he knew. I could not understand it. But badgers have always been misunderstood or at least misjudged.

Edward Gower
(January 1955)

THE 'LOST SLIPPER' OF THE DALES

Botanists maintain a discreet silence as to whether the exquisite Lady's Slipper Orchid still survives in a secret location in the Dales. Thomas Hey related the melancholy story of its decline and fall.

WHEN BUSES and private motoring opened up the Dales to thousands of weekend trippers, many floral treasures began to vanish. I can recall the slopes of Buckhaw Brow, beyond Settle, thickly-carpeted with primroses, but they have been uprooted down the years and you'd be lucky to pluck a buttonhole anywhere near that road today. And how many of the little pink bird's-eye primulas have also been taken from the hills to languish in town gardens? (After all, this lovely plant is usually marked at 1s. 6d. in the rock plant specialist's catalogue.) But the 'lost slipper' of the Dales – the Lady's Slipper Orchis (*Cypripedium calceolus*) – was not a victim of the tripper with the trowel. It vanished long before cars and buses invaded the Dales. It was the calculating collector who robbed the hills of West Yorkshire of this beautiful plant.

About forty years ago it was still clinging to its old haunts, as Reginald Farrer tells us. Writing from his famous Ingleton

garden, he said: 'The essential glory of our district is, of course, *Cypripedium calceolus*. Wickednesses untold have been perpetrated upon this plant, but even so, it still lingers unsuspected in the high hill valleys, nestling into the steep copses under the cliff. Only last year a clump was discovered in its old station in the Arncliffe Valley under Penyghent, and was duly chronicled by the *Strand* magazine.'

That was around 1909. There have been occasional reports in more recent years that the Lady's Slipper still survived in these hills. Whether by some miracle an odd plant still remains it is impossible to say, for the botanists who may know wisely keep silent. Only once did any direct evidence come my way that the Lady's Slipper may still survive in the Dales. I was at my desk in Bradford one June evening in 1933 when an Airedale countryman called in to describe some episode concerning foxes, Cononley way. But I soon discovered that he had brought far more interesting news than that – he had chapter and verse of the existence of *Cypripedium calceolus* in the Grassington neighbourhood. I will not disclose the precise spot, but he left me with the notes of the history of those few plants over three years – how many had flowered, how cattle had nibbled back two of them, and how he was certain they still survived. If his story was true, and if those particular plants have escaped the collector's grasp in the intervening years, then assuredly the Lady's Slipper is still there. But I must say that I could not find it when I searched.

Here we must leave the question of the survival or otherwise of the Lady's Slipper today. It is its melancholy past that mainly concerns me in this article – the story of how the orchid has steadily dwindled to vanishing point during the 300 years since

the first Yorkshire records were made by John Parkinson, Herbalist to Charles I, apothecary to James I and a director of Hampton Court Gardens, and by John Ray in 1670. It is a story with its dramatic as well as sad episodes. There was the day, about fifty years ago when a factory girl out for a treat came innocently back to tea with a bunch of forget-me-nots and in the middle of them were two blooms of the Lady's Slipper. A year or two later a child on the way to school near Settle found another plant. But neither factory girl nor child could ever take the eager botanists to the spots where they picked the rare blooms.

Again, surveying the history of the orchid in the Arncliffe Valley, we have a delightful picture of Archdeacon Boyd, the vicar, keeping guard over one plant for many years. Every year he cut off the flowers before they expanded, so that collectors or visitors would pass it by as a lily-of-the-valley (though by this method he unfortunately prevented any chance of it propagating itself by seed). But the vicar fell ill, or was away from the valley. The orchid put forth its showy bloom – and promptly was dug up.

I looked up Archdeacon Boyd's little book on Littondale when I was in the British Museum the other day: it was a spotless copy – it looked as though it had never before been taken from the shelves since the day it was placed there in 1893. The Archdeacon tells how a professor of botany at Edinburgh University offered one guinea for a root of the orchid, and that was its death blow. Looking back on this episode, Farrer cannot contain himself. 'Accursed for evermore, into the lowest of the Eight Hot Hells, be all reckless uprooters of rarities, from professors downwards,' he explodes.

It is worth glancing at the downward progress of the Lady's Slipper through the centuries. First came Parkinson's record in his Theatre of Botany in 1640 – 'In a wood called the Helkes . . . neere the border of Yorkshire.' Then follows Ray's record of it growing at the end of the same wood in 1695. When Dawson Turner searched for it there nearly 100 years later, he could find nothing. And a little later the editor of Withering's list of plants wrote: 'I searched for it in vain in Helks Wood, a gardener of Ingleton having eradicated every plant for sale.' (That gardener is not spared by Farrer as I shall soon show.) In 1746 a Mr Thornbeck, an Ingleton surgeon, found the Slipper in Friar Wood, Chapel-le-Dale, at the foot of Ingleborough, and it was also reported 'sparsely in woods about Clapham' in 1762. But by 1838 the plant was 'now hardly ever met with'.

In Wharfedale much the same dismal tale can be told. It was recorded in 'woods and hilly pastures about Kilnsey' in 1732, and 'about Arncliffe, Litten and Kettlewell' in 1805. The Settle botanist, J. Windsor, whose old flora is open before me as I write, says: 'About 1804 or 1805 a few specimens of this rare and beautiful plant were pointed out to me in this locality by a relative of my own, Miss Petty, of Arncliffe. Whether it still exists as it formerly did in Helks Wood I do not know.'

In 1847 Archdeacon Boyd appears in the records reporting the orchid 'really wild' at Arncliffe; it was in Grass Woods, Grassington, between 1875–81; in 1883 one plant was found in a wood at Kettlewell – again reported by Archdeacon Boyd. 'It was carried off,' he adds. Long after the Lady's Slipper was virtually a plant lost to Yorkshire, it could be seen growing in the garden of the Falcon Inn at Arncliffe – presumably the plants had been trans-

planted from the neighbouring countryside at some time. They flourished in the garden, tended by the mother of Mr Marmaduke Miller, mine host at the inn today, and one year there were eighteen blooms, four of them in pairs on two stems. After this big effort at flowering, the plants seemed to deteriorate and finally vanished. Whether they died naturally, or were taken by some collector, is not certain, but with their disappearance perhaps the last living link with the race of *Cypripediums* in the Dales was broken.

It is clear from the old records that Helks Wood, near Ingleton, must go down in history as one of the last main strongholds of the Lady's Slipper. That Helks Wood episode set Farrer on his war horse again when he studied the records. Here he is in full charge: 'Even in the days when gorgeous Elizabeth was going down in gloom to the grave, Parkinson tells how the *Calceolus Mariae* (earlier scientific name for the Lady's Slipper) abounded in the 'Helks Wood by Ingleton under Ingleborough, the highest hill in England' and had often (Oh shame!) been sent up to him, root and all, by Mistress Tomasin Tunstall, 'a worthy Gentlewoman and a great lover of these delights, who dwelleth at Bull Bank, nigh

unto Hornby Castle in those parts.'

'A worthy Gentlewoman indeed,' continues Farrer. 'O Mistress Tomasin, if only you had loved these delights a little less ruinously for future generations! Do you sleep, you worthy gentlewoman, in Tunstall Church, or does your uneasy sprite still haunt the Helks Wood in vain longing to undo the wrong you did? And after Mistress Tomasin had long been dead as the *Cypripediums* she sent up to Parkinson, there came a market gardener, a base soul, animated only by love of lucre (and thus damned to a far lower Hell than the worthy if over-zealous gentlewoman), who grubbed up all the *Cypripediums* she had left and potted them up for sale.'

And so, adds Farrer sadly: 'Helks Wood is now an oyster for ever robbed of its pearl – unless, unless in some unsuspected nook somewhere, one gold-and-purple flower is yearly mocking at the Memories of Mistress Tomasin and the wicked gardener both.' Would he dare to hope as much writing today, forty years after? It is very doubtful – but as I say, the botanists who may know whether the Dales oyster has lost its pearl for ever, keep their silence.

(August 1949)

10

LIFE AND TRADITION

DOWNSTAIRS AT HAREWOOD HOUSE

Elsie Thynne fascinated Dalesman *readers with her true 'Upstairs Downstairs' account of the period from February 1928 to September 1930 when she was 'in service' at one of Yorkshire's great stately homes.*

I WAS born and brought up in a mining area. When it came time to leave school there wasn't much in the way of work for girls so I went 'into service'. My first place was what we would call today a large detached house. The lady was elderly and spent most of her time in bed. There was just a cook-housekeeper and myself. I was very happy until eventually the lady died.

Her niece managed all her affairs and

Harewood House. (*Bertram Unne*)

one day she said to me: 'You will need a new place Elsie.' I said. 'Yes madam' and she said she would look for something for me. Sure enough, one day she told me that in *The Yorkshire Post* there was an advertisement for a fourth housemaid of five required at Harewood House at £26 per annum. This was of course the Earl and Countess's home near Leeds and she wrote about the position for me. The housekeeper replied, and I was 'engaged' as they called it.

I went by train to Leeds station and was

met there by Mr Twinn, who had been a coachman but now drove the 'Black Maria'. It looked just like the one used by the police but this one carried produce from the gardens to Leeds Market. Off we went, along Boar Lane and into Vicar Lane, where Mr Twinn stopped at the *Harewood Hotel* for his refreshment. I wondered whatever was going to happen to me and longed for the safety of mum and dad at home. There was no need to worry. Off we went to Harewood, down the mile-long drive, passing the front of the house to the side door where Mr Twinn rang the bell. (Those bells were on long wires and clanged when rung. You had to make a beeline when they went off to see which one was ringing.)

Herbert, one of the odd job men, answered the door and took me to the housekeeper, Mrs Wilson, who had a suite of rooms in the basement though her window looked out over the parkland. She was not really a 'Mrs', you understand, but senior staff used that title. She had a talk to me, then took me along basement passages to the housemaids' sitting room where I met the head housemaid, Agnes, Peggy the second and Nan the third – all Scots. I was fourth and Doris Bakewell fifth. There were two girls called Doris in the household so she was always known as 'Bakey'.

There were twenty-five inside staff – a butler, two footmen, boy, two odd job men, kitchen staff, valet, ladies' maid and Norah, the Still Room maid. The Still Room was where jams and marmalades were made; the trays were collected there and she made afternoon teas. On a Sunday morning, Norah used to love to see us because she said we rustled in our fresh uniforms. Occasionally I helped the housekeeper when Norah was away and I remember that the tables were scrubbed with sand. The Princess Royal once asked me how we kept them so spotless.

When I arrived at Harewood the Earl and Countess were away. They used to go off for six months, during which time we did the spring cleaning. Agnes, the head housemaid, was first class and trained us all well. We went on to board wages and had 17s. (85p) a week for our keep. We pooled the money and shared out what was left at the weekend. During the rest of the year, we saved sugar, so we didn't need to buy any when on 'board wages'. We were provided with lamb and rabbits but exchanged the lamb for beef or pork at the local butchers. We shopped at the local grocers and a boy got us fish on Tuesdays and Fridays. We took it in turns to cook. Agnes taught us how to clean steels, with rough emery paper, fine emery paper and burnishers.

A burnisher is a piece of leather with steel loops on like a chain. All fire irons were polished up in this way then wrapped up and put away for when the people came back. All the bric-a-brac was washed and notes placed inside each piece stating exactly where it stood. It was returned there in due course.

Many of the fireplaces had crests which needed black leading, after which paper then sticks and finally coal was heaped up ready for lighting later. The top pieces of coal had to be touched up with the black lead brush. We had to beat beds with the old-fashioned beaters – not just any old how, but in time, one at one side, one at the other in a sort of rhythm.

Visitors to Harewood House see a lovely gallery, music room, dining room and library. Nan and I had to clean the floor in the gallery, we went down on our hands and knees and were supervised by the head housemaid. There were fires to light in bedrooms and endless cans of hot water to carry, there being no hand basins then. In the evening we had to go round the house, 'shutting it up', as it were, each of us having a section to attend. All windows and shutters had to be fastened. The housekeeper went round later to check that everything was in order. After tea we were allowed to leave the House. We would meet some of the gardeners who lived in a bothy. One of them had a guitar and played *Ramona*. There were three sets of stairs in the house and we three younger ones had to wash them. One of the young men said we should stand at the top and throw the water down. We used to reply that Agnes would be sure to be at the bottom!

There was a church in the grounds and as we attended it the estate workers pelted us with toffee papers. Once Peggy put a has-sock in the aisle so that the man taking the collection would trip over it. One Sunday afternoon Peggy and I went to Wetherby – and missed the bus back. We got one to Collingham and were then resigned to walking the remaining miles. Well, Peggy didn't care for the devil or the deep blue sea. She saw two young men on bikes outside the Barley Mow, on Wetherby Road, and asked them to lend us their bikes. She did get the use of a bike. The other young man got on his and I rode on the step. We left the bikes at the gates and got in just before our ten o'clock deadline.

Time came when the people returned. Lord Harewood was in poor health and Lady Harewood would go to see him in his room every morning about 7.30. The pattern changed, and now we had our meals, except afternoon tea, in the servants' hall. The butler would be at the head of the table – no talking was allowed – and the footmen would serve the vegetables. The senior staff then retired to the housekeeper's room for their sweet. We called it the 'Pugs Parlour'. It was the same name at all the places I worked, though I never knew why. We used to love to watch the gentry go down to dinner and see the gorgeous dresses and jewellery. We were caught peering over the balustrade one evening by a guest but she didn't report us.

The Earl of Harewood died one Sunday at about 4 p.m. We prepared the house for family and visitors, airing beds and lighting many fires. The Duke of Windsor arrived. Everything was valued and Lady Harewood went to London to live. H.R.H. Princess Royal and the new Earl took over. They still lived at Goldsborough but came often. New rooms were to be built in the roof space for the maids but meantime we were moved downstairs to sleep. I was made equal third housemaid with Nan.

Mrs Wilson sent for us and spoke about all the workmen who were coming to the house to carry out alterations. There were 200 in all. Despite all the hard work, we had endless fun. Plumbers came from London, one of them, John Hicks, having a beautiful singing voice. He sang *Tiptoe through the tulips* and *If I had a talking picture of you*. There were presents from the men for letting them make tea in our sitting room. We used to get out on the roof and bask in the sun. I remember an odd job man called Herbert who had turned-up toes through washing floors on his hands and knees. Another character was Johnny Horner, who among other things swept the staff chimneys. He was once caught doing the walls – with the same brush – and explained he was just helping the maids!

Lasting impressions of Harewood include snow in the parkland; shepherds looking for lambs during a severe late winter; and the gamekeeper sitting on the front steps in the evening, popping off the rats (the basement flags had been taken up and they lived under them). I recall a man who came from Leeds to wind the clocks on a Saturday. The job took from half past nine until one o'clock. My memories of Harewood are endless. It's all the fun I remember and not the hard work! A controller was appointed to take over above Mrs Wilson. She decided to leave and that unsettled us all, so we left too, Agnes to Petworth House, Norah to Buckingham Palace, Peggy to London, Nan to Scotland, Bakey to Welbeck Abbey, Doris to go into nursing and me to Briery Close, Windermere. That's another story.

(November 1985)

DEW PONDS

(or why Jack and Jill went *up* the hill)

Arthur Raistrick, outstanding scholar of the Dales and one of the country's leading industrial archaeologists, has contributed many Dalesman *articles of major importance. They have generally been spread over several issues and of such erudition and length as to defy inclusion of extracts in an anthology of this nature – several have in fact subsequently been published as books which have become standard works. This much shorter treatise with its allusion to a popular nursery rhyme was not typical but nevertheless displays a masterly grasp of its subject.*

'We have no waters to delight our broad and brookless vales –
Only the dew-pond on the height unfed, that never fails,
Whereby no tattered herbage tells which way the season flies –
Only our close-bit thyme that smells like dawn in Paradise.'

[164]

S UCH IS Kipling's description of part of the Sussex Downs, and the words will apply without alteration to parts of west and north Yorkshire. On many of the broad stretches of limestone pasture that lie round the head of the Dales, over most of Craven and a good part of Wensleydale the dew-pond is a familiar sight. A shallow bowl-shaped depression three or four yards in diameter, and possibly two or three feet deep at its centre, circular, and now mostly grass grown, the typical dew-pond is stumbled across in many a quiet hollow on the fells. Occasionally the pond is really a pond with a pool of water to which faint sheep tracks lead from a good distance round

Arthur Raistrick (left), in conversation with Mike Harding. (G. *Bosnyak*)

about. In a few cases the hollow stares blankly skyward in a dry circle of grey concrete, with grass and nettles growing out of its many cracks.

The name 'dew-pond' is only of mid-19th-century origin though the ponds are often of considerable antiquity; writers have been happy to wrap the ponds in mystery, to ascribe them to the work of craftsmen whose art has long been lost, and to relate their capacity for containing water in the driest seasons, to some mysterious property not now understood.

Dew-ponds are common on the Chalk Downs of England, and on some of the areas of thick limestone – in fact on any upland where the nature and structure of the rock is such that the normal drainage is by underground and not surface streams.

The problem of watering sheep and cattle on such areas which are generally areas of fine pasture, has existed from the earliest time when man tried to domesticate sheep or to live himself on these dry uplands. Associated with many of the earthworks, 'camps' and village sites of prehistoric times on the Downs, there are ponds, mostly now dry, on some of which ancient cattle and sheep paths as well as habitation sites, converge. On our limestone pastures of Craven, ancient dew-ponds are abundant in the areas of Iron-age and Romano-British camps, and so frequent is the coincidence of them, that we are almost justified in regarding them as part and parcel of the same culture. There are of course many dew-ponds of fairly recent construction as well as of intermediate ages sufficient to suggest a very long continuity of their use and construction.

When closely examined (several have been partially excavated both for examination and for repair) they are found to consist essentially of the bowl-shaped hollow cut in the soil and subsoil, usually in the middle of an area of shallow depression which may extend to a few acres. The hollow is lined with thick clay puddle well trampled into position. In the very few references we have made to dew-ponds, it is clear that the common way was to carry up clay for puddle, spread it over the hollow and then 'temper' it by driving cattle back and forth across it until the whole was worked into a first class waterproof bed. To prevent the cattle hooves doing damage to the puddle skin while it was being formed straw or rushes were generally thrown in with the clay to form a tough mat. In the course of a comparatively short time, the straw decays, and plays no real part in the final efficiency of the pond. To protect the puddle after the pond comes into use, the whole hollow is paved out with large stones right to the edge of the clay and a little beyond. In the abandoned ponds this pavement is often to be seen under the grass cover that now fills them.

The name dew-pond was given in the mid-19th century because it was then thought that all the water that collected in the pond was received directly by the deposition of a heavy dew over the pond area. This simple explanation is not sufficient and recent investigations suggest a multiple source for the water. When the pond has been properly made, it is found that during the drier summer months, the pond will often receive four or five inches depth of water during a still, clear night, and will maintain a useful level of water even through prolonged drought, when all other sources fail. The position of the dew-pond in a natural hollow however shallow, ensures that what little rain does fall, drains into the pond and is thus saved. During very hot weather, the evaporation of moisture from the earth is great during the day, and at night the air has a high water vapour content. There is a certain temperature, called the dew-point, at which the atmosphere will cease to hold all the water vapour it contains, and some of it will be condensed on cold surfaces as dew. On a clear cloudless night following a clear day of heat, radiation of heat from the surface of the ground will be at a maximum. Where a dew-pond is in good condition, the puddled circle acts as an insulator preventing the radiation of heat from its area, and so remains, in comparison with the surrounding ground, a cold spot. Over this cold spot air currents tend to descend and flow outwards at ground level, and a considerable flowage may be set up. If the air is already near the dew-point it is nearly saturated with water vapour which can condense on the cold spot around the pond, and so renew supplies. Any objects round the pond – low thorn bushes are fairly frequent, heaps of stones, thick grass – will all help condensation of dew, and a moderate amount of water will be obtained in this way. When weather conditions are such that low cloud or mist lies on the fells, these 'cold-spot' hollows will tend to hold cloud and mist longer than other parts – indeed I have frequently seen the remnants of heavy Scotch mist flowing down the sides of a hollow and accumulating over a dew-pond site. Again the drenching condensation from such a mist drains into the area of the pond and may refill it on a day when the lower ground has had no rain at all. The supplies are thus drawn in part from heavy dews, from condensation of mists, and from the rains falling in the small drainage area of the pond.

When a pond is old and neglected, grass will grow in the crannies between the paving, the roots penetrate the puddle and allow the escape of water, and the pond dries out. The cracking of the puddle soon follows, and the pond changes from a dew-pond to a wet weather pool, and before long even the wettest weather fails to maintain a pool in what has become an upland seive. During the last forty years many farmers have resorted to concrete as a convenient waterproofing, but a thin skim of concrete has only inferior insulation value compared with the thick puddle and stone, and sooner rather than later, frost will crack the concrete and destroy the value of the pond.

Of the West Yorkshire dew-ponds there is a small proportion that by their very close association with the Iron Age camps can safely be referred to that age, though none of these is still known by me to be in use. There are many finely built larger diameter stone-paved ponds of the 16th and 17th centuries, when sheep pasturage came into its own. Many of these were made before or during the Enclosure walling, as walls frequently diverge from the direct line in order to pass over a dew-pond and so give water to two enclosures. Occasional boundary ridings refer to dew-ponds as boundary marks in the 17th century.

Whatever be the date of the dew-ponds, they will always have an air of mystery and will carry the mind back to the dim past when some observant Neolithic cattlemen noticed that when his cattle puddled the ground at a camp entrance or near an occasional spring, the hollow so formed, held water after rain. Generations must have used cattle-puddled hollows before the daring idea of making an 'artificial' puddle was born. The final working out of the art of making dew-ponds extended through periods for which we have no written history but only folk memory and tradition. The old nursery rhyme, *Jack and Jill went UP the hill to fetch a pail of water*, has always seemed wrong. It is general experience, ever since the settlement of most of our villages, that people go *down* the hill to the springs or rivers for water. If Jack and Jill were members of an Iron-age hillside community, they would certainly avoid the boggy, danger-infested valley bottom, and climb the limestone scars uphill to dip their pail in the hilltop dew-pond. We shall never know, but it may not be too absurd to think that Jack and Jill were early prototypes of our Dales shepherd folk, and that they could probably have told us much about the making of dew-ponds that all our research today fails to reveal.

(November 1944)

[167]

BRASS BANDS AND CHEESECAKES

Arthur Percival, one-time leader of the Hallé Orchestra, had both literary and musical gifts. He spent his childhood in Wensleydale when the brass band contests at Hardraw Scar were a highlight of his life.

AYE, AH cu' frae Wensiddill: born an' bred theer, an' christened i' Aysgarth church. Me father wor a country fiddler, wen 'e wern't farmin'. Nivver played out o' t' first position in 'is life; but 'e could play sike a reel as wud have med our Sir John Barbirolli reel reight off 'is rostrum!'

Never were those country fiddlers held up for the need of a bow re-hairing. 'Thi bow's wearin' a bit thin, lad. Pop ower into yon field, an' 'elp thisen: there's plenty more 'airs were these cum fro, in th' 'ossie's tail!' As for fiddles, 'weel wa' reckon nowt much o' sum on 'em: them lile foreign fiddles: they's nobbut middlin': not enough *tone* in 'em, wi' nobbut *one* soundposst in their belly: sound like a lile moorbird squakin', does sum on 'em! 'As tha ivver 'eard young Jason's fiddle? By, lad! Tha wants to 'ear young Jason's fiddle: 'e's putten *fower* sound-possts in. Tha can 'ear it all ower t'dale!'

There was plenty of music to be heard 'all ower t'dale' in the days of my childhood. I had my first violin out of my Christmas stocking when I was rising five, 'an it fair glissen'd, wi' orange-coloured varnish!' Wear and tear necessitated that it should be replaced on each subsequent Christmas for several years, and each 'new' treasure gleamed and glistened as brightly as its predecessor. I can *still* recall the smell of that varnish! Each new violin was fresh from the factory in Czechoslovakia and also bore a label inside: 'Guaranteed Strad. Model, made in 1741!'

It was one of my infantile boasts that I could *play* one voice-part on my fiddle, and *sing* a different one simultaneously! Whatever in this world the result must have sounded like, I cannot bear to think. But those were happy days! One of the happiest days was when I heard my first brass band. The impact was terrific. I can remember literally tingling with the sheer thrill and excitement of it.

Hardraw Scar was the scene of a great annual band contest. From far and wide they came: fine, rough, loyal bandsmen of the north. And their supporters came too, travelling the steep, winding roads in ponytraps and wagonettes. When the road went *down*, we all sat tight; when the road went *up*, 'us young 'uns all got out an *pushed*: to give t'pony a lift.' The Scar was one of nature's good gifts to the music-loving Dalesfolk – a perfect amphitheatre for the listeners with a green-turfed arena in the centre for the performers. There was also room for the tents, one for the adjudicators; one for the performers, and one . . . for the eatables. That tea-tent was a sight to behold, with ham-and-egg pasty, Wensleydale cheesecakes – pride of the district, 'all on 'em homemade, lad: non' o' yer bowt-stuff 'ere!'

Once the contest had got under way attention was riveted; prowess was assessed; and the process of elimination evident. Margins became narrower, and loyalties were taxed. Even a very small boy could feel the mounting tension and excitement, all to be released in heartfelt good-natured

Poster advertising the 1885 contest, complete
with 'Glee' and 'Grand Gala'.
(*W.R. Mitchell*)

Heyday of the brass band concerts at
Hardraw Scar, 1902.

roars, once the winners had been proclaimed. And when the hugging and the back-slapping was over, came the bustle and commotion of departure. Many in that great company were 'locals'; others had come from the neighbouring dales. 'Aye – cum be train, and t'train wouldn't wait . . .' So off they all tramped, the whole company, to Hawes Junction, and there that hearty, happy to-do reached its natural and spontaneous climax. The hymn was *Rimington* and the valleys rang again with the grand sound. The 'foreigners' packed into the train and were away, we 'locals' squashing into wagonettes.

I remember I went to my last band contest proudly arrayed in my brand-new Boy Scout uniform, so by that time I must have reached the ripe old age of eleven years. As the pony-trap wound its way round the twisty roads in the golden evening light, through peaceful, lovely country, I fell to day-dreaming. I thought of the winners of the contest, of how proud they would be feeling, and how they would be praised and honoured on their next public appearance. I tried to frame a speech in their honour.

The two farmers facing me were also talking about the winners. 'Ow dosta think they played, John?' said one.

John went on puffing his pipe, staring at the road ahead. 'It's a bonny bit o' road, this, Dave: snod as an apple.'

'Ah,' said Dave, 'that it is . . . 'ow dosta think they played?'

Further long silence, then: 'Verra weel. I think they played verra weel. I reckon yon lot's middlin' musical. Aye . . . verra musical.'

(January 1971)

MY BEST-EVER MEAL

Yorkshire folk are certainly fond of their food, and thus it is not surprising that a competition inviting readers to describe their best-ever meal attracted a huge response. These mouth-watering entries were the three winners.

Breakfast

The best meal I ever had in Yorkshire was in the Spring of 1910 at The Hill Inn, Chapel-le-Dale. I was one of a party of about a dozen students who arrived by train at Ribblehead station late one Friday afternoon and walked the two miles to the inn – the luggage to follow by horse-and-cart. We were to spend the Saturday botanising on Whernside, and on Sunday to climb Ingleboro' to find alpine plants at the summit.

The first morning we came down early, already shod in heavy boots over thick woollen stockings, and gathered round the big oblong table. Each was served with a bowl of porridge, and took a generous helping of fresh cream from a quart jug. Then, in came Mrs Kilburn with a huge dish of ham and eggs. This sounds ordinary, but never before or since have I enjoyed such fare: the thick juicy, sweet, sizzling rashers cut from one of the home-cured hams that hung from the rafters of the big old kitchen, and with each succulent portion a fresh egg frizzled in the tasty dripping, light and frothy with browned, curled edge. Then we 'filled in the corners' with home-made bread and honey and unstinted fresh farm butter.

To little Johnny Kilburn this was all in the day's work, and, of course, we had such a breakfast on the next two mornings, but there has been no breakfast in my long life, in many countries, to equal that memorable one of over fifty years ago.

E.M. Blackwell

Dinner

The best meal I ever had in Yorkshire was at my Granny's cottage at Catwick in the East Riding of Yorkshire. My Grandad had

pulled fresh peas and dug up small new potatoes, while my Granny had a large piece of thick rib of beef in the oven. I can still see, yes, indeed I can still smell the aroma from, two blue-and-white tureens piled high with lovely fresh vegetables, the blue-and-white Wedgwood meat dish bearing the succulent joint, and the matching gravyboat full of rich brown gravy. Of course, there were crisp, golden Yorkshire puddings with gravy first, to be followed by the meat and vegetables. Lastly, there was a deep gooseberry pie with a very 'short' crust topped with real cream.

My Granny and Grandad, Mother and Father had a cup of tea after their meal, but my brother and I had a glass of water in our own red glasses which Granny kept specially for us. My dear Grandparents are

(*Ionicus*)

now dead but how I wish my own little boy could have a memory of a Yorkshire meal in the same surroundings which he could treasure as I do.

B.M. Robinson

Tea

Kippers, newly-baked bread, newly-churned butter. More bread and butter with lashings of moorland honey. Raspberries and cream. A curious conglomeration of food? Maybe, but to this day, forty years on, I know I have never tasted more delicious food.

I was in my early teens and was on holiday in Robin Hood's Bay. The day had started with my brother and I taking half a dozen loaves of bread to be baked in the communal ovens. We had arranged to walk into Hawsker to visit a farmer friend, but first we had to wait for a certain caller. The caller turned out to be a tall, thin old lady dressed in black from head to heel. On her head, she balanced a basket of kippers which emitted an exciting, hunger provoking tang. Her carriage, I remember was that of a Hartnell model (we called them mannequins in those days) and her speech curiously dignified – a dignity which I was to learn in later years was the dignity of labour and honest dealings. As she drank her tea, we helped ourselves to kippers, and what beauties they were! So large and shiny and so plump!

We came back from Hawsker rich with spoils. Farmhouse butter that we had helped to churn. A honeycomb from the moors. Raspberries that we had picked and a bottle of cream to complement them. It didn't take long to prepare tea. I can still smell that bread as my brother brought it in, still savour those rich succulent morsels of kipper meat, still recall the sweetness of the sticky honey on those thick doorsteps of crusty bread. The memory of those raspberries, still warm with the July sun, wrapped in the cloying smoothness of the cream, still titillates my palate, especially when I think of my slimming diet.

R. Meadows

(October 1962)

'Life and Tradition' embraces a multitude of topics, and it would have been possible to fill this entire book five times over with appropriate articles and snippets. The remaining chosen extracts are at least diverse, ranging from the feudal system to simple pleasures and from Nidderdale to Holderness.

COURT LEET

WE WERE all taught at school that what is known as the feudal system (later they explained to us that it wasn't really a system at all) was done for by the time that Henry VIII came to the throne. In the twenty-odd years of his rule his father demolished the entire structure – social, economic, political – of which the realm was built in the shape of a pyramid. The lowest tier consisted of some thousands of manors, the smallest social unit in the hierarchy, the cells of a body politic which worked on the basis of land tenure by service and defended itself from external enemies on the basis of personal following ('suit') by all freemen of manorial lords who were landlords in peace and a sort of platoon commanders in war.

By the time Henry VII had won his war to make England a land fit for Welshmen to live in, he had already set about the demolition process. I remember criticising an excellent historical novel about Danby Dale (*This Freedom* by Brenda English) on the grounds of anachronism. It showed the Court Leet of Danby Manor functioning as in feudal times, attended by all landholders in the manor, some freemen, some servile. Endless debate took place about what was to be done or not to be done in accordance with the Custom of the Manor, and the book referred to the heart-searchings of one of the principal characters as to whether or not he should accept the office of Reeve (a sort of agricultural foreman). Acceptance would be tantamount to acknowledging that he was a serf, since this office could not be held by a freeman.

This novel was set about the time of the Dissolution of the Monasteries, and I reckoned it was about half a century out of date in its portrayal of the social set-up. How wrong I was appeared last autumn after we had come to occupy a holding near Stormy Hall, just within the Manor of Danby. The great truth that Danby is Different burst on me when I received a summons in form and manner following:

	THE Court Leet and Court
Manor of	Baron of the Right Honour-
Danby	able JOHN VISCOUNT DOWNE,
	Lord of the said Manor.

By Virtue of a Precept under the hand and Seal of BENJAMIN CHARLESWORTH RALPH DODSWORTH, Gentleman, Steward of the said Court, to me directed, you are hereby summoned personally to be and appear at the next Court, to be holden at DANBY CASTLE in and for the said Manor, on THURSDAY the 30TH day of OCTOBER next, at ONE o'clock then and there to do and perform your Suit and Services, according to the Custom of the said Manor.

Dated this 16TH day of OCTOBER 1975.
To: MR. A. DENT, WEST CLIFF, DANBY.

F. RAW
Bailiff.

If it comes to the crunch, I suppose 'suit' means following my lord to the wars. Nine times out of ten, in these parts, this meant the wars against the Scots. It has not troubled Danby men much since about 1603, but I suppose if devolution goes much further we shall have to reckon with that possibility again, at least if this holding is among those responsible for furnishing an hable man with horse and harneys when the powers of the shire are levied. But then, I reflect, my sixtieth birthday fell two days before the court was due to be holden: moreover my old mare, though perfectly hable in outward appearance, is not altogether sound in the wind. I suppose we should have to fall in behind my lord and proceed to the tryst at Langbaurgh under the shadow of Roseberry Topping, to muster with the other contingents comprising the wapentake band. I have every confidence the muster-master would not pass us as hable and sufficient. So not to worry.

It's the services that worry me. I don't know, yet, what the Custom of Danby requires in this line, but I have read the

Customal of Hackness when that manor was a fief of the Abbot of Whitby, and my heart quails at the services demanded, from which mere age does not seem to have granted exemption. They included such chores as catching all the mares and foals running in the woods over there beyond Harwooddale, sorting out the Abbot's own stock from those of the villeins and cottars and other occupiers, and branding the young stock. Besides being allowed to cut turf and fern and rushes on their own account, and to gather estovers, the suitors of Hackness had to get in a certain quota of these useful by-products for the lord's use: and they also had to do some quarrying, and to dig clay and line fishponds and repair milldams. I don't feel much like a rodeo, nor like a dig-in of that nature.

When I got to the Castle I found the court assembling in the hall. It's quite small for the Great Hall of a genuine medieval castle, even if the latter has been a farmhouse, and nothing but, ever since the Civil War, in which it was thoroughly 'slighted'. The sun shines fitfully on the Esk, winding slowly between high clay banks through innumerable ox-bow curves, to pass, directly below us, under Duck Bridge. A bright light burns in the restored hearth of the hall, and trestle benches covered with ex-government blankets are arranged in rows: well, not actually trestles, but planks resting on empty diesel cans. But at one end of the hall is an impressive piece of furniture with a linen-fold panel back, somewhat like a cathedral stall, and comprising three seats with a desk or lectern in front. This accommodates the Steward, the Bailiff, and one other, to be mentioned hereinafter. After the Steward has intoned the ritual Oyez and invited all persons having to do, etc., to draw near and attend, the routine busi-ness opens with a terrible lot of swearing. In fact I haven't heard so much swearing since father sat on the hot stove.

All the officers of the court are sworn in, except the Steward (why?), including twelve Jurymen who perform the routine business of the courts both Leet and Baron, at monthly sessions. In some ways it is vaguely military, since a roll is called, interminably, of all the suitors. It is all rather confusing, as about half of them seem to be called Welford or Raw or Tindall. In the body of the hall there must be about twenty-five people present, all suitors or their representatives. New suitors also take an oath. To do what? To honour our Sovereign Lady the Queen and the lord of this manor, and to perform all services due from them. The routine business done, the Steward inquires what extraordinary matters are to be dealt with.

If I had hoped to see someone amerced for not paying heriot on the death of the head of a household, or for not paying merchet on the marriage of his daughter with the lord's permission – or Heaven knows what fine on her marriage without the said permission – I was disappointed. There was no extraordinary business, except that certain parties paid a penny into court. There lay the heart of the matter. Looking round me to discover what made one a suitor, I recognised many neighbours. They were not all tenants, and not all freeholders. The qualification is that one holds a property which comprises the shooting rights ('freewarren') and the right to fish in Danby Beck or the Esk or other tributaries, and stray on Danby Moor (High or Low) for ewes – in our case fifty. These rights are not inherent in the free-hold itself, but are derived from the man-orial right. The grazing on the moor extends, not over what social historians call the Common Waste, but the Lord's Waste, probably because all the Common Waste was enclosed long ago.

This court is not entirely functionless or toothless. Most of the duties are of a negative nature, such as not dumping any more rubbish in the disused pit near Didderhowe at the top end of Castleton which is a township of Danby, and not letting any stock stray on the moor in excess of the fifty ewes or whatever is allowed. But there are circumstances under which more positive action might be required of a suitor. Today's session is attended by the Lord of the Manor in person and this, the Steward remarks, is something that does not seem to have happened within living memory. No doubt that is why we are honoured with a Press photographer this time. The Steward closes the court with a resounding 'God save the Queen and the Lord of the Manor,' echoed in a respectful mumble by all present.

I walk down in the autumn sunshine into Ainthorpe and the 20th century, musing that I never liked that Lancastrian king, and I am glad his work is not quite done, after nearly five centuries. Long may this court sit.

Anthony Dent
(March 1976)

VILLAGE STORE

D ESPITE THE creeping invasion of modern shops and houses, the little village of Patrington retains much of its old charm. It is easy to trace the layout of the village as it was long ago, with the village green and the manor, and its magnificent church to which even today all roads lead. There are street names full of interest too. Pump Row was once a row of cottages built of narrow red bricks. They had pantile roofs and short stumpy chimneys. They were all slightly different, but in the ends of the gables the bricks were all set diagonally. The village pump stood here and further along on the village green were the stocks.

The grass has long since gone, some of the cottages have been pulled down. A fine big window transforms the parlour of one of the remaining ones into a shop. It is an exciting little shop, kept by a delightful little lady. She sells everything from cotton reels to men's shirts, from babies' bootees to 'beaver' lined leatherette jackets to keep out the cold. It can be very cold up here, when storms of wind and rain come battering in from the coast, with neither hill nor tree to break them. She sells bright coloured pinafores too, for no village shop in Yorkshire would be complete without this much used garment. There are shelves from top to bottom of the walls, and all are stacked with goods. The shelves on one side of the shop are completely filled with knitting wools. There are wools of every conceivable colour and texture for the people up here are great knitters. There are bales of materials piled on the counter.

When you buy a length of cloth the little lady of the shop takes her huge scissors,

and, holding them wide open, propels them straight through without moving the blades. There are bundles of goods piled up on the only chair, and bundles lie all over the floor. You must stand and point to anything you require on the other side of the shop, for you would have a hazardous journey if you tried to cross that floor. This shop is the collecting house for the village laundry, though any old inhabitant would be aghast at the idea of sending her clothes to 'one o' them places wheer the' puts iv'thing i' th' tub together wi' other folkses.' Besides it would not be Monday morning without that line full of spotless washing blowing cheerfully in the wind.

As you enter the shop, the door opens with a jerk, and you hear the jangle of a bell. In a moment our little lady emerges from the room beyond. One morning a delicious smell of cooking filled the shop as she came in.

'Good morning,' I said, 'you are busy cooking?'

'Ohr aye, I be makin' a bit o' cheese cake.'

'How lovely, I've always wanted to know how a real curd cheese cake was made. I wish you would tell me.'

'Oh, that's 'asy.'

'I expect it is really, but how do you do it?'

'Ohr, well, yer jis mixes t' curd and stuff and beats it all up. I tell yer it's 'asy.'

(Arthur Bent)

'Well how much of everything do you use?'

'Ohr well now, yer jes gets a nice bit o' treacle an' some sugar, an' a couple o' eggs, I allus uses two eggs, I likes plenty eggs in it, and a bit o' ground rice an' some currants, and beat 'em all up till its nice an smooth, an' a lump o' butter.'

'But how much butter?'

'Ohr, a nice bit – it maks it goods and rich.'

'And how much sugar?'

'Ohr a nice 'elpin' if yer likes it sweet.'

'And how much rice?'

'Well jes a sprinklin'.'

'And how much treacle?'

'Ohr now ye can put a nice spoonful o' treacle in: It maks it rale nice t' treacle does.'

I went home and had a try, and it certainly was 'rale nice'. It was delicious, in fact.

Olive Cort
(August 1963)

Corner Shop

We have some somewhere, luv, I know
I had 'em in my hand, by gow.
Eh, Florrie, hasta seen them nails?
Them half-inch 'uns we sell from t' scales?
Tha what? In't bath? Then cum on down,
Ah've got shop full. Put on thy gown.
Ah'll see to thee, lad – what's thi pleasure?
A yard of beadin'. That's good measure.
Now lass, an' how's thi mam today?
Ah'm reet put out to hear that – nay,
I thowt that she were pullin' round.
Come on, Florrie – he wants a pound.
And Winnie here wants one o' they
Pink pan scrubs, they were in a tray.
Tha's put 'em on't top shelf, by heck,
Tha's bahn to hev me brek mi neck!
The supermarket may be quicker
But I enjoy my top shop bicker.

CLARE PIERSON
(March 1977)

SIMPLE PLEASURES IN THE DALES

Seeing

Cloud shadows chasing across open hill country.

Golden sunbeams swinging through piled grey clouds across a wide landscape.

The blue shadows of sunlit snow.

A full moon bathing the roofs and lanes of a sleeping village on a still frosty night.

Rainbows.

The striding patterns of dry-stone walls in Pennine moorlands and daleheads.

Hearing

The running waters of rocky streams.

The *distant* noise of railway trains, now puffing and clanking up, now rattling down, a long incline.

The ringing of an anvil under the hammer of a skilled blacksmith.

The piping and crying of curlews.

The song of the willow-warbler and of the skylark.

A winter gale howling round the house at

'Hearing the running waters of rocky streams' – one of the 'Simple Pleasures' captured in this wood engraving by the famous Malhamdale artist Joan Hassall.

night when I am snug in bed or by the fire.

Smelling

On the moors: heather in full bloom as I brush through it on a dry, warm day.

In the fields: broad beans in flower; new-mown hay.

In the garden: old-fashioned roses; mignonette; night-scented stocks; lilies-of-the-valley.

Indoors: peat fires; baking day.

Coming unexpectedly on the smell of wood-smoke in the open-air.

The earthy smell of kitchen gardens and lawns when heavy rain follows dry summer weather.

Tasting

Very cold water from a moorland spring.

Ripe Victoria plums straight from the tree.

A farmhouse tea of home-cured ham with eggs and fresh white bread after a long walk.

Junket and cream from a cool larder.

Oven-bottom-cake still warm from the oven, with farmhouse butter.

Well-matured Yorkshire parkin.

Feeling

A wet west wind in my face when ridge-walking on the high moors.

The glow on my face and neck and hands after a long day out in the sun and the wind.

Getting my boots and stockings squelch-ingly wet when fishing or shooting or cross-country walking (so long as my feet inside them stay warm!)

Getting into – and by stages lying right down in – a steaming hot bath, just as hot as I can bear.

Yawning when I get up in the morning.

Laughing immoderately, till my eyes water and my ribs ache.

Doing

The relief of trotting effortlessly downhill after a long stiff climb.

Steady digging of good garden earth.

Breaking and chopping dry branches into kindling and small logs.

Free-wheeling my bicycle down a long, winding and preferably switch-back hill.

Playing 'ducks and drakes' with flat stones on still water.

Sharpening pencils, if the knife be apt.

John Dower
(December 1944)

NUTTING IN NIDDERDALE

IN LOWER Nidderdale many of the hedges are of hazel. It seems to like the soil and climate here. But the nut crop is definitely not what it once was. No longer can you walk along the quiet country roads or field paths and stretch out your arm to pick a cluster of nuts to crack as you walk along, or fill a basket with the smooth, shining, honey-coloured shells, which are such a contrast to the two rough, grey-green 'leaves' that form the cup.

It is easy to tell why. On the roadside the farmers keep the hedges clipped well back and low, to give motorists a better view at corners and more room. No longer are the quiet roads dappled with the shade of overhanging branches and leaves. On the field paths, much more frequented than in the past, especially near our market town, schoolchildren and weekend visitors pick the nuts before they are ripe. If you want a basket or a pocket full you must seek out a secluded spot, like the one by the edge of a wood I know. The nut trees grow on the outer fringe, high and leafy, overhanging the surrounding fields. The farmer doesn't trouble to clip them back, and here you may find the sweet, sunwarmed nuts.

Nutting parties must have been quite the thing in the past, and nuts, of course, are an essential part of Hallowe'en festivities. There is a strange story of nutting connected with the small village of Thorpe, near Little Ouseburn, in Lower Nidderdale. A funeral party was following the bier to church, and on the way walked down a leafy lane of hazels. It was autumn and the nuts were particularly abundant, in thick, rich clusters – too good to pass by. With one accord the mourners dumped the bier by a field gate and dispersed to go 'a-nutting'. When they returned several hours later, the bier and coffin had disappeared. For many years afterwards the gate in the lane was called 'Corpse Yat'.

M.A. McManners
(November 1960)

11

TRAVEL AND TRANSPORT

THE CORPSE WAY

Until the advent of adequate roads, carrying the dead in 'crude wicker baskets' from the head of Swaledale to the nearest church at Grinton was a two-day journey. Edmund Cooper described some of the perils which beset mourners and pall-bearers.

CROSSING Kisdon Hill between Keld and Muker, then fording the Swale and continuing up Iveletside, high up along the north slope of Swaledale, runs an ancient track which is now known as the 'corpse-way'. It was used by funeral parties when they carried their dead from the dale-head to a final resting place at the parish church of Grinton. There is little doubt but that it is one of the oldest roads in the dale. Flint arrow heads found along its route point to the fact that it was trodden by prehistoric man. The original path or 'trod' avoided the wet marshy land in the valley bottom and the tangled forest which covered the lower slopes. Following the sunnier and warmer side of the dale, it was natural that when men came to settle in the valley of the Swale they built their farms and hamlets on or near its course. Thus it became a link between one settlement and another.

Itinerant packmen, 'badgers' and 'higglers' journeying on foot or on ponies used it. They carried salt, corn and cloth. When lead-mining became the most important industry in the dale, it rang to the tread of the miners' clogs and the clopping of pony trains laden with smelted lead for Richmond and beyond. There were, of course, old bridle-ways on the other side of the valley. As two sides were linked by 'waths'

Upper Swaledale near Keld. (*Bertram Unne*)

or fords, these routes were probably used as alternative ways of getting to Grinton, depending largely upon the state of the river.

Dr Whitaker, writing 150 years ago, said that 'before interments began to take place at Muker, the bodies of the dead were conveyed for burial upon men's shoulders upwards of twelve miles to the parish church, not in coffins, but in rude wicker baskets.'

As described above, funerals from Keld and Birkdale passed over Kisdon to Muker, but those from West Stonesdale, Frith, Smithyholme and Ravenseat kept to the left bank of the Swale and joined the 'corpse-way' at Calvert Houses. Two pall-bearers were supplied from each of these hamlets in addition to the family bearers, so that the carrying could be done in relays. Before the procession began, watch was kept over the body by each of the relatives in turn. Special biscuits and wine were handed over the wicker-coffin to the guests as they arrived. All the neighbours were 'bidden' by personal calls, and sometimes as many as 200 would attend the service. When a shepherd died a fleece of wool was placed in his coffin. His occupation could thus be proved on Judgement Day, so that his irregular attendance at church would be forgiven.

While the journey lasted the funeral guests lived at the expense of the bereaved. At intervals along the route the body was laid upon stone slats or resting-stones whilst the cortege halted for a while. There is still to be seen at the north approach to Ivelet Bridge a flat, elongated slab, which is pointed out as one of these old 'coffin-stones'. However, it may be argued that it owes its name not to the use made of it, but to its striking likeness to the shape of a coffin. Travelling from the head of Swale-dale to Grinton would take at least two days, depending upon the state of the weather. Funeral parties are said to have stayed the night at Shoregill Head, near Ivelet, which must have been a farm-cum-inn in those days. Calvert Houses had a beer tavern called *The Travellers Rest*. Feetham was another half-way house. Just above this village are the ruined foundations of a building known as the 'dead-house', where the wicker-coffins were left in safety while the procession slipped down to what is now the Punch Bowl, to rest and refresh themselves.

There is a tale told that once two funeral parties were using the wayside mortuary at the same time and that it was only after the burial service had taken place and when the effects of the 'refreshment' had worn off that the bearers realised that the bodies had been interred in the wrong graves. As there were no bridges in the dale until the end of the 16th century, ponies were used to carry the wicker-coffins over the fords. Especially was this necessary when the rivers and becks were in spate. Many an accident must have occurred at such times involving a bearer in a worse fate than just a wetting.

After the new chapel and burial ground at Muker was consecrated in 1580, corpses from the dale-head and downwards as far as Gunnerside were carried to Muker. Those dying below Gunnerside continued to be taken on to Grinton as before. The custom of providing meat and drink for funeral parties continued. The Queen's Head at Muker, near the church, catered for them up to quite recent times. Here a sum of money called a 'shot' was paid to the landlord by the dead man's relatives, to provide drinks to all the guests who called until the 'shot' was exhausted. They drank out of special 'funeral mugs', which, when not in use, hung from the ceiling joists of the inn kitchen. When the Queen's Head was sold after the first world war and

became a private house, the 'gaily-decorated' mugs were dispersed.

During the 17th century an Act of Parliament was passed forbidding the use of linen shrouds or winding sheets, and ordering that the dead should be 'buried in woollen'. This was done in order to stimulate England's wool trade. This law was often evaded by the well-to-do, who gladly paid the statutory fine of five pounds. In fact, the continuance of the time-honoured custom of burying in linen almost became a licensed practice, the fine being regarded as a sort of fee permitting the use of linen sheets. The use of wicker carriers was certainly in vogue in 1716 when the curate of Muker gave notice that he would bury no more corpses without a coffin. Whether this ended the use of wicker baskets is not known. Heavier wooden coffins would certainly have made these journeys more arduous, and it is likely that sledges would be used. In 1828, William Hunter, aged ninety-one, was drawn to his grave by his mare, aged thirty-two.

Towards the end of the 18th century better roads were made; bridges were built by public subscription, and wheeled traffic began to supersede the old pack-horse trains. A hearse was bought by the parish of Muker in 1836, a box-like structure on four wheels. The driver sat on a seat fixed to the front end and the wheels were lined with leather to deaden their sound. On either side of the slightly domed roof were three black plumes or tassels. Sixpence was the usual fee for its use for persons residing in the Muker township, but outsiders paid 6d. a mile. It was the custom to stop the cortege at the school. The coffin was then hauled out through the back of the hearse and lifted upon the shoulders of the pall-bearers. Then, with the mourners chanting a solemn dirge, the procession proceeded up the village street to the church.

(July 1963)

BESIDE THE FIVE RISE LOCKS

One of the unsung engineering triumphs of northern England is the Leeds & Liverpool Canal, wending its way through the industrial Aire Valley and then the rolling countryside west of Skipton. William Hodgson worked on the canal for fifty-one years, latterly as length foreman, before retiring to live at the top of Bingley's famous Five Rise Locks. Clifford S. Scott sought his recollections.

WILLIAM Hodgson will tell you that when the staircase of five locks was being built at Bingley, the holes were excavated by local labour with pick and shovel. The men were paid threepence halfpenny for every cubic yard (one ton) removed.

There was a strata of limestone – washed down in the glacial age – and this was burned in part by using coal underlying the limestone. The slaked lime was used in building the locks from stone – mainly outcrop – taken from surrounding land. Each lock holds approximately 80,000 gallons of water and quantity was estimated in lockfuls, not in gallons. The main supply of water is from Winterburn reservoir, which holds 300 million gallons according to the reckoning of Mr Hodgson who carried out the sum for the information of school-children. Some water is supplied from streams. Factories at the side of the canal and drawing water from it had to pay a standard rate. Farmers with land alongside the canal, whose cattle drank from it, paid for the estimated consumption of each beast. Inexperienced users of pleasure craft were responsible for very considerable wastage.

Mr Hodgson relates that in the heyday of commercial traffic on the canal, life was hard and labour not very well paid. The bargee (boatman) and his wife (or mistress as was often the case) lived on the boat in a cabin which was small and, in most instances, little larger than a modern bath-room. On many barges the cabins were spotlessly clean and tidy, but others were dirty and untidy, even to the point of being verminous. Keeping check on conditions was the responsibility of the Health Department of local authorities.

The men were hard workers and invari-ably hard drinkers. Their way of life was frequently referred to as gipsies of the waterways. This was resented but Mr Hod-gson would say that perhaps they had much in common. Wearing of gold ear-rings by the men was a fashion both adopted. Young children were 'tethered' dog-like by rope to a wooden chimney coming through the deck, a practice followed to reduce the risk of drowning tragedies. When travelling without cargo the children could play safely in the hold of the barge. Older children went to school for two or three days while a cargo was being unloaded and schools had separate registers for such scholars. When on the move children, not yet in their teens, walked with the towing horse along the towpath.

In tunnels, such as near Foulridge, horses could not be used and men propelled the boat by a method known as 'legging'. This necessitated lying on one's back and using a walking motion on the roof of the tunnel. 'Legging Boards' were also used to 'walk' in the same manner along the sides of the tunnel. One man, well-known to Mr Hodgson, made his living as a 'legger' and estimated he 'walked' a distance equal to twice round the world in fifty years. There was also a livelihood for unloaders of the cargoes of coal, wool, wheat, flour and a whole host of other commodities.

No tea-breaks were taken. Meal times were organised in turn by the two men who usually comprised the crew. Horses fed from nosebags while boats were negotiating the locks. Heated arguments often took place when barges arrived, almost simul-taneously, at the top and bottom. A horse 'first past the post' was considered to earn first use of the locks for its boat. The posts, white-painted and 100 yards from the Five Rise Locks, are still there. The 'lock-ahoy'

call could be heard up to a mile away.

Halts for the night were made at stables strategically placed and if one was full the bargees had to push along until accommodation could be found. This led to various subterfuges. To gain an advantage one bargee would slip his boat past another in the darkness at one of the wider parts of the canal. To deaden the sound corn sacks were wrapped round the horse's feet. If the usual stabling could not be found, it was not uncommon for the horse to be put into a nearby field or even into the stable on a canal-side farm. If discovered the bargee would meet the cost with a barrow-load of coal. Who was to miss that amount from a cargo of fifty tons? (A barrow-load would be worth about sixpence at the time). Such quantities were bartered for eggs, a roasting chicken or boiling fowl. Dogs were not allowed but most boats had one – usually a lurcher type which earned its keep.

It was compulsory for all barges to be equipped with a stock-whip – short-handled with a long lash. The whip had many uses and was manipulated with great skill. A claim was that, properly cracked, the sound could be heard up to a mile away. Often a whip was used to urge the horse to move a little faster. When approaching a 'blind' bend the whip was cracked 'to give audible warning of approach' – a term embodied in the bye-laws. By this means it was found possible to estimate who was the nearer to a bend where boats were approaching from opposite directions and collision had to be avoided. The sound invariably called a lock-keeper from his office. This whip was also used as a lasso to catch an unsuspecting wild (or even a tame) duck. Quick as lightning the bird was on deck. So tomorrow's dinner was assured.

Commercial traffic on the canal has now disappeared. It has become of great recreational value to cruiser owners. 'I still assist many of these week-end sailors to negotiate the locks, and have to tell them they are not fit to be out with a peggy-tub,' was Mr Hodgson's final quip.

(June 1975)

NIGHT EXPRESS OVER AIS GILL

The Settle–Carlisle line, at various times lost cause, neglected backwater, England's greatest scenic route, third wonder of northern England and a political shuttlecock, has inevitably featured in The Dalesman *more often than any other railway. Desmond Heap captured the essence of the route when it was still a proper main line, conveying sleeping car expresses from Scotland to London.*

ALONGSIDE the dimly-lit departure platform at St Enoch Station, Glasgow, stands a long line of dark coaches. Inside, the compartments are well lit but heavily curtained. The bruising and scarring of the panelling in the narrow corridors show that three years of war and the carrying of loads and luggage of a kind for which they were never constructed have had their effect. The maroon livery of the LMS Company, with which the outside of the coaches is finished, is concealed beneath layers of grime save in those oval and circular patches where the dirt has been cleaned off to reveal the class of a compartment – first or third – or the serial number of coach. At the head of the coaches, suffused in a thin cloud of steam, stands a locomotive of the latest LMS, 4–6–0 type.

This is the London Train – the night express to St Pancras. There are sleeping berths to be had (provided members of the Cabinet haven't booked them all in advance) if you like sleeping in trains. Personally I don't, but in any case I have other designs for this journey. It is a frosty winter's night with a full moon and there has been snow.

The starting signal glows green and at 9.15 p.m. precisely the London Train pulls out of St Enoch and curves its way round the bend and over the Clyde. Nearly three hours later, at midnight, the train runs into the smoking jaws of Carlisle station, that fabulous place, into which, in the days before 1922, seven different companies sent their trains. The stop at Carlisle is short and soon we are running up the Eden valley towards Appleby. The compartment is very full and, by now, very stuffy, owing principally to the fact that all the other travellers prefer to journey in hermetically sealed containers and have done their best, by manipulating the ventilators which I had covertly opened before we left Glasgow, to bring about this state of affairs.

Nearing Kirkby Stephen I am very glad to quit the compartment and walk to the end of the coach where, through the open windows on either side, it is possible to get both air and a sight of the country. The full

moon rides high in a cloudless sky and the whole of the snow-swept land is bathed in pale light. This is Mallerstang Common. There is no wind and the sound of the engine comes strong and clear through the still night as it labours up the gradient towards the summit at Ais Gill where at over 1,100 feet above sea level we shall be, I believe, at the highest point on any main line in the country. Ais Gill is the little stream running beneath the track at a point just over three miles north of the Moorcock Inn at Garsdale Head and as we reach the crest I look back towards the ruins of Pendragon Castle and see the wide expanse of the Common spreading before me.

Now the long climb is ended and the London Train gathers speed. Soon we are over the curving viaduct across the Hawes road and running along Garsdale. The valley is suddenly shut off as we turn into the tunnel and the sound of the bogie wheels, almost immediately beneath me, comes like thunder through the open window. Bursting forth into the moonlight again we are into Dent station in a trice. The double row of screens holds back the drifted banks of snow which else would swamp the track. The Station Master's house stands four-square to whatever winds may blow and a gaunt, lonely, snowbound citadel it looks this night. We seem to be on top of the world here as the train threads its way along the narrow ledge of the terraced railway and I look down into the length of Dentdale, that intimate valley with its stripling river, lying far below and striking out from the foot of the perilous station hill towards Sedbergh.

Now we are crossing Arten Gill viaduct, one of the most graceful in the district, its lofty piers towering into the sky when seen from the valley below, as I have seen them,

Ais Gill summit in spectacular winter setting is stormed by the Cumbrian Mountain Express. (*Peter Fox*)

in the days when they supported the *Thames-Clyde* express around three o'clock in the afternoon on her journey north. The inky blackness and the thunder of the Blea Moor tunnel come and go and now at ever increasing speed, we are heading for the long viaduct at Ribblehead and the prospect opens wide on either side of the line. It is this I especially wanted to see for this, to me, is a magic land . . .

Over the brow towards the Hill Inn following the valley of the infant Greta goes the road to Ingleton. In the other direction I can see nearly as far as Gearstones, the narrow track where a snow plough has been at work opening up the way to Newby Head and Wensleydale. Nearby, their twin sources within a stone's throw of each other, rise Wharfe and

Ribble to flow their divergent courses to the seas. Behind us now is Whernside; to the right the hump of Simon Fell and flat-browed Ingleborough; to the left, furthest away but most distinctive of all, Pen-y-ghent, the very form of the heraldic lion couchant. Seen in the night with the moon full upon them the great hills and spaces of this land assume an awful majesty as they pass, unfolded by the racing train, in stupendous succession before the traveller's enraptured eye.

The tiny hamlet of Selside is swiftly passed. The train is now approaching Horton-in-Ribblesdale and the speed is over seventy miles per hour. Along its single street the village straggles in the snow, a river bridge and an inn at either end; the low square tower of the ancient church rises sturdily out of the drifts and in the background is Pen-y-ghent, nearer now and more like the lion than ever. With a wake of flying snow flakes the train goes swirling through the station and as we pass the signal box the sound of the telegraph bell is heard momentarily above the roar of the express – we are being handed on to 'Helwith Bridge'. At the cluster of dwellings which is Studfold I see again the spot where the Horton road dips almost to the river – the spot where, on a winter's night not long ago, I drove a car into two feet of flood water having been assured, on enquiring at Settle, that the road, impassable for several days, was open again. Masked headlamps and flood water should not be had together.

The rythmic 'tickerty-tick' of the bogie wheels is suddenly broken into a clattering cacophony as the train surges over the points and cross-overs at Helwith Bridge sidings and then enters, with the river, into the narrow gorge leading to the two Stainforths. In my mind's eye I look beyond the rocky cutting and see again the lovely pack horse bridge over the Ribble and the waterfall and Stainforth pool itself, the best bathing place in Yorkshire if you arrive there on a pedal bicycle from the Hart's Head at Giggleswick at six o'clock on a June morning (as I happen to know). Standing on its eminence comes the domed chapel of Giggleswick School and I am glad that on this occasion I view it alone so that for once in a while I may pass this landmark without having to hear misinformed travellers, referring to it in the most categorical terms, explaining to their untaught companions the wonders of 'the Observatory'.

We have passed through Settle and now are met by the shining metals of the line from Morecambe and Carnforth whilst out towards Rathmell, wriggling its way through a flattish land, goes the Ribble, now swollen to the proportions of a grown river and reflecting the full moon in its spreading waters. This is the last view of the Ribble tonight. The engine throttle has been opened. The long, down-hill run is ended and we are leaving the magic land and taking the rising gradient that will lead us to Hellifield and the engine sheds. I return to my compartment. I do not wish to see Hellifield and the engine sheds . . .

The rest of my journey over this well-known route is *felt* rather than seen. A pronounced check in speed followed by a left-hand lurch indicates that we have taken Shipley junction and are now running down the valley into Leeds. There comes the thunder of Apperley tunnel and the swing of the coach, now left, now right, as the train takes the reverse curves through Calverley, Horsforth and Newlay. We are nearing Kirkstall. It occurs to me that the ruined Abbey should be looking well tonight in the snow and the moonlight but I have no time to look out again. Personal luggage has to be extricated from the 4,763 other articles cramming the racks. There is a general restlessness in the compartment. Waking bodies, whose last recollection was a cup of tea at Carlisle, ask sleepily, yet hopefully, if it is St Pancras. No, it is not St Pancras. It will not be St Pancras for another six and a half hours.

There comes a check as we pass through the rocky canyon in which lies Armley station. Ahead, at Holbeck, stands the great signal gantry, its banks of red and orange lights burning steadily against the night sky. A single red light hanging just above our track turns green. Brakes are released and a minute or two later the London Train slides, with surprisingly little sound, into City Station, Leeds. Slightly more than half its journey is done.

(January 1945)

[187]

CYCLING IN THE DALES

W. Hill recalled the pleasures of half-a-century of riding a tandem uphill and downdale.

I WAS eleven years old when, in 1915, my parents bought me my first bicycle. Father taught me how to ride the machine on what at that time was the only piece of tarmac road in Colne – the level piece between the tip of Langroyd and Langroyd Hall. One of my earliest recollections was being taken to Barden Tower and the Strid, in Wharfedale. Another outing which I thought a great adventure at the time was to see the village of Stocks-in-Bowland before it was 'drowned' by the new reservoir. That day we returned over the then stony track crossing Bowland Knotts. I felt a real cyclist after that expedition!

We moved to Barnoldswick, where father had a clog shop at the bottom of Manchester Road, and it was in our house adjoining the shop that, in 1923, the Barnoldswick Clarion Cycling Club was formed, with six people present. I was the youngest member – 'Little Willie'. Now, as the only surviving member of those early days, they call me 'Owd Bill'. My father rode with the club until he was killed in a collision with a milk lorry at Higher Hodder Bridge. The club erected a memorial seat near Bracewell to his memory, and the inscription above the seat ends with the following couplet: 'Friend of man. Friend of truth. Friend of age and Guide of Youth.'

OPPOSITE

The traverse from one dale to another can often be made by cycle along ancient green tracks – Malham Tarn is in the background of this picture.
(H. S. *Parker*)

The Dales and the Lake District became my happy hunting grounds. There was little traffic on the roads, and I remember many delightful rides home from Upper Wharfedale or Littondale with the bright lights of our acetylene lamps reflected on white limestone dale roads. Another feature of cycling in the Dales in the 1920s and 1930s was the availability of food and refreshments at most inns and many farms or cottages. One could buy pots of tea to eat with one's own sandwiches. In fact, in those lean times of the depression, 'Tea only' was all we could afford. Many farmer's wives did 'bed and breakast' to supplement their income, and I have enjoyed many such for 5s. a night.

My wife and I rode a tandem for fifty years and spent many week-ends in the Dales. Swaledale was one of our favourite areas, and our favourite 'b & b' place in the Dale was at the home of Mr and Mrs David Harker, who lived at South View, near Muker church. Nellie said it was really home from home. It was, in more ways than one, for Muker churchyard was full of her ancestors (the Hoggarths and Aldersons). Using Muker as a base, we explored the hills and Dales. One wild weekend we went up to Swaledale. It had been our intention to go over the Stake Pass and then down to Semerwater on our way to Swaledale, but the wild weather and torrential rain decided us to use Bishopdale to Aysgarth road before going over the hills again to Swaledale. We stopped for a drink of tea in Aysgarth, before turning up the Dale into the teeth of the gale to Askrigg.

By now it was pitch dark. It was a

struggle against wind and rain to reach the village and undertake the long walk to the top of Askrigg Common. At the summit, the wind was blowing the rain horizontally as it screamed across the fells. We had three attempts to get on to the tandem before we could start to ride, and when we at last got to Swaledale, it seemed comparatively quiet. It was with relief that we knocked on Mr and Mrs Harker's door. He answered the knock, and when he saw us, bedraggled and wet, he exclaimed: 'Good God. Ha nivver thowt anybody 'ud turn up a neet like this.' Mrs Harker's voice came from the kitchen: 'Who is it David?'

He answered: 'It's Bill and Nellie, tha'

knaws, them fra Colne wi t'tandem.' There was a slight pause and she said: 'Bring 'em in.' Once inside the warm cosy kitchen, with the fire burning bright, it seemed another world.

As the years went on, and traffic on the roads increased, we turned more and more to the 'green' roads of the Pennines. Nellie and I had always liked to get off 'the beaten track', and we enjoyed what cyclists call 'Rough Stuff'. In fact, in the late 1950s, we joined an organisation called the 'Rough Stuff Fellowship', a band of cyclists who loved the byways. Happy Days!

(October 1982)

BUS TO MALHAM

Travelling on the first bus services in the Dales was a never-to-be-forgotten experience. C. Senior rode on a conveyance that included a breakfast stop!

IT WAS not until after the First World War that properly organised motor bus services gave the many Craven villages daily reliable links with the large towns. True, Silsden had it special service to the railway station a mile from the town itself, and the famous pioneer service of Ezra Laycock connecting Cowling with East Lancashire and Cross Hills had long established itself. The Keighley Corporation had given Steeton, Sutton and Cross Hills motor bus and trolley bus connections with the town. Still, the many villages on the north side of Skipton had little or nothing in the way of passenger transport. When the buses did come, the initial operators were, in the main, local individuals with a

spirit of enterprise behind them. Many good stories could be told of those services.

As one who lost his heart to Malham as a boy, I was delighted when in the twenties a service was started between Skipton and Malham. Pleasant though the five-mile walk from Bell Busk station by road and riverside to Malham had been, the prospect of being able to get to Malham more quickly was sufficient to tempt me to patronise the new service. I shall never forget that first journey. The service was operated, I believe, by Messrs Parker Bros. of Airton. I boarded the bus in High Street, Skipton and found that the driver was also the conductor, and that his duties included the conveyance of parcels, messages and letters for people on the route and other duties which certainly are not the lot of bus employees today.

The bus left Skipton at 9.30 a.m. with a fairly full load and was soon in Gargrave. Here there was a short stop which saw the driver get rid of some of his parcels and letters and collect a few more. At Eshton we dropped a woman passenger who arranged with him that on his return journey in the evening he would collect her. The journey was then resumed and just beyond the village green at Airton the bus went to the offside of the road and pulled up opposite the moorland road to Settle. 'Have we broken down?' asked one of the passengers. The driver promptly responded 'No, we have not; I'm barn to have a bit o' breakfast. S'an't be long.' He promptly left the bus, went into a cottage opposite to where the bus had stopped, and through the window the passengers were able to see him do full and quick justice to a meal which entailed the use of a knife and fork.

He kept us waiting no more than five minutes. When he emerged, he rubbed his hand across his mouth and with a comment to himself, 'That's better', put his bus in gear and we resumed the journey to Malham. My companion that day was a London friend paying his first visit to Yorkshire. To this day he talks of that bus journey. He was impressed with the majestic sweep of Malham Cove and of the grandeur of Gordale Scar but he has never forgotten the 'bus that stayed for breakfast'.

When we returned in the evening, the driver did not forget to go personally to the little house near Eshton and fetch the woman he had left there in the morning. My London friend, cradled in the highly organised bus system of the Metropolis, was vastly amused by such a high standard of public service, wondering what would happen in London if a passenger-collection service was initiated.

(May 1965)

THE DAY WE FLEW BLIND

Flying open-cockpit, propellor-driven biplanes from Yeadon in the 1930s was fun but could also be hair-raising. R. Dove just made it back to base.

LOOKING back on life to when I left school in 1930, I now know how it all started. I was a timid, shy, unheroic type, scared of heights, scared of the dark. I did not like to be hurt. I must have been subconsciously influenced by these failings that were submerged out of sight and out of mind in my subconsciousness, and chose a career of compensation. At school I knew pilots held top heroic status in those days of leather flying helmets. I would learn to fly and become a pilot.

With some inherited money I bought my way into a college of aeronautical engineering, got an 'A' flying licence and later became a draughtsman designing wooden aircraft at Reading at 15s. per week, then a progress chaser at Southampton. Even-

tually, in reply to an advertisement, I landed a job with the Arrow Aircraft Company at Yeadon Aerodrome. Flying open cockpit propeller-driven biplanes had its fun, once I got used to the terrifying, roaring, rushing hurricane round the head at take-off, and the sight of the ground getting lower and lower. It was grand fun, looping the loop and trying to hit the bump of the slip-stream where the plane had flown a few seconds before, or trying to touch down on a handkerchief laid on the grass, on three points at once.

Parachutes had only recently been invented. I got a parachute packer's licence, and was honour-bound to test my skill. I did three drops. It cost £1 to be taken up to over 1,000 feet. The job at Supermarine Aviation at Southampton was great fun. I was progress chaser, mustering all the parts that went to building the prototype Spitfire fighter, and at the nearby Hamble airfield I witnessed the first flight of an autogyro, the forerunner of the helicopter. It was invented by a Spaniard, a Mr Seivera, I think.

At Yeadon I again flew. The most memorable flights were at night over Leeds and Bradford – as targets. Territorial Army gunners picked us up with search-lights, and they practised sighting their guns on us. There were stars above and stars below, miles and miles of them in lovely clusters and lines, twinkling from street lights and cars, all trying to confuse us and make us lose our sense of direction as we twisted and turned away from the great searchlight beams pivoting from points on blackness. The most difficult time was finding tiny Yeadon airfield and coming in smoothly on to the ill-lit grass from the darkness above.

Another memorable flight was from Brough on the Humber to Yeadon with an acquaintance who had just bought a second-hand two-seater biplane. Neither of us had flown by instrument, and my co-pilot had never been to Yeadon. We had only the compass and altimeter and airspeed indicator for navigation. We started into a clear sky in autumn sunshine, but soon reached cloud patches and had to fly lower to keep below the cloud layer. Beyond the A1 we were just above pylon height, following road and river. I discovered my co-pilot was not knowledgeable when, from the forward cockpit, he asked if I would do the map reading. Without folding the map properly, he tried to pass it back, but the slipstream snatched it from his hand and it was gone. He said nothing into the intercom. His head sunk out of my sight. As he had taken hands and feet off the dual controls, the plane was mine!

We had just crossed the A1 and the ground was barely visible close below, so I turned the plane round and flew back until we found this major road again, following north to the Wharfe. I then turned west, with the river below. I should have turned east and tried to get back to the Humber and Brough, but visibility improved for a minute or two and I flew on, wondering what I should do. Soon we were in thick cloud, so I nosed down slowly until the ground showed vaguely below. Pool railway viaduct flashed under us for a second and was gone. I did a tight right hand turn, crossed back over the viaduct again and then made a wide left hand turn. The railway showed up. I flew back southwards over it until the viaduct showed, and then pulled the stick up and climbed into cloud at full throttle, with my eyes on the compass, trying to keep the course steady. It was quite dark in the cloud. I levelled out and slowed up when I judged we were high enough above Arthington.

I had flown at night before and gone through odd clouds but now I was not to know which way up we were. The compass needle began to wander. I could feel 'tilt'. I tried to get the compass dial back on course, but it made things worse. In desperation I looked down into the mist, concentrating my mind on what the tilt of my body would feel, when suddenly a round black blob showed for a fraction of a second and I felt a faint air bump. It was a ventilation shaft from the tunnel below us under Pool Bank. The shaft rose out of the fields like a wide squat chimney, and the warm air from it had melted the fog and caused the bump. We must have been hardly 100 feet above its black opening, heading for Bradford. I made rapid adjustments to the aircraft's trim. Next second the mist grew suddenly darker and we were over grass.

I closed the throttle, and lifted the nose, letting the plane sink lower till it touched down in a perfect three-pointer. At the touch of the wheels my co-pilot's head came up from the cockpit – I had forgotten he was there. When the plane stopped, the faint bulk of the Arrow Aircraft factory showed at the edge of the aerodrome.

(February 1974)

12

HALF-A-CENTURY OF CHANGE

ALL QUIET IN THE DALES

The most dramatic change in the fifty years of The Dalesman *occurred when the magazine was just six months old and the country was plunged into war. The atmosphere in the higher dales during the first few months of war was beautifully captured by Alfred J. Brown, author of such memorable books as* Striding through Yorkshire *and* Fair North Riding.

DUSK WAS falling when I reached Buckden on a mild October evening to take what might be my last chance of a weekend in the high Dales during wartime.

When I had made sure of a room at a farm under Buckden Pike and enjoyed a prodigious supper, I strolled up the road that skirts the fells and leads to Bishopdale; but resisting the lure of the friendly White Lion at Cray, I turned down the by-lane to the tiny hamlet of Hubberholme, groping my way in the black-out by the light of the stars. There was no moon but the few stars seemed to shine with unwonted brilliance, giving promise of a frosty night and a bright morning. As I reached the bridge that separates the ancient church from the inn, that twin constellation which seems to comprise nearly all Hubberholme, I stopped for a few moments to listen to the song of the Wharfe as it glides down the Beckermonds through quiet Langstrothdale. It is a song I first heard twenty odd years ago when the last war had already caught me in its toils; and it is a song which in one way and another has coloured my whole life.

My first big walk was to follow the Wharfe to its source, and the revelation so fired my blood that I could not rest thereafter until I had explored every dale and river in Yorkshire; and though there are many nooks and corners in the County that call one back again and again, I find myself turning more and more frequently to that green valley where Wharfe begins its high career.

When I groped my way into the inn I found the tiny parlour comparatively 'crowded' with visitors. Half a dozen Dalesmen were playing dominoes and drinking ale, and two or three visitors were keeping them company at the table. There was only just room to squeeze into a corner seat by the fire and listen to the familiar dialect and good-humoured banter of the players while I joined them in a pint of mild. Nothing unusual happened beyond the immemorial argument as to the shortest distance between two points: the two points in this case being two inns: the George at Hubberholme and the Queen's in neighbouring Littondale, with a small obstacle in the shape of Old Cote Moor Top 2,000 feet high, between. But trivial

[194]

as the argument was, the homely talk acted like a soothing balm. War seemed a million years away, until someone in a still smaller inner room turned on the wireless and the 'B.B.C. Home Service' filled the air with a different kind of talk whereupon I stepped forth into the keen night air again.

It seemed blacker than ever outside, yet some farmlad rode by me on a bicycle without any light, shouting me a friendly greeting as he passed, possibly to reassure me that he was a human being and not a boggart as I imagined. Gradually the eyes became accustomed to the night and the vague shape of farms and shippons loomed out of the darkness; and Wharfe made music at my side. As I approached Buckden again, the comforting smell of wood fires filled the air, and soon I was warming myself by one in the farm before turning in to bed.

I was up betimes next morning to take a stroll before breakfast. After the commotion in the city it was a relief to find no evidence of A.R.P. precautions in the village: no feverish work on air raid shelters seemed to be in progress: no tin helmets were visible, no gasmasks, sandbags: nothing. But the cocks were crowing as usual, and a bull bellowed defiance in a distant field, otherwise the sirens were silent. Scores of evacuees *may* have been slumbering in the deepest farms, but they were certainly not wandering about the streets yet. On the contrary, everything seemed to be perfectly normal and just as I wanted it to be. The little village post office at the corner looked as tranquil as ever, and the old Buck inn as secure. Late roses, gorgeous dahlias and meek Michaelmas daisies graced the cottage gardens, and the comforting sign of 'Ham and Eggs' greeted me from my farmhouse window as I turned back for a traditional Dales breakfast before starting the serious pleasure of the day.

Fortified by another heroic meal, I set out to climb Buckden Pike as a prelude to the day. There are, of course, several ways of climbing the Pike; the approach I like best starts from Cray and leads straight up the steepest shoulder, but this time I followed the green track which starts from Buckden, crosses the beck and ascends the hill by easy stages. When I reached the lower woods I turned round for a last look at the village and the valley. There was something peculiarly satisfying about those grey stone farms and cottages; something reassuring about the way the blue smoke curled from the chimneys; and something so solid and durable about the whole village that was singularly comforting. It was the best answer I had seen to the fulminations of the dictators: and the vaunted strength of the Siegfried Line. For how many wars have devastated Europe since Buckden first appeared on the scene and how little it has changed through the centuries. This war may be different from all the preceding wars, but I fancy Buckden will look precisely the same when the tumult and the shouting dies again, and the men march back. Away over in nearby Littondale, there is a tablet in Arncliffe church commemorating the names of the Dalesmen from this very valley who fought for England at Floddenfield, and another commemorating those who fought in the last Great War. Probably there will be a third tablet when this war is ended; but still the Dales life goes on unchanged and will go on, I trust, when Hitlerism and Communism are long forgotten.

When I reached the summit of the Pike, a snell wind was blowing from the east, but the air was so invigorating that I had a mind to spend the day on the tops rather than to descend to one of the neighbouring

valleys. There is nothing spectacular about the Pike itself; it is just a shaggy giant of the early world – a great lump of a mountain – but the view from the top is enchanting. On Buckden Pike one can see at various points: Langstrothdale, Bishopdale, Coverdale, Wensleydale and, close at hand, delectable Waldendale. With such a plethora of dales it is difficult to decide which to explore, but I solved the problem by making a circuit of the great plateau, walking first towards Bishopdale Edge.

In those high solitudes it is a rare thing to meet a human being but as I approached the most desolate part of the moor, a shepherd came over the brow of the hill whistling up his two dogs. Stopping for a moment to exchange greetings and to admire the cunning of his dogs as they rounded up the scattered flock, I rejoiced in the thought that this simple ceremony too had gone on unchanged through the centuries. From Bishopdale Edge, one can see half Wensleydale at one's feet; perhaps the fairest dale of all, dominated by Castle Bolton which stands remote and austere in the middle distance, overlooking a scene which can have changed little since Mary Queen of Scots was imprisoned there. I lunched under a wall high above the dale in order to enjoy this superb view, and then turned towards Waldendale.

It is many years since I first set eyes on Walden, one of the most secluded and, in

(D. C. Smith)

its upper reaches, wildest of the smaller dales. On this occasion I approached it from the plateau above Walden Head to find it bathed in the afternoon sunlight; and I have never seen it look lovelier and more peaceful. Unable to resist the lure of that lonely green valley, I dropped down to the dalehead, crossed the beck and then climbed halfway up the opposite ridge which looks over to Coverdale. But as my time was limited, I followed the course of Walden Beck past the falls until I reached the boundary fence which leads over the watershed towards Langstrothdale again. There is a very boggy stretch of evil quagmire and peaty moor between Walden Head and Wharfedale which cannot be circumvented or commended; but once you cross it and reach the dividing wall, you are rewarded by an enchanting view of Starbotton nestling in the dale below. Cam Beck leads directly to that Arcadian village, but I had a desire to drop straight into Buckden again to complete the full circle, so I kept to the high land until I reached the shoulder of the Pike, and then made a beeline for the village.

As I approached it, the sun was just sinking behind the hills, but the village was basking in sunshine and the serenity of evening lay about it. Smoke was still curling from the chimneys and again there was that delicious smell of wood fires in the air, and as I came nearer the music of the beck became more and more insistent as it hurried down to join the river. The old stone cottages looked as sleepy as ever.

An uneventful day perhaps! Certainly nothing sensational had happened: which was precisely why I had gone there and why I will always remember it during the troubled days ahead.

(January 1940)

PRESERVING THE LANDSCAPE

John Dower, gifted architect and planner, was invalided out of the Royal Engineers at the start of the war and given the enormous task of preparing a report on the establishment of National Parks in England and Wales. Written while he was living in Kirkby Malham, this report led directly to the passing of the historic National Parks and Access to the Countryside Act of 1949. At the same time, John Dower wrote a series of astonishingly prophetic Dalesman *articles on post-war reconstruction, including one on open-air recreation:*

NEXT TO farming among the users of the Dales country comes recreation – *open-air* recreation in its broadest sense, both active and passive, both through walking and other outdoor exercise and through the contemplative enjoyment of natural beauty. To the large and growing body of visitors, from neighbouring industrial areas and further afield, this recreational value will, indeed, appear supreme; though a little consideration should show them that the aspect and delight of the countrysides they visit are everywhere dependent on the maintenance of farming use. To the Dalesfolk themselves the pleasures of their native moors and valleys are no less dear because they are more familiar. To visitors and residents alike, the Dales are a reservoir of physical, mental and spiritual refreshment – a natural refuge of priceless worth from the strain, clatter, congestion and artificiality of our machine-ridden civilisation. It is a beautiful country which must be kept beautiful. It is a country well-fitted and already, in considerable measure, by custom freely open for rambling and other forms of enjoyment, which must be made progressively more fully and widely open on an assured basis of public right.

To keep the Dales beautiful – do not let us underestimate the magnitude and diffi-culty of the task. We may stoutly deny the pessimists who tell us that England's beauty must perish, that we fight a losing battle against the forces of disfigurement and destruction: against the ubiquitous motor-car, with its accompaniment of noise, roadside advertisements and petrol-pumps, and against the type of 'country-lovers' who express their affection for unspoilt countrysides by spotting them with pink-roofed week-end bungalows and decorating them with trails of litter. But we must as stoutly resist the optimists who hold that, since the beauty of our country (or what's left of it) has survived till now, it will automatically go on surviving, and who blindly trusts that, if some preventive action is found necessary, 'they' will take care of it – *they* being Westminster or Whitehall, or anyway, somebody other than ourselves! In truth, the task is urgent, heavy and never-ending, but it can be done: and, however much the local and central 'planning' authorities may provide the powers and the machinery, it is primarily for us, the people of the Dales, to do it.

It is broadly true to say that, while we enjoy beautiful landscapes in the mass, we make or mar, preserve or destroy them in detail. It is the whole effect of a harmonious view, the general impression of a picturesque village, even the sum of a

The traditional Dales landscape, as seen near Castle Bolton in winter. (*P. Walshaw*)

succession of views as we pass along a valley or across a moor, that quickens our appreciation and lives in our memory. But every scene, every piece of Dales country that our eyes and minds so instinctively unify, is in fact a complex assembly of varied features, natural and man-made – the wild almost always in some degree moulded by man, the artificial as time passes coloured and clothed by weather and vegetation. If we would preserve the scene, we must preserve its significant features and we must ensure that no discordant new features intrude upon it. It is not, of course, a question of preventing *all* alteration. Nor is the job by any means entirely negative and restrictive; the positive and creative side may in practice bulk less

large, but it is not the less important. Merely to maintain rural beauty, and the fertility on which it depends, needs constant attention and frequent effort, not least in the care and replacement of woodlands and hedge-row trees. With rare exceptions, it is far better that timber should be felled when mature than that it should be kept on into stag-headed and lop-limbed decay; but for every tree that is cut down at least two should be planted – or better still should *have been* planted in some nearby position well in advance. There are plenty of places, especially in the lower valley land, where we could go further and, like the 'improving' landlords of the 18th and early 19th centuries, deliberately enrich the landscape for the benefit of future generations by skilful new planting and other adjustments. Many more detail changes essential or desirable on other grounds can be fitted into their surroundings without harm and even with enrichment, provided their position and forms are carefully and sympathetically designed.

There remains, however, a wide variety of all-too-likely 'developments' which must be firmly resisted. We want no more roadside advertisements (and all existing ones, which outlast the war, cleared away as soon as possible thereafter); no more festooning of pylons, poles and overhead cables (long-term policy should be to get them *all* underground): no more spiked iron-railings, concrete fence-posts, kerbs and footpaths, or other road 'furniture' of incongruous urban type: no more unsightly rubbish-tips or dumps of worn-out cars: no more shack cafes and vulgar roadhouses: no more weekend bungalows or other non-agricultural buildings outside the immediate neighbourhood of towns and villages: and no more ugly buildings, of clumsy design or unsuitable materials, anywhere. In sum, we want to give as much thought to the appearance as to the utility and profitability of all that we do 'on the face of the land', to make landscape values, next to and in association with farming values, the dominant criterion – the yardstick – by which we judge, allow, modify or reject every proposed change . . .

Preservation of the landscape (and of the farming on which it depends), freedom and facilities for open-air recreation, and protection of wildlife in the best of Britain's larger stretches of beautiful, wilder country; these are precisely the purposes of the 'National Parks' which the people so widely desire, and which government seems at last to regard with favour as an element in post-war reconstruction. There is no magic in the name. It means simply a national decision and national as well as local powers, organisation and funds to ensure that these purposes are dominant in the selected areas. No selection has yet been made, though few would deny the Lake District pride of place: after that 'Every man to his taste'. But surely we may claim that a substantial part of the Dales – covering at the least Wharfedale down to Bolton Abbey, Malhamdale and Upper Ribblesdale, with the fells topped by Whernside, Ingleborough, Penyghent, Buckden Pike and Great Whernside – should come high on any list? Surely, though we will do all we can to preserve our country, unaided if need be, we can fairly hope for some national help in maintaining for the nation's enjoyment so fine a piece of our common inheritance?

(August 1942)

URBAN MINDS IN THE COUNTRY

WITH THE start of a new holiday season comes the old problem of the misuse of our countryside by those who come into it for relaxation and recreation, misuse that includes everything from using our fell tops as litter bins to enjoying a picnic in a field of growing corn.

A delightful story of a north country

farmer's reprisal for damages by trespass was told recently in a leaflet issued by the Cheshire N.F.U. Discovering a man complete with family making free use of his land, this farmer took their name and address, and on the following Sunday the farmer turned up with his own family and camped for the afternoon on the trespasser's lawn. There is an air of poetic justice about this which will commend it. I do not suggest that even in these days of direct action your Yorkshire farmers should start a campaign of reprisal and retaliation in this form, but they are troubled by the damage to crops and livestock caused by trespass. Like farmers everywhere in areas which are by nature playgrounds and centres of recreation for industrial districts, they suffer from the thoughtlessness of townsfolk. And they might well be pardoned for taking bold measures to induce consideration of their sufferings among those who cause them.

This thoughtlessness is a comparatively new thing. A century ago three-quarters of our people lived on the land and only a quarter in towns and cities. And even that quarter had close enough links with the land to have always in mind its importance and its needs. They looked at the land through the farmer's eyes and had a sense of his problems. They felt for the land and knew the ways of its creatures. We were a rural people with a countryman's outlook. Today the proportions are reversed. Only a quarter of our people are on the land, the remainder live in towns and cities. And, what is worse, they are slowly losing their inherited memory of the land and their recognition of its claims. We are becoming an urban nation with an urban outlook.

No one who felt for the land would allow his dog to chase sheep and cattle, and particularly in-calf cattle. He would know the cost both in suffering to the animal and in financial loss to the farmer. Nor would he leave open field gates or scatter bottles over hedges into pastures. Every instinct would be against it. He would refrain by nature as he would from striking matches on his own sitting room wall or from discarding household rubbish into his front garden. Yet how urban-minded we have become is shown by the fact that in those parts of our countryside near built-up areas worrying by dogs has made impossible the keeping of breeding sheep. Indeed, in some districts it is impracticable to keep sheep at all. If the townsman protests that he cannot always be responsible for the actions of his dog, any Dalesman would be shocked, for the thought of a dog out of control is amazing to him. On the rare occasions where a sheep dog goes wrong and becomes a sheep-worrier the owner of the dog would be the first to shoot his own animal if the dog was caught in the act.

Most of the damage done or allowed to be done by the townsman in the countryside is not the result of deliberate intent; it is done because the townsman has forgotten what he would once have remembered instinctively, that a field of mowing grass is the winter bread-and-butter of the farmer, the sheep and cattle in a pasture are his capital assets to be treated as carefully as a precision machine or a shop-keeper's stock, and that to break a fence or wall is tantamount to breaking a shop window. That is why the problem of persuading the townsman to observe common decencies of the countryside is so difficult; it calls for the revival of an ancient memory, for the re-creation of the old love and appreciation of our rural areas, for a realisation of the

OPPOSITE
Town comes to country – overflowing litter basket at Buckden in Wharfedale. (*Clifford Robinson*)

importance of country to town and of town to country.

There are those who would barricade the countryside against the man from the town. They would put up 'No trespassing' notices everywhere, they would throw away all plans for National Parks, more footpaths, and bigger and better Youth Hostels, and they would discourage any interest the townsman might show in their territory – unless it had a cash basis. Such a policy would leave the real problem untouched, for modern transport, present-day notions of recreation, and in fact all existing social policy inevitably means the continuing invasion of the country by the town. We are fast reversing Dr Johnson's dictum that:

'No wise man will go to live in the country unless he has something to do which can be better done in the country.'

We seek to do even urban things in the rural areas.

Perhaps the very urgency of this will bring about that mutual understanding which is so desirable. For some three generations past the two civilisations – rural and urban – have distrusted the other and each has exploited the other. Now both of them are thrown together again and find that they have something to offer in the building of the future. The townsman will remember that he cannot have milk, meat, and other products in abundance if his dog chases every animal it sees in the countryside. The farmer will realise that by inviting the townsman to walk along footpaths through his fields he is ensuring a greater regard in the future for his needs and his well-being.

Dalesman's Diary (May 1964)

NEW BUILDINGS FOR OLD

Post-war urban renewal has in many cases been a saga of lost opportunities and a misguided effort to be progressive. Derek Linstrum looked with dismay at the larger cities of the West Riding but found hope in a few smaller towns.

THE POST-WAR rebuilding of the larger towns and cities in the West Riding is a dismal story. Unimaginative layouts, often no more than the widening of existing roads, have been filled in with an apparently unco-ordinated series of buildings. Often no regard appears to have been paid to neighbouring buildings, old or new. Consequently important streets, such as Park Row and South and East Parades in Leeds, have lost their character as entities while individual replacements have been,

on the whole, distressingly mediocre. The insipidity of a large new building in Park Row is a poor replacement for the colour and richness of its predecessor. While some of the new buildings in East Parade have merit, they are of such diverse character in materials and window proportions that the street as a whole is meaningless now.

Old village centres in Leeds and Bradford, now embedded in the urban sprawl, have been destroyed although there is an encouragingly imaginative proposal for the rebuilding of part of Chapel Allerton. The new centre of Bradford has been severely criticised for its lack of human values, its sacrifice of the pedestrian to the motor car, and the mixture of pretentiousness and shoddiness in its standard buildings. Wakefield has widened its roads and left its architecture to a developer; it has lost every opportunity of improvement by neglecting to preserve any of its fine old buildings or to make a space of any distinction in the centre of the town. This melancholy story of the larger towns is relieved only by the example of Huddersfield. An

New buildings for old. Many Dales' barns have been converted into houses, as seen in this better-than-average conversion at Feizor, near Settle. (*H. S. Parker*)

excellent plan has been commissioned by the Council and when it has been realised the town centre is likely to be greatly improved without losing its essential character.

The smaller towns in the West Riding have changed less drastically, although there have been some regrettable developments; they should benefit by a conscientious application of the requirements and intentions of the Act. There has already been some action by the County Council in this direction and a development plan for Haworth has been prepared which includes the control of building materials, heights and window proportions. This type of control need not lead to architectural pastiche and it can prevent the squandering of the individual character of towns

as diverse as Knaresborough and Holm-firth, Skipton and Heptonstall, Bawtry and Sedbergh. It is not a question of bow windows, shutters and carriage lamps but of the fundamentals of architecture. A town's character has been formed by its siting and climate, the occupations and interests of its inhabitants and the availability of building materials. If all these are considered new buildings can enhance the character and improve the appearance of the town. A lead has been given by the County Council, whose architects and planners have often shown a great concern to maintain the local character in their own developments.

In the Market Place at Knaresborough, an area which the local authority has deprived of its cobbled surface, a new library has taken its place without any self-consciousness in the surrounding groups of varied buildings. The High Street and the Market Place are excellent examples of Conservation Areas which, with sensitive architectural control, could be immeasurably improved. The pattern of streets linking the Castle with these areas could be exploited more fully by careful development and the replacement of some nondescript buildings.

Wetherby is a town that lacks the architectural distinction of Knaresborough but it has a potentially rewarding pattern of streets from the bridge, through the market place and towards Harrogate, which is not realised in the existing buildings. In such a town a new character can be developed from its vernacular, and again it is the new library that suggests a possible form. The colour and texture of the materials harmonise with the traditional buildings but the new building has an added scale and quality which, if they were continued in the market place, would create an enclosure of some distinction.

The most familiar part of Skipton is the long market place leading up to the church and castle. It is a memorable view, containing pleasant but essentially modest buildings, a context which could be disastrously disrupted by the introduction of a large-scale building. The new Health Centre succeeds in adding a comparatively large piece to the existing pattern without destroying the scale of the enclosure; the sympathetic materials add, without disturbing, to the harmonious mixture of materials and textures.

These are all successful and praiseworthy developments; they are not the only ones in the huge West Riding area. Unfortunately they are not typical. Too many proposals are rootless and alien in their context, conceived in a misguided effort to be progressive. Our environment has always been the expression of ourselves, each generation contributing to the experience of the past.

(January 1968)

LOOKING AHEAD IN THE DALES

R.T. Fieldhouse, the then Organising Tutor for the Dales Area of the Workers' Educational Association, pinpointed some of the problems caused by rural depopulation and increased visitor levels – and suggested possible solutions.

THE YORKSHIRE Dales are faced with a declining population and an increase in the number of trippers and visitors. Both these facts bring their problems. Depopulation leaves the villages empty and without means to provide modern amenities and improve living conditions; unable to support a public transport system. They are left further and further behind; they become 'olde worlde' relics of a previous century. If this suits the visitors and the retired people in the Dales, it does not suit

Farming may be in decline but agricultural shows lose none of their popularity – as demonstrated by the Upper Wharfedale show at Kilnsey on Summer Bank Holiday Tuesday. (*Clifford Robinson*)

the young people. They leave for more up-to-date places, causing further depopulation. In the present century the losses of population have been in the fifteen to forty age group; the number of older people has actually increased. If the trend continues, many Dales villages will slowly grow old and die and the Dales themselves become mere recreation parks filled with choking cars belching out petrol fumes and litter and transistorised music . . .

The low level of real incomes and the lack of a choice of jobs is the major cause of migration. While wage levels are low it is a fallacy that it is cheaper to live in the countryside. Any solution to the problem

of depopulation must be related to the provision of a wider choice of jobs. In the past it was believed that improvements in agricultural prosperity would solve the problem of rural depopulation. In the Dales in the last hundred years the main trend has been the amalgamation of farms; the number of farms in the Dales is only about a third of the number in 1871 . . .

Afforestation of parts of the Dales could provide more jobs than agriculture. A study of a similar Welsh hill area in the 1950s predicted that forestry could employ three or four times as many men as hill farming, even before the trees were ready for cutting. In upper North Tynedale and Redesdale, one of Britain's major post-war afforestation areas, there has been the unusual phenomenon of net immigration into a rural area and population figures have been maintained. Forestry could provide more jobs for the Dales. Of course it would change their landscape, but it is debatable whether tree-covered hills are any less beautiful than heather-clad ones. And the Forestry Commission is now experimenting with ways of opening its forests to the public. In time, afforestation also gives rise to ancillary industries such as sawmills, pulp and paper mills and others like the chipboard plant at Hexham. It should also be remembered that any increase in employment in an area breathes new life into the community and gives rise to further demands and opportunities. The service industries – the retail trade, transport, building, repair and maintenance work – would all be revived. As depopulation reduces the potential of an area, so new jobs will lead to repopulation.

Regional development has not helped the Dales: it has concentrated growth in the North East, on Tyneside and Teesside. In the future, with better communications,

perhaps by giant helicopter air-buses or hovercraft, people may be able to live in the Dales and work on Teesside. But the immediate need is for more varied and plentiful jobs in the market towns – Hawes, Leyburn, Reeth, Richmond. It is frequently argued that young people are right to leave the Dales and widen their experience, which is true at the present time, with the Dales offering so little to young people. If the Dales were more populated they would be able to provide more facilities and amenities and opportunities: there would not be the same need to seek the wider world.

It is also objected that industry would spoil the nature of the Dales, but agricultural and forestry ancillary industries and other light industries and 'white collar' administrative offices situated in the market towns or nearby need gush no smoke over the surrounding countryside. People living in villages of not less than 200 inhabitants in the Dales could travel to these employment centres each day. These key-settlement villages would act as nuclei for repopulation and would be large enough to provide better amenities and living conditions. What is the alternative? There is no virtue in preserving a corpse.

Meanwhile the Dales are faced with that other problem – an ever increasing number of motorised visitors pouring into their confined spaces, changing the nature of the Dales. The creation of the National Park has often been blamed for this, but in fact tourists are bound to come as communications improve. The number of cars in this country has doubled since 1955. There are now seven million on the roads. By AD 2000 it is estimated that there will be thirty million. At the same time, it can be expected that the average working week will be cut from forty-two hours to thirty hours. More leisure time and more cars will surely increase the number of visitors . . .

This raises the question: for whom is the nation preserving the natural beauty of the Dales? For the ever decreasing local population? For the weekend cottagers and the grouse shooters? For ramblers? For posterity? Surely a national heritage – a National Park – should be enjoyed by as many people as possible. It is the aim of the National Parks authorities to preserve the Dales with as little interference to the inhabitants as possible, but at the same time it must be recognised that they are attractive to many people who are less fortunate in where they live, and these people have a right to enjoy the National Parks. More will have to be done in the future to accommodate the visitors, both the walking and the driving variety.

(September 1966)

A DIFFERENT WORLD

Marie Hartley has made an immense contribution to Dales literature by recording a now vanished way-of-life in her books, written in collaboration with firstly Ella Pontefract and then Joan Ingilby. For The Dalesman's *fortieth anniversary she reflected on the far-reaching changes that have occurred in the area since the 1930s. She began by recalling a prescient letter which Ella received one day in February 1939.*

I REMEMBER a letter coming to Ella from W.L. Andrews, then Editor of *The Leeds Mercury*, and later to become Sir Linton Andrews and Editor of the *Yorkshire Post*. He asked if she would support 'a small journalistic project of a friend of mine, Harry J. Scott', who was hoping to start a monthly magazine to be called *The Yorkshire Dalesman*. After a visit from Mr Scott himself, and further correspondence, an article on 'Dales Folk' was prepared for the first number and regular monthly contributions from us were arranged. I am thus carried back to the 1930s before the dread date 3 September 1939, dragged us all into war. In that peaceful decade Ella Pontefract and I had written our first books, *Swaledale*, published in 1934, *Wensleydale* in 1936, and *Wharfedale* in 1938, and we were completing a fourth entitled *Yorkshire Tour*. Many people had written to us, and we were able to send Harry Scott lists of their names and addresses.

It was a different world and they were different dales from those which we inhabit now. Dalesfolk lived in comparative isolation. Buses there certainly were, but cars were few and far between, and television had not arrived to take a hold on people and affect their lives as it has now. An unhibited zest in their everyday life was evident, and colourful dialect words and phrases were to be heard in those days before people were rendered self-conscious by the presence of many strangers or radio commentators or, as now, by television crews. (Authors hardly count.)

We spent the month of June 1932, in a rented furnished cottage at Angram, near Keld. I recall the wonderful calm sunny

[207]

Marie Hartley (left) and Joan Ingilby, photographed in their cottage at Askrigg about 1950. (*Bertram Unne*)

weather. We attended Keld Sports, a long defunct event, and visited Tan Hill Pit, then working. Later in the year we climbed Great Shunnor Fell and Water Crag, and talked to elderly farmers at what were the remnants of Thwaite Fair. But what was remarkable that June, never mind October, was the almost total absence of visitors. It was possible to walk Dales roads and lanes all day and see no one but the occasional farmer going about his work. Only the buzz of a bee, the rustling of grasses, the sad bleating of sheep, and the bubbling call of the curlew disturbed the absolute silence. In the 1970s the sound of tractors (and sometimes heavy lorries) is everywhere, and in haytime there is the thud and whirr of machinery in action.

In the 1930s, all the farmhouses in the small branch valleys were occupied by different farming families. Now almost all have been deserted and are taken over as country cottages or have fallen into ruin, whilst the dales themselves have partially been planted with conifers. Not that the thirties were a time of plenty. Whenever we attended a sheep sale, or talked of the price of wool, we heard a sorry story. Lambs then sold at 10s. each and wool was 6d. a pound. It is very different today. Lambs may well sell at £30 each and wool at 40p a pound. Most people except the elderly and retired have a car, and farming flourishes.

In the villages, hamlets and market towns were Dalespeople with their own characteristics and idiosyncrasies. Their memories readily took them back to traditional ways of life which, at any rate in the heads of the Dales, were still continuing. Oatcake in the old style was still baked over the fire on a bakestone. Peat was cut on the moors and stored for winter fuel. (It burnt well with the poor quality coal from Tan Hill.) Clogs were commonplace, and saddlers flourished at Hawes, Richmond and Settle. Hay-making proceeded as it had always done, slowly with horses and wooden sledges and sweeps. Elderly men who had worked in their youth in the lead-mines were still living in the villages or, after exile to find work, had returned to

their native places in old age. Although we did record many old customs (and I have done so since with Joan Ingilby). I greatly regret that we did not seek out the lead-miners, for very little has been recorded of their actual recollections.

When Sir Linton wrote to Ella in 1939 he ended his letter with the sentence: 'The Dalesfolk ought to regard you as a great benefactress in helping to bring so many visitors'. Except for the many who benefit from the influx of people, we now would dispute this sentiment, and say that too many come. It is a popular exercise to blame the National Park for this, although many factors contribute to it. In 1978 over 4,000 people arrived in the village of Askrigg on the Summer Bank Holiday Saturday. This was not typical, but it illustrates the change. So, as I look

Gunnerside, Swaledale. (*Marie Hartley*)

Winter at Arncliffe. (*Marmaduke Miller*)

through my first copy of *The Yorkshire Dalesman*, as it was then called, I cannot but be reminded of the host of Dalespeople I have known. Sadly, very many have gone. For me the Dales are not the same, as these elderly people with their kindliness, warmth of heart, interest in our work and ready hospitality are not easily replaced. I miss, too, some of the contributors to the first numbers: my colleague Ella Pontefract, Phyllis Bentley, Dorothy Una Ratcliffe, J. Fairfax-Blakeborough, A. J. Brown, M'Duke Miller and others. Harry Scott is no longer in the room in his own home at Clapham, which he used as an office, and where we used to be given tea by Mrs Scott.

From my own point of view I note, too, that a poem in the second number of *The Yorkshire Dalesman* is by Joan Ingilby, whom I did not then know, but who has so happily worked with me since Ella's death in 1945. I also note that *The Dalesman* from the first number in 1939 survived the outbreak of the war, about which Harry Scott wrote to us in dismay, and has grown into a large publishing concern. Continuity is reassuring in these changing times.

(March 1979)

INDEX

Note: page numbers for illustrations are given in italics.